# JOIN THE
# CONVERSATION

# JOIN THE CONVERSATION

How to Engage Marketing-Weary
Consumers with the Power of
Community, Dialogue, and Partnership

JOSEPH JAFFE

John Wiley & Sons, Inc.

Published by John Wiley & Sons, Inc., Hoboken, New Jersey.
Published simultaneously in Canada.

Wiley Bicentennial Logo: Richard J. Pacifico

For general information on our other products and services or for technical support, please contact our Customer Care Department within the United States at (800) 762-2974, outside the United States at (317) 572-3993, or fax (317) 572-4002.

Wiley also publishes its books in a variety of electronic formats. Some content that appears in print may not be available in electronic books. For more information about Wiley products, visit our web site at www.wiley.com.

*Library of Congress Cataloging-in-Publication Data:*

Jaffe, Joseph, 1970–
    Join the conversation : how to engage marketing-weary consumers with the power of community, dialogue, and partnership / Joseph Jaffe.
        p.  cm.
    "Published simultaneously in Canada."
    ISBN 978-0-470-13732-1 (cloth)
Customer relations.  2. Business communication.  3. Relationship marketing.  4. Marketing  I. Title.
    HF5415.5.J34  2008
    658.8'343 — dc22

                                                              2007015889

Printed in the United States of America

10  9  8  7  6  5  4  3  2  1

*Dedicated to my incredible family — my wife Terri and my children, Amber, Aaron, and Jack. This book is all about conversation, and lately I've been doing all my conversing with you from airports and hotel rooms. I'll rectify this sooner than later (or bring you with me).*

*Thank you all for your unconditional belief, support, and love.*

# Contents

# Foreword

It's a new day.

We live, play, and work at a time when change is the only constant. If your daytime activities involve making brands famous, attracting new customers, or navigating the proliferation of new media, hardly a week goes by without a startling development clouding your view of what used to work best.

How much is changing is not what is terrifying the CMO today. The scary part is the pace of change itself. You barely adjust to Web 2.0—or watch from the sidelines as it passes you by—and here come the astonishingly intricate interactions of Web 3.0.

Don't say you weren't warned.

Cisco ads in big, bold type proclaim a time when Web applications mash together to create experiences never imagined previously—a time when everyone connected to the human network taps into a collaborative intelligence (think Wikipedia) to make the most of whatever comes along next.

Did you read Joseph Jaffe's earlier book, *Life After the 30-Second Spot*? Jaffe was first to look at what lies ahead now that the 30-second commercial has seen its best days. His book sounded the alarm. He told us that we were about to be hit by a perfect storm rapidly gaining strength, velocity, intent, and momentum. What you could expect was "an ever-increasing digital arsenal governed by the ability to create countless synergies that result in a dynamic never witnessed before."

Life in the fast lane for marketers didn't always move at such a frenetic pace. During the golden years of mass marketing, ads changed very little over almost half a century. From the moment in the 1950s and 1960s when a mesmerizing black box arrived in everyone's home, watching intrusive 30-second commercials became the price paid for free entertainment. Given enough reach and frequency, it was relatively easy for "hidden persuaders" with deep pockets to turn their brand into household words.

Nothing lasts forever. The explosive growth of cable, specialized magazines, and endless line extensions opened the way for mass marketers to master the art of targeting segments and reaching out to niche markets. By the 1990s we were ready to welcome a new age of one-to-one marketing. We began to pursue a more rewarding, data-driven relationship with our best customers.

Such terms as ROI and lifetime customer value now reside in the CMO's vocabulary. The race to build massive customer databases in the 1990s became a race to benefit from the direct marketing model while remaining a multichannel marketer. Throughout the years of the age of one-to-one marketing, talk on Madison Avenue focused on building profitable relationships with known customers. But, sad to say, big-time marketers never strayed very far from a traditional view of the media world. They kept themselves busy switching from one underperforming agency to another equally underperforming substitute. They never seemed to get the point that squandering huge budgets on mainly ineffective "above the line" measured media was not the best way to place your bets in the age of one-to-one marketing.

Never underestimate the power of the advertising/media/Neilsen complex to protect and expand its hold on the big bucks in most marketing plans.

With the age of mass marketing and the age of one-to-one marketing behind us, it's time to think about what the next stage in the aging of marketing will be. So . . . what's next? William Gibson, the popular science fiction author, tells us: "The future is already here. It's just unevenly distributed."

What's next is everything you'll be discovering in the pages of this book. It is the embodiment of what was promised and never fully delivered during the age of one-to-one marketing. It's the most efficient means of creating, saving, and building brands seen on this planet since the heyday of the age of mass marketing.

So, what's next?

It's the new age of engagement—the perfect time to gain a competitive advantage with Joseph Jaffe's new concept of conversational marketing. What you now can do as a marketer to get close to your customers is almost too good to be true. Maybe that's why so many marketers fail to take full advantage of a new era in which anything imaginable is doable.

The age of engagement arrived in earnest two years ago when we reached the halfway mark in bringing broadband access to Internet households. An incredible transformation in human behavior has followed in just 24 months! The numbers are mind-boggling. Tom Anderson, one of the founders of MySpace, has 190 million friends pitching their tents on his MySpace page. There are 43,000,000 unique visitors a month downloading or viewing the wild, wacky, and, at times, wonderful videos on YouTube. Virtual worlds for children, teens, and adults are popping up every week, with avatars cavorting in make-believe second and third lives. It's a time when the virtual and real worlds are coming together in every more surprising ways.

With more and more people getting engaged with one another by sharing mutual interests online, marketers eagerly seek to build their own face-to-face relationships. The long-standing separation between buyer and seller is replaced by the miracle of infinite shared space ready to be transformed into countless formats staking out common ground on the World Wide Web. To be a successful marketer in the age of engagement, there are four fundamentals to keep in mind:

1. The Internet is the center of the universe.
2. The experience is the brand differentiator.
3. The database is the primary marketplace.
4. The technology is the explosive ingredient.

We are living in a time populated by what jaffe identifies as the new "i" generation—a network of communities with no one in charge (forget all that nonsense about the consumer being in control). Jaffe tells us it's a generation that is not defined by age but rather by the mind-set of anyone currently in the first decade of life to the eighth decade, or the ninth decade and beyond. The "i" generation is "anyone young at heart, any person with a zest and zeal for life (after the 30-second spot), any human that feels empowered by the social side of the new media."

Each new period of marketing spawns its own gurus. They are the thinkers and leaders who help us make sense of all these astonishing changes taking place. My favorite guru of the age of engagement, arguable the most bewildering, rapid-fire turnaround ever seen by consumer and B-to-B marketers, is Joseph Jaffe. Like all true marketing gurus, Jaffe's insights and fervent beliefs grow out of his own personal immersion in almost every aspect of what is happening right now.

Thousands of marketers regularly click onto Jaffe's insightful, shoot-from-the-hip blog. One of the chapters in this book was written online by his linked-in Web friends. The podcasts jaffe makes available for downloading are great for listening while on the treadmill or out for an early morning jog. The inspirational in-house training provided to Fortune 100 clients is welcomed by traditionalists hungry to grasp the new realities.

Long before brand marketers discovered how to connect with the early adopters of the virtual world experience, Jaffe's avatar established the headquarters of his consulting group, *crayon*, on Second Life on the island of crayonville (www.crayonvillesecondlife.com). You can drop by any Thursday at 9:00 A.M. EST for the weekly get-together over virtual coffee at their open house.

Right now is the perfect moment for Joseph Jaffe to be sharing his keen insights and clear-eyed view into the workings of the new conversational marketing. If the book came out any sooner, the advertising establishment would still be in denial at the tried-and-true beliefs of twentieth-century marketing are crumbling rapidly. If we missed the publication date, a moment may have passed when you could be among the first to get your arms around what counts most in marketing today.

Bob Garfield, the must-read columnist in *Advertising Age*, recently told us in a front-page article that we are living in the post-advertising age. According to Garfield, "it's a post-apocalyptic media world substantially devoid of brand advertising as we have long known it." He has it right as far as the article goes but never tells us what advertising becomes once it no longer is what we have long known. Is there a new role for the 30-second commercial and its kid brother, the 15-second commercial, when getting connected is at the heart of the marketing process? You bet there is.

Brand advertising's role in the age of engagement is to take the viewer or reader by the hand and bring them to an amazing and memorable experience at a sticky web site. Getting across the brand positioning and opening up a deeply engaging experience are totally compatible goals.

As this book goes to press, there is nothing to indicate that the pace of change is about to slacken. Actually, the contrary is true. Mike Vehviläinen, chief operating officer at Nokia Siemens Networks, wants to know if we will be ready to connect with five billion people before too long. Yes, that's five billion. He points out, "Like the distant collision of two spiral galaxies, the Internet and the world's telecom networks are merging unstoppably . . . nearly all of us on this planet will always be in touch by 2015 through a broadband IP connection, the engine that enables the Internet to become the predominant platform connecting all those people."

How far along are you in mastering the new constellation of communications available to reach out to five billion people waiting for you in an interconnected world only 100 months away?

Read on. *Join the conversation.*

You may not agree with everything Joseph Jaffe has to say, but one thing is certain. You won't be bored and the positive consequences for your career could be substantial.

—Stan Rapp
Chairman, ENGAUGE Associates
www.engauge.com

# Preface

The revolution in marketing happening right now was summed up in two announcements at the 2007 AAAA media conference. First, Procter & Gamble's global chief marketing officer, Jim Stengel, declared the end of "telling and selling." Second, Microsoft's Mich Matthews announced that the global software and technology giant would be shifting significant ad dollars to digital media. Indeed, "we're actually pretty confident," Matthews said, "that by 2010 the majority of our media mix will shift to digital."

Of course, by 2010 the majority of TV will be digital too (and Microsoft certainly intends to remain a dominant player in the ubiquitous video space if Xbox, MSN, Windows Media Player, Windows Media Center, Vista, CE, and so on, are any indication), but don't let that take anything away from the enormity of the two announcements. Matthews was describing Microsoft's new marketing strategy called "the Era of Customer Participation" and the company's intention to shift from "informing, persuading, and reminding" to "demonstrating, involving, and empowering."

It's taken Microsoft and the rest of us only 2,000-odd years to come to the realization that open and honest conversation trumps communication each and every time. As Chapter 11 reveals, we can trace the art of great conversation back to Plato and Cicero. Perhaps people were listening then, but can corporations and brands start listening now? The purpose of this book is to explain how marketers can "join the conversation."

Madame de Staël, an intellectual and conversationalist of the French Ancien Régime, called conversation "a means of reciprocally and rapidly giving one another pleasure." But how much reciprocal pleasure is there in today's cluttered "marketing-place?" Contrast that arena to the bizarre bazaars of the past, where passionate crowds of buyers and sellers noisily fed on each other's intensity. Today there is noise all right, but it is an unbearable noise of one-way traffic . . .

and what happened to the crowds? The wise crowds have scattered, fragmented, and reappeared in the new digitally infused marketplace.

Your grandfather's communication is no longer the currency of this new marketplace; this marketplace takes place on a level playing field where all transactions are two-way. The billion-dollar question is this: How well will you fare in a game in which you no longer control the shots? In which the best-case scenario is to be invited to participate as an equal and the worst-case scenario is to be ignored or forgotten?

A critical principle of *cooperation in speaking* is not so much to get a point across but to find out what others think.[1] The English luminary Samuel Johnson defined conversation as "talk beyond that which is necessary to the purposes of actual business."

## THE FIREWORKS ANALOGY

Marketing today is like a giant fireworks display: The sky lights up with explosions of sounds and spectacular color. People gaze up and gasp in awe and amazement. They are enraptured—almost mesmerized—with the kind of performance that has them hypnotized with delight. And then, after the grand finale, the light dims; the sound fades; and there is . . . nothing. The sky is dark. The sky is black. The crickets are chirping.

That, ladies and gentlemen, is your typical marketing campaign. Pop and fizzle. Big bang followed by an anemic whimper. Zero follow-through. This is communication at both its best and worst. The bigger the explosion, the bigger the letdown when there is nothing to sustain the impact and maintain or even build on the momentum.

Conversation, by constrast, follows what I call the "short head" (as opposed to long tail). Irrespective of the size of the launch, it is

---

[1]A point illuminated by Penelope Brown and Steven Levinson in their 1987 "politeness theory"; for a discussion, see "Chattering Classes," *The Economist*, December 19, 2006.

what comes next that will define the potential, impact, and staying power of the idea and commensurate value proposition.

It reminds me of an old joke, where a husband comes home and finds his wife of 50+ years of marriage packing her bags. "Are we going on vacation?" he asks. "No," she replies. "Well, why then are you packing your bags?" he inquires. "I'm leaving you and heading to Vegas," she explains. "I heard that a woman can earn $250 a pop in exchange for selling her body." Suddenly, his frown is replaced with a broad smile. "Let me help you pack," he says. "Why the sudden change of heart?" she asks. "I want to see someone survive on $250 a year!" he exclaims.

It is time to determine whether you are in the one-trick-pony Fourth of July fireworks display business or in fact in the kind of relationship-building business that can endure even the occasional Vegas wobbly! The choice is yours. Read on and make your decision.

Consumers are no longer passive recipients, targets, empty vessels waiting to be filled with marketing messages, products, and services. They are connectors—nodes that connect the dots and enhance the conversation. As content creators, they are literally creating the world . . . a world in which you just need to find your place.

With the full spectrum of nontraditional and conversational approaches to harness, Microsoft and P&G are starting the inevitable voyage from communication to conversation. How about you?

In *Join the Conversation*, I'll take you into that new world where consumers and marketers can peacefully and productively coexist. I'll show you how much opportunity comes knocking on your door on a daily basis and how you can fine-tune your marketing efforts by listening first, responding second, and then—and only then—implementing or initiating your own marketing efforts.

Can a book be a conversation? This one already is. In addition to the typical case studies, insights, and examples of conversation you'll find in it, I've engaged the marketing community for input and contributions, from the book's cover design to Chapter 10, a unique community-powered chapter created and edited by interested parties. To my knowledge, no book has left an entire chapter up to—and in the hands of—its readers.

I also reached out to the more visually inclined to help design the jacket of this book. In the end—and after a communal vote—I went with an initiative called the "2000 bloggers" (more on that later), which essentially documented the world's most diverse mash-up of passion, perspective, and engagement. This was not only the face (2000 of them) of the conversation and with it the new influencers, but more importantly the faces of *your* customers.

You can join the conversation around this book via the book's web site (www.jointheconversation.us) or blog (www.jointheconversation.us/blog). In fact, you can become a co-author for the blog if you like by registering on the site. You can call 1-206-203-3255 and leave a message or ask a question which I'll answer on the next episode of my podcast, Jaffe Juice (www.jaffejuice.com). There's also a Facebook "Join the Conversation" group for you to join and connect with one another.

If a book can be a conversation, then why not your marketing? Read on, speak on, join in!

Finally, it is wholly conceivable that many companies mentioned in this book will no longer exist by the time you read this text (generally due to being swallowed up into the belly of a beast—for example YouTube and Google). I sure hope that is the case. At the end of the day, this book is about change, evolution, adaptation, and experimentation. How that could ever happen against a backdrop of status quo and stability would be beyond me.

In such cases, take the names as contextual signposts and look beyond the company toward the category or even the spirit of innovation as your directional guideline or benchmark.

# Acknowledgments

I'd like to thank my fellow *crayonistas*—most notably Aaron Greenberger, who assisted me on many book-related fronts—for their contributions and support along the way.

Again, my thanks to Richard Narramore at Wiley and the rest of the Wiley team for believing in me a second time and also for the numerous deadline extensions.

I am eternally grateful to each of the Chapter 10 wiki contributors, as well as to those who helped design the cover for the book. You all stepped up to the plate and made this particular conversation richer and more meaningful.

The wealth of data supplied would not be possible without my friends Jennifer McClure of the Society for New Communication Research and Tudor Williams of TWI Surveys Inc.

I'd also like to take this opportunity to acknowledge every single reader of and listener to my blog and podcast (formerly called Across the Sound), Jaffe Juice (www.jaffejuice.com). You are the wisest of crowds, and your feedback has made me smarter. Many of your thoughts are reflected in this book and are presented here irrespective of your status, title, or blog size, but only on the basis of the strength of your ideas.

Most importantly, I'd like to thank each of the 2,000 bloggers not just for helping with the book cover but for doing what you do and for being the faces, voices, hearts, and souls of the conversation.

Finally, once again, I'd like to thank my mom for anything and everything.

# 1

## Talking "At" Versus Talking "With"

In my first book, *Life After the 30-Second Spot*, I introduced a no-holds-barred hypothesis about the demise of traditional advertising—led by its poster child, the 30-second spot—and in its place the rise of non-traditional, emerging, alternative, or "new marketing" approaches.

Yet today, several years after that book was published, everything has changed and nothing has changed:

- The rate of change and innovation from within the marketing and communications industry is still less than the rate of change and innovation outside of it.
- The relative gap or disconnect between marketer (sender) and consumer (receiver) is widening.

I've had the pleasure of talking to scores of marketing professionals in countries from Singapore to South Africa, in cities from Antwerp to Ann Arbor, and at companies from Pioneer to Procter & Gamble.

The reaction is always the same. The consensus is always the same. The message is always the same.

With one exception . . . and to illustrate it I'll recount a conversation at a trendy boutique hotel in SoHo, New York, with an executive from an international communications holding company: "Hey, Jaffe . . . I gotta hand it to you, mate. You do a great job on-stage *performing* in front of a crowd, but I gotta ask you: Is it all an act (if so, it's bloody good), or do you really believe what you say?" I paused, thought for a moment, and then said, "It's not an act, and every day I believe it more and more."

In fact, the other day I asked a small group of senior marketing executives the following question: "How many of you in this room believe that advertising in five years will look anything like it looks today?" As you probably would guess, nary a hand was raised.

Ever heard of a five-year plan? What's yours? How are you planning and preparing for five years from now? What are you doing today in order to be ready for tomorrow? Are you more focused on updating your brand or updating your resume?

While we're at it, perhaps we should bring in not just advertising (media) for questioning, but indeed all of marketing communications—including the much more visible PR industry.

Today consumers view marketing and PR as the same and lump it all into the same bucket of manure.

And while we're on the subject, let me throw in one final quotation to help us understand our situation. It was the legendary advertising creative Lee Clow, grandfather of many of the dusty advertising campaigns in our Hall of Fame, who said:

---

**Ninety percent of advertising is crap.**

---

Seeing this quote again got me to thinking, and so I turned to my muses—my kids. Ever notice that if the smallest kid makes the smallest poop in the largest pool, we still drain the entire thing? Using Clow's guesstimate would mean that we're gleefully swimming (or expecting our consumers to swim) in a pool that is 90 percent polluted with irrelevant, insulting, unnecessary, and hyped communications.

And so, if the pool for attention, engagement, or connection is so muddied and murky, why are we not thinking about draining the pool or moving to a new one?

Because here's the thing. Our consumers are departing in droves to the cleaner, clearer, and more meaningful waters of "conversation."

At this point, let me define and very clearly separate the two spheres:

*Communication* is the very distinct process of marketer-generated or -initiated messaging, often without any concern or consideration for the intended recipient. Communication is one-way, unidirectional, and carefully controlled in its implementation.

*Conversation*, on the other hand, is a two-way dialogue or a stream of messaging between two or more parties with like-minded or shared beliefs, wants, needs, passions, or interests. Conversation is not initiated by any one person, side, or organization. It is organic, nonlinear, unpredictable, and natural.

---

Are you in the communication or conversation business? Join the conversation at www.jointheconversation.us/blog

---

## ISN'T CONVERSATION THE SAME AS WORD OF MOUTH?

No.

Next question.

Okay, you want some elaboration? Fine, then.

Word of mouth is an industry term for the fact that human beings have mouths and tend to use them. Go figure. Word of mouth is what humanoids do when they talk to other humanoids (and sometimes even web sites) about each other, as well as about products, brands, and services.

Word of mouth is neither artistic nor scientific. However inaccurate, emotional, personal, or misappropriated it may be, it is relatively authentic. And because of these authentic attributes, it tends to be a lot more believable. Perhaps because there is not much skin in the game other than genuinely wanting to help in some way, shape, or form.

Word of mouth is suddenly every marketer's wet dream because:

1. Mainstream marketing is failing.
2. Consumers have an exponentially enlarged palate of opportunities to converse and trade war and love stories, as well as share these stories with a "million of their closest strangers."
3. Marketers have newfound metrics to measure the prolific nature and extent of this chatter.

And along with everything pure and innocent come the bottom feeders who sadly attempt to manipulate, pervert, influence, and buy word-of-mouth opinions, recommendations, and exchanges.

Conversation, however, is so much bigger than just word-of-mouth recommendations for buying stuff. It is about life, love, laughter, sadness, frustration, nothing, everything, all of the above, and none of the above. It's about how "just doing it" changed my life as much as it's about how little Aaron (gratuitous plug of my son's name) scored the winning goal in his soccer game. (Oh, did I mention that Nike sponsors his team's jerseys?)

Conversation is so much bigger than word of mouth because it is all-encompassing, providing the bucket that collects everything from influence to recommendations; from viral referrals to idle banter; from random encounters to planned discussions; from publicity to, yes, marketing communications . . . and in all cases we're talking about a two-way street—and perhaps the difference between a web site and a blog, or a blog with comments turned on versus one with comments turned off.

## ISN'T CONVERSATION THE SAME AS BUZZ?

Now you got me going down the whole viral spiral. Viral marketing is the lazy marketer's guide to new marketing. In today's world, anything *good enough* is going to be viral—and by viral I mean whatever it is that people naturally want to talk about, share, and spread around. The problem is that marketers believe they can buy viral success and manufacture it, just like . . . the 30-second spot.

Buzz is even worse than formalizing and bastardizing word of mouth. Take the heinous Orville Redenbacher campaign, which was aptly dubbed "Orville DEADenbacher."[1] This creepy and disturbing reenactment from the grave generated buzz all right—*negative* buzz. According to brand sources, some 33 million PR impressions were allegedly generated based on this negative buzz. The agency creative director even dared to insinuate that this was exactly what they had planned all along and that future sales would justify this move.

[1]*Ad Age*, January 22, 2007.

I say, "Huh?" For starters, associating a decaying corpse with a product that is supposed to pride itself on "freshness" is a disconnect. Provoking consumers as a strategy seems almost as twisted. And even if sales moved in the right direction, is this a price worth paying? Is this the way we want to be breaking through the clutter? What next? Shooting gerbils out of cannons? Oh wait, that's been done before.[2] By the way, the agency in question subsequently lost the account. I hate to say, "I told you so," but I told you so.

Karl Long put together the following pretty good list of five rules and implications for measuring viral and social media:

1. *Number of views bare little relation to reach or impact of Viral Marketing*—this is one of the most important lessons in terms of understanding the mechanics and economics of conversation. The game of influence and authority is a *quality* game. For this reason, we need to focus on key conversations and their *bonviveurs*, as opposed to a blanket smothering of our message. Whereas the latter is nothing more than a cheaper substitute for the status quo, the former is a much more effective means of seeding a galvanizing idea amongst those who count.

2. *Success bares no relation to investment*—Following on from the previous point is the notion of "disproportionate and exponential lift and traction" from what is typically a much smaller investment. This should not be an invitation to justify the minimal commitment. Often times, success will lie somewhere between dipping your toes in the water and diving in head first. On the flip side, be prepared to liberally reward performance based on over-delivery.

3. *Viral Marketing does not have a timeline*—This book contains several examples that are by many standards old. They worked, and are *still* working.

4. *In social media, everyone is a critic*—This is a critical point and one which you're just going to have to come to terms with. You're

---

[2]In Outpost.com commercials. And in case you were wondering, the company doesn't exist anymore.

just never going to please everyone all the time, and your real test will be in how you deal with the critics and dissidents. In fact, I would go so far as to say that how you deal with this element of conversation might very well define you (your career) and your brand.

5. *Virals are unpredictable, so pay attention*—The tide can turn on a dime, and based on how closely you're monitoring and maintaining the conversation and dialogue respectively, will determine how well you cope with curve-balls, speed-bumps, and moments of truth. Exercise viral stewardship.[3]

## WHY CONVERSATION? WHY NOW? WHY NOT!

You just read a term in Karl Long's list that nowadays gets bandied about liberally—"social media." An interesting concept if you think about it—essentially an oxymoron. "Media" comes from the word "medium" . . . as in "middle" . . . as in stuck in the middle . . . as in an unnecessary layer that just adds complexity, ambiguity, and the kind of impersonal touch that says, "Your call is important to us. Your estimated wait time is 25 minutes."

Today the distribution and consumption of media are largely solitary and isolated experiences.

The traditionally famous water cooler has both literally and figuratively become a relic—an exhibit at the Natural History Museum (or perhaps the Museum of Television and Radio)—and been replaced with bottled water and bimodal conversation such as through integrated text messaging applications like Twitter, Jaiku, or Pownce.

Social networks such as Facebook, MySpace and LinkedIn have given rise to communal experiences; video sharing sites—led by YouTube (now owned by Google)—have demonstrated that consumption is best served in a crowd; blogs and podcasts are powered

---

[3]See "Five Implications for the Social Media Agency," at Karl Long's blog ExperienceCurve, http://blog.experiencecurve.com/archives/five-implications-for-the-social-media-agency-inspired-from-agencycom-youtube-pitch.

by a technology called Really Simple Syndication (RSS), which allows a thought, meme, or idea to be beamed instantaneously around the world with the click of a mouse; and virtual worlds like Second Life have joined together thousands of disparate islands by invisible bonds of uniformity. (And the teleporting thing doesn't exactly hurt it, either.)

Which brings us to the all-important question: *Can media be social?*

Media are ultimately vehicles through which to deliver communication (marketer-originated messages to unsuspecting targets). Social media, however, give targets the opportunity to turn the tables and set *their* sites on those who once called the shots. The hunters become the hunted.

There's no question that the very definition of "media" is changing (quickly). In fact, it may behoove us to abolish the term completely in favor of the more familiar term "content."

Be that as it may, whether or not you believe media can be social, and whether you prefer the term "media," "content," "storytelling," or another buzzword of the month, perhaps the real questions should be:

- Can brands participate in social media?
- Can brands be a part of the conversation?
- Can brands afford *not* to be a part of the conversation?

The landmark text *The Cluetrain Manifesto* posits that markets are conversations.[4] Literally. To illustrate this point, the authors take their readers back to the ancient bazaars of days of yore.

You can picture the scene right now, can't you? In a slice of life right out of Aladdin's time, the market is teaming with activity and life is bursting at the seams. You see agreement, disagreement, and shrieks of amazement and disbelief over the performances of fire-breathing jugglers and sleight-of-hand magicians. Everywhere there's negotiation, deal-making, haggling.

---

[4]See Christopher Locke, Rick Levine, Doc Searls, and David Weinberger, *The Cluetrain Manifesto: The End of Business as Usual* (Perseus Books, 2000).

Monty Python captured the patter in *Life of Brian*:

> BRIAN:
> How much? Quick.
>
> HARRY THE HAGGLER:
> Oh. Uh, twenty shekels.
>
> BRIAN:
> Right.
>
> HARRY THE HAGGLER:
> What?
>
> BRIAN:
> There you are.
>
> HARRY THE HAGGLER:
> Wait a minute.
>
> BRIAN:
> What?
>
> HARRY THE HAGGLER:
> Well, we're—we're supposed to haggle.
>
> BRIAN:
> No, no, no. I've got to get—
>
> HARRY THE HAGGLER:
> What do you mean, "no, no, no"?
>
> BRIAN:
> I haven't got time. I've got—
>
> HARRY THE HAGGLER:
> Well, give it back, then.
>
> BRIAN:
> All right. Do we have to?
>
> HARRY THE HAGGLER:
> Now, look. I want twenty for that.

BRIAN:

I—I just gave you twenty.

HARRY THE HAGGLER:

Now are you telling me that's not worth twenty shekels?

BRIAN:

No.

HARRY THE HAGGLER:

Look at it. Feel the quality. That's none of your goat.

BRIAN:

All right. I'll give you nineteen, then.

HARRY THE HAGGLER:

No, no, no. Come on. Do it properly.

BRIAN:

What?

HARRY THE HAGGLER:

Haggle properly. This isn't worth nineteen.

BRIAN:

Huh. All right. I'll give you ten.

HARRY THE HAGGLER:

That's more like it. Ten?! Are you trying to insult me?! Me, with a poor dying grandmother?! Ten?!

BRIAN:

All right. I'll give you eleven.

HARRY THE HAGGLER:

Now you're gettin' it. Eleven?! Did I hear you right?! Eleven?! This cost me twelve. You want to ruin me?!

In contrast, the only question asked in today's marketplace is: Where's the beef?

Markets are no longer conversations but cold, sterile, and largely lifeless shrines to the glory of "the brand." Today it seems like standard operating procedure to erect a pristine and over-the-top edifice (The Apple Store, Sony Style, NikeTown . . . I can't wait for Durexville), counterbalanced with an even more one-dimensional e-commerce counterpart, which is about as welcoming and warm as the Kazakhstan government's feelings toward Sacha Baron Cohen.

Customer service is either completely AWOL or painfully misinformed, aloof, and in some cases arrogant.

Quarterly results, Wall Street, and venture capital expectations have essentially poisoned what little humanity is left in the ability to engage with consumers in a meaningful, authentic, and considered way.

So cast yourself back to your now-scarred image of the bustling ancient bazaar. Today the bazaar is barren—automated, calculated, and not a whole lot of fun.

However (and this is a *big* however), don't you dare believe that there is no conversation going on at all. Au contraire. There are plenty of conversations going on . . . they're just not with you.

Today we have an organization called WOMMA—the Word of Mouth Marketing Association. On the one hand, it is laughable that there could be an official organization that formalizes the ultimate *informal* and natural form of communication. On the other hand, it is a sign of the times, especially if you look at the growth of this organization coupled with the upwardly mobile trajectory of word of mouth on *most* companies' priority lists. It also represents an overdue acknowledgment of the oldest confession in the book of selling: the vast superiority of conversation over communication.

Simple as that. Advertising is less credible, less influential, and less persuasive than Jane Smith from next door.

## CONVERSATION IS YOUR IMMUNITY IDOL

An Association of National Advertisers (ANA) study from 2004 revealed the three top priorities of CEOs:

1. Creating sustainable competitive differentiation and advantage
2. Maintaining corporate growth
3. Staying close to the company's customers

The same study revealed the top three priorities of chief marketing officers (CMOs), which were not only embarrassingly misaligned with the CEOs' agendas but also hopelessly antiquated and traditional. And they wonder why CMO's can't hold on to their jobs.

But I digress.

Let's go back for a moment to the priority of staying close to the company's customers. How exactly do you do that? Focus groups? Research? The occasional drive-by "Hey, how you doing?" in a randomly selected store? Whatever the norm or status quo is today, it's just not working. Case in point: A Burson-Marsteller study reveals that 129 CEOs changed mahogany desks in 2005 (a record), up from 57 in 2000 and 98 in 2004. (*Source:* Burson-Marseller, 2005 CEO Tracking Survey.) It's a domino effect from that point on—CEO churn leads to CMO burn, followed by agency turn.

Ultimately the buck starts beyond the client and even the board level—or perhaps that should be "bored" level. The status quo and relative stagnation translate into Wall Street woes, and in this day and age of transparency, accountability, and the relentless pursuit of differentiation, growth, and competitive advantage, stakeholders are impatient and unforgiving.

While "ROI or die" may be the rallying cry among corporations, there is a logical precursor to the ability to generate increased sales, satisfaction, and repeat patronage: empathy, emotional connectivity, relationship . . . in other words, conversation.

# 2

# The Many-to-Many Model

To understand where the world is going, perhaps we should take a couple of steps back to ascertain where we've come from and gain some much-needed context. (See Figure 2.1.)

## PHASE 1: ONE-TO-MANY (BLITZKRIEG)

This is the familiar spray-and-pray method, the command-and-control approach, or, as I recently coined it, the drag-and-drop. Mass marketing and media reign supreme in the one-to-many approach of marketers attempting to be all things to all people and ending up being nothing to nobody.

This shotgun method (also affectionately known as the Dick Cheney approach) originates from one central source and then distributes en masse. (In a bizarre and ironic twist, you might see some viral/influencer resonance, but don't get the two mixed up or confused just yet.)

As my doodle illustrates, the pellets of the shotgun disperse rapidly but hit only one of the targets while, in the process, maiming scores of disinterested innocent bystanders. Call it the collateral damage associated with the biz.

The rationale of those who still perpetuate this outmoded way of doing business might be something like: "My heart bleeds lumpy custard for you unappreciative brats. You're getting your content for free, so stop complaining."

One-to-many is an idea whose time came and subsequently went, and laziness is the only reason it remains prevalent today.

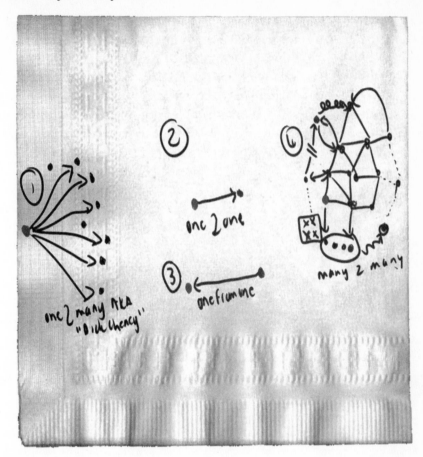

Figure 2.1   The Evolution of Marketing Communication

One-to-many assumes that it *is* possible to divide and categorize human beings into generalist buckets, using artificial variables such as age, sex (yes, please), occupation or education, and, to a lesser extent, attitudes, interests, and opinions.

Demographics and psychographics play their part but arguably are too simplistic for a world that is so deep, complex, and fragmented. I don't know about you, but I am just not going to put my future or my brand's future in a confident assertion that all 35-year-old women with a college education, 1.3 pets, 2.7 children, and a love of Oprah are created equal, nor am I going to contend even remotely that I understand her and what makes her tick. Heaven knows I struggle to figure out the one who married me!

At this point, if you work for a large advertising agency or get some kind of cocoa-bean high from guzzling M&Ms as you peer at other humans from behind a one-way mirror, you are probably fuming. Angrily waving your fist in the air, you may be cursing the upstart author who dares to challenge your grasp of the consumer you feel you know so well.

But do you? Do you really know your consumer? Do you know her name? Do you know what keeps her up at night and what gets her out of bed in the morning? When was the last time you actually talked with her? Or to ask the sort of questions raised in *this* book: Do you know what she is talking about, who she is talking about, and when she last spoke about *you*?

One last question: If you really know her so well, why do you insist on talking to her so impersonally and lumping her together with so many others who are so different from her?

Just askin', [insert your name here, customer #327658].


## PHASE 2: ONE-TO-ONE (FROM SHOTGUN TO RIFLE)

Don Peppers and Martha Rogers (both of whom I have seen in action) coined one of the most important evolutionary philosophies: one-to-one marketing. Arguably the entire CRM (Customer Relationship Management) field has some kind of root in the belief that a brand or company can be millions of different things to millions of different people.

Grounded in the reality that each and every one of us is different, one-to-one marketing utilizes these nuances, differences, and distinctions to present a more personal, valuable, and relevant message.

One-to-one is not without its problems, though, largely owing to the idea being a little ahead of its time, the investment in money and time being exorbitant, and the learning curve being a little too steep

. . . and oh yes, that laziness thing all over again. Too much data, too little time. . . .

But don't write one-to-one off just yet. It is making its comeback in a big way as the world becomes more accountable, the metrics more pronounced, and the implementation methodologies more succinct and deployable.

There isn't a pair of marketing eyes that doesn't light up at the prospect of being able to take the guesswork (see phase 1) out of attempts to go to market with a more efficient and effective solution.

## PHASE 3: ONE-FROM-ONE (MAKE LOVE, NOT WAR)

From a chronological and perhaps also evolutionary standpoint, next comes one-*from*-one: in this model, consumers are just as likely to initiate or drive the "communication" or the contact as the marketer.[1] In this reversal of roles, the sender becomes the receiver, and the receiver the sender. It is profound in that it completely turns the profession of marketing on its head and forces those in ivory towers to add an in-box to their already cluttered out-box.

In practical terms (if you haven't guessed already), this is *search* personified. Judging by the size of the search market right now, search is real . . . *very* real. Search has been called many things by many people. One term for it is "pull"-based marketing—or, in effect, permission-based marketing in that the consumer is in the driver's seat. This makes search—especially when coupled with a business model that has essentially built-in relevance and a performance-based compensation system as reward—an almost unbeatable proposition.

But search is just one small piece of the ever-growing puzzle (although Google would have you believe otherwise). For starters, search is oversimplified to a fault. It has no emotion, no richness,

---

[1]Attributed to G. M. O'Connell, founder of Interactive Agency, Modem Media.

no context, no depth. What-you-see-is-what-you-get only gets you so far.

There is life after the text link.

One-from-one could also be the story of one consumer telling another consumer about a product, or conveying one message, which then gets picked up by an army of Davids (Glenn Reynolds, Nelson Current) and spreads from there.

One-from-one could be the story of Vincent Ferrari, who had an unsatisfactory experience (a euphemism along the lines of Hurricane Katrina being a pesky wind) with the customer service folk over at AOL. Vincent tried at length and in vain to cancel his AOL ISP service, but unlike so many others who had gone down the same painful path of sucky service, he recorded the conversation and posted it on his blog, "insignificant thoughts" (as if!).

His post accumulated "Diggs" (3,162 times), and Vincent became an overnight press sensation. He was interviewed on NBC, and the video was uploaded to YouTube. Even the *New York Times* got in on the act (*Gee, I wonder what would happen if I tried to cancel my* New York Times *subscription, assuming I had one*). Finally, AOL apologized, but it was too little, too late. . . .

One disgruntled consumer. One customer service representative. One major headache (okay, migraine) for AOL.


## PHASE 4: MANY-TO-MANY (BURN YOUR BRAS)

The truth is that Vincent's experience is part of the many-to-many model, which is really the central premise of this book. No start. No end. No sender. No receiver. Just fluidity. Continuity. Subconversations amid webs of larger conversations. Multiple shape-shifting roles, with today's sender becoming tomorrow's receiver, this morning's influencer this afternoon's influenced.

In the many-to-many model, Vincent—the protagonist—plays his role as a catalyst by exploding an ordinary (unfortunately) experience with a lousy service provider and, in doing so, doesn't simply expose the obvious but allows dozens of others just like him to nod their heads in vociferous agreement and take action.

Is it any coincidence that Vincent's 15 streams of fame (June 21, 2006) and AOL's announcement that it would be phasing out the paid ISP revenue stream (August 2, 2006) were so close together? Let the conspiracy theories continue. . . .

Or perhaps Vincent was not the catalyst at all. After all (with apologies to Vincent), he was a nobody before and a nobody afterwards. Perhaps his blog was the catalyst, or perhaps his *Today Show* interview served as the accelerant—after it was posted on YouTube and other video-sharing web sites and received over 750,000 views.

The many-to-many model is like mercury, which peacefully coexists in the three separate states of solid, liquid, and gas across a sea of fragmented globules that can become a pulsing mass of *quicksilver* in a split second.

In Vincent's case, he was the solid—together with his first-person account of his story on his blog—to his social network (one pixel of separation) and in his first-person interviews. The links and trackbacks[2] to his blogs were the liquid, as was the ensuing conversation that directly followed the actual event. The gas was the aftertaste that blended into the environment and stuck around for a long, long time.

If you go to Google today and type in "AOL account," two of the top three results are about canceling the account. Or how about "AOL customer service"? That search reveals that out of 4,210,000 hits, the top result is the story of . . . you guessed it: Vincent Ferrari.

In the many-to-many model, there is no dominant player, but there are influencers. Malcolm Gladwell would call them connectors. When they sink their teeth into a juicy piece of meat, they don't let go.

Take Jim Dubois and Ethan Chandler, the two alleged employees of Bank of America who got so psyched up at a company

---

[2]See Wikipedia for a definition of "trackback" (http://en.wikipedia.org/wiki/Trackback).

The International Association of Nobodies was formed after a main-stream media editor by the name of David Murray called out a blogger by the name of Alan Jenkins.*

"One day I was reading his stupidly named blog, 'Desirable Roasted Coffee.' I read his blog a lot, *despite the fact that Jenkins is pretty much a nobody in the communication business*. I read it because he's smart and unpredictable and rude sometimes. I like it when he's rude. In a vaguely kinky way, I even like it when Jenkins is rude to me."

Nobody Jenkins, together with Nobody Eric Eggertson and a cast of countless others, got together to form a community of interest to cele-brate their *un*-noteworthy *un*-status.

While each member of IAN is most certainly a somebody to the other members and a prominent participant in the ongoing conversa-tion, it is an ironic role reversal that Murray, in effect, *is invisible to the online world*. Makes you wonder how an important somebody can look so much like a nobody online.†

The International Association of Nobodies

*See "I'm Nobody ... Who Are You," http://allanjenkins.typepad.com/nobody/.

†A point eloquently articulated by Eric Eggertson at Mutually Inclusive PR, http://mutually-inclusive.typepad.com/weblog/2006/04/im_a_nobody_in_.html.

off-site about the merger between Bank of America and MBNA that they felt the urge to butcher the living daylights out of U2's "One," much to the shock and awe of their fellow balding colleagues.

*It is even better*
*Now that we're the same*
*Two great companies come together*
*Now MBNA is B of A.*

*And it's one bank*
*One card*
*One name that's known all over the world*
*One spirit*
*We get to share it*
*Leading us all to higher staaaaaaaaaaaandards Oh OHHH*
*UMMMMMMM.*

*Have you come to meet Bruce Evans?*
*Have you come to meet Liam McGee?*
*Have you heard about Michelle Shepard?*
*She's leading the team in the Northeast.*

*And we've got Bank One*
*On the run.*
*What's in your wallet?*
*It's not Capital One.*

*One bank*
*Working every day*
*To bring higher standards, higher standards . . .*
*OOONNNNEEE OONNEEE YEAHHH.*
*We are OONNEEE bank.*

When I found out about this, I posted quickly and decisively, imploring my readers to help get these two *American Idol* or *Pop Idol* wannabes on TV. I also podcasted a karaoke tribute to this song! (Masochists proceed to www.jointheconversation.us/one.) What followed was a litany of press coverage, countless spoofs, and, yes, even a token cease-and-desist from Universal Music.

By the way, did you know BofA and MBNA merged? Many didn't until they joined *this* conversation.

Some contended that this was a viral marketing exercise. For argument's sake, what if Dubois and Chandler were indeed staging a ruse? If so, it could very well have backfired—the comments that made their way to the blogs, the YouTube videos, and so on, were largely negative, echoing the poor customer service and cultish insider Kool-Aid overdose that plagues the banking industry.

Either way, who cares? People were talking about Bank of America. Can you remember one of its television commercials? Nope. Invisible advertising.

I am in fact a Bank of America customer, and I wonder now if I will love them more or love them less—maybe not because of what happened, but because of what didn't happen. There was no Bank of America response. No fight-back. No B-side follow-up. No *Pop Idol* auditions for the dynamic duo. No self-deprecating acknowledgment that maybe—just maybe—could have added a little bit of humanity to an industry fundamentally devoid of life.

Kodak took a healthy dose of self-deprecating medicine with its video *Winds of Change*. The feedback and buzz was overwhelmingly positive. You can view this video by visiting www.jointheconversation .us/windsofchange

And if you work for any of the other banks, don't think you're off the hook. Where the hell were you in this story? Nowhere. You just sat on the sidelines like the spectators you are, either pointing fingers and laughing in ridicule or letting your lawyers frantically deploy your employee-spying software to check whether any rogue cover versions of "Imagine" by John Lennon were circulating on your intranet talking about paperless billing, zero-fee checking accounts, and rewarding affinity programs (very, very, very rewarding).

"Oh, it's off-brand," you say. "It doesn't fit the brand persona. It gives off the impression that we don't take banking seriously, and the last thing we would want is for our customers to lose faith in us and actually think of us as human beings instead of cold, faceless number-crunchers."

You—one and all—are setting yourselves up beautifully for what Virgin did to the airline industry.

And what about the Vincent Ferrari incident? Same thing. Nada from AOL. Squat from all of the ISPs (assuming there are any left out there).

Or how about Kevin McCormick?

Kevin is an ordinary guy (a consumer, if you will) who realized an extraordinary accomplishment in the form of a web site called Dress Kevin (www.dresskevin.com) and a succinct and simple tagline, "I didn't know what to wear, so I made a web site." (See Figure 2.2.) Indeed. A web site that has been featured on CNN, *Good Morning America*, and the CBS *Early Show*!

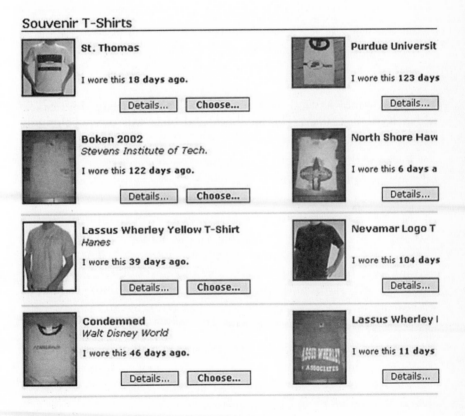

Figure 2.2    Screenshot from Dress Kevin

Kevin put a web site together based on the simple insight that he—like millions of other clueless males (especially the ones without wives and/or taste)—wasn't all that good at the tough decisions in life, like, you know, dressing to impress and dressing for success.

So, long story short, every day he turns to a community to make the decision for him, and he wears the clothes that have been selected for him.

Once again, where were the brands? Gap? Banana Republic? J Crew? Hell, even the casino Golden Palace, which advertises on boxers' backs and pregnant bellies? At a time when spontaneous and opportunistic trumps linear and predictable every time, it is this kind of 15 minutes of fame that can give brands the staying power they need to stay above the fold.

---

You can listen to my podcast interview with Kevin at www.jointhe conversation.us/kevinmccormick

---

Kevin could have given far more back to Gap than Joss Stone or any of the other celebrity endorsers the clothing retailer has leaned on for way too long.

Perhaps the "Bank of Opportunity" could have learned a thing or two from the folks over at Onitsuka Tiger, manufacturers of the Injector DX Football Shoe.

In this very cute effort, 22 actual head office employees who actually manufacture the shoe shared their love for football and karaoke with a truly forgettable ode to the brand. Their music-making is a little shaky, but that's the point—consumers could challenge the choir with their own version of the track. Simon Cowell might not have been amused, but Onitsuka Tiger's customers sure were. (See Figure 2.3.)

You are going to see an irrepressibly strong common theme throughout this book that runs along these lines: *There's a series of endlessly rich, dynamic, gratifying, robust, authentic, and meaningful conversations going on out there. Isn't it time you joined in?*

Figure 2.3    Screenshot from Onitsuka Lovely Football

## THE POWER OF ONE HUMAN VERSUS THE IMPOTENCE OF A FACELESS CORPORATION

Persuasion is overrated. At least in advertising. Duping consumers with promises of sex, drugs, and rock 'n' roll is just not what it used to be. We've never met that smiling cashier at McDonald's, empathetic flight attendant on a United flight, or caring adviser at Citi. We've never encountered the black silhouettes against multicolored backgrounds selling iPods, run into fairies hawking General Motors cars, or stumbled upon the repository of beautiful people who seem to hang out exclusively at Target (as spoofed on NBC's *Saturday Night Live*).

There's got to be something else. There's got to be something more. Surely additional forces are in play that persuade and convince with assurance, conviction, and experience. There are. One such force is called Dan. Dan the Man. Dan the dude in IT who knows his stuff when it comes to PCs. He's the guy who told you

not to buy Sony (unless of course you like using your laptop as a barbecue).[3] There's Jeff (Jarvis), the snarky blogger on Buzz Machine
(www.buzzmachine.com) who went on a personal rampage against
Dell, and his self-branded "Dell Hell" haunts the beleaguered elec-
tronics company to this day. There's Adam Curry, the "podfather"
who convinced this author to fly Virgin upper-class. (PS: Make sure
you ask for an espresso or latte, which are made to order.)

Where does advertising figure in this story? Nowhere. It is less
than visible. It is invisible. Forget necessary or unnecessary evil. It
doesn't even exist in a world where conversation prevails and marketing fails.

And make no mistake—the aforementioned brands spend millions upon millions of dollars to interrupt, disrupt, intervene, and intercede on the off chance that you're in the mood to buy.

Quite sad really, but not utterly hopeless. No one (least of all
me) ever said that marketing has no place in the equation. It does.

---

[3]In 2006, stories circulated quickly about a massive recall of defective Sony laptop batteries
that were responsible for several computer models—including Apple, Sony, and Dell—bursting
into flames.

# 3

# Can Marketing Be a Conversation?

In *Life After the 30-Second Spot*, I took a pretty tough position on the beleaguered television commercial as a pretty inclusive metaphor for a certain way of doing business. As time continued, I distanced myself further and further away from advertising—all advertising. I began to set my sights on "interactive—the new traditional," with its cacophony of cheap imitations and neutered attempts to replicate the broadcast model on the homepages of your typical portal like Yahoo! The 2007 departures of CEO Terry Semel and Chief Sales Officer Wenda Harris Millard—and the demise of advertising seems conveniently related, do they not?

Then there are the latest attempts from the lemminglike industry which add up to a hodgepodge of misses. Most are ill-advised efforts to embrace new marketing, either in some kind of diminished or hedged fashion or, worse, with a completely retro-massed approach.

Some brands have attempted, for example, to retrofit new marketing within the confines of the 30-second spot: MasterCard asks its viewers to complete the commercial or fill in the blanks (more on that later). Others have challenged consumers to create their own 30-second spots, the best of which would run on the Super Bowl or Academy Awards broadcasts.

Then there are those sinners like Wal-Mart, Sony, and McDonald's that do the opposite—instead of cramming new marketing into old marketing, they take the worst of old marketing and attempt to deceive their way through new marketing with fake blogs (a.k.a. flogs or frogs).

Finally, a burgeoning cacophony of new thinkers are taking one step back for every two steps forward as they explore nontraditional opportunities but fall short when it counts. Starwood launched its new "aloft" hotel in the virtual world of Second Life, but failed to sustain it. This was a classic case of communication versus conversation (more on that later).

Not all of these attempts were necessarily misguided, but for better or worse, Consumer Nation lumps them all together, anyway.

With each of these examples—all of which will be covered in greater depth throughout the pages of this book—we're seeing fairly incremental revisions (some larger than others) of otherwise traditional, mainstream, or predictable approaches that all begin in "communication" and proceed from there.

At best, they are examples of starting a conversation.

At face value, they are examples of forcing a conversation.

At worst, they are examples of faking a conversation.

Back to my hit list: From 30-second spots to advertising to "traditional interactive" to half-pregnant new marketing, there's one more fateful step on the downward ladder to hell—marketing itself.

In October 2006, I launched a company called *crayon* dedicated to new marketing—to conversation and transformation *above* communication. When we launched the company from within the virtual world called Second Life (you can view photographs, audio transcripts, and a video montage at www.jointheconversation.us/crayoninsecondlife), we encountered a degree of resistance from the installed residents because of our marketing association.

Second Life is a microcosm (think snow globe meets crystal ball) of what has come and what is yet to come in the changing marketing and media space. The experience with Second Life made me realize that all of marketing is arguably under attack. The pressure is not confined to advertising or media but is being applied to anything that bears the mark of the devil.


## ROI: THE NEW 666?

We're living in direct marketing hell. Wall Street has taken over from the money-thirsty venture capitalists of dot-com days. CFOs, purchasing, and procurement have confused the hell out of marketing folk, who have had to go from completely unaccountable to completely accountable.

It makes for a pretty volatile cocktail. More like a Molotov cocktail, if you ask me.

Make no mistake: Return on investment is no less important than the power of the clichéd "big idea," but by that I mean, when *wasn't* it important? When wasn't the primary and overriding goal of marketing to make money? When last I checked, corporations were not in the charity business (although increasingly they should be).

My point is that we're now so confused and befuddled by the need to justify our efforts that we've become a little desperate. We are that guy who walks into the bar and proposes to the first woman he comes in contact with that they go back to "his place" for a "good time." We are also the guy who wakes up the next day with an ice pack on his groin.

Marketing used to be an art. Today it is a science. The only problem is that science doesn't exactly do well with the kind of chemistry that deals with intangibles, emotions, illogical drivers, and fallibility . . . in other words, humanity.

Today marketing is a red flag that consumers see a mile away, and its predictable approach is like Homer reaching out to touch an electrified doughnut. Marketing's "buy now or else (I'm going to be fired)" pleas are falling on deaf ears. There are just too many viable alternatives for consumers to give a damn anymore.

Marketing is no longer any fun. Consumers aren't digging it — unless of course they "Digg" it (www.digg.com), in which case it's probably in a disparaging way. Those trapped within the walls of the industry are having even less fun.

Perhaps the problem all along has been that marketing is too intently focused on communication, but not enough (or even at all) on conversation.

Marketing simply has to evolve. But is it realistic to think that it can become part of the conversation? Of course it can. Dove's Campaign for Real Beauty is the perfect example of how a brand became a conversation and how a bar of soap became a badge of pride.

Or how about HSBC's Your Point of View campaign, which asks: "Who knows what you'll see when you see someone else's point of view?" (See Figure 3.1.)

HSBC's Your Point of View campaign (www.yourpointofview .com) was not only on-strategy, it was also on-conversation. According to its web site, "We at HSBC, the world's local bank, strongly believe in the potential of difference. In a world of increasing sameness, we believe it's important to value different points of view and there should be somewhere everyone can air these views and see the views of others." Bravo.

And while HSBC's ubiquitous advertising (see below) teed up the idea, it was the web site that really activated the means for people to come together and celebrate diversity of opinion. In other words: discussion. It also brought HSBC's tagline to life, reflecting the global melting pot of perspective through a very personal and local lens.

Today, for example, the topic du jour is global warming: Leaves you cold or gets you hot under the collar?

As Linda Richman, the colorful host of "Coffee Talk" on *Satur-*

Figure 3.1   HSBC's Your Point of View

*day Night Live* (played by Mike Myers), would have said: "Rhode Island is neither a road nor an island. Discuss."

Conversation, which couldn't be more necessary today, points up a very important distinction between old marketing and new marketing. Whereas the former puts the brand on a pedestal and expects consumers to worship it, covet it, aspire to it, and ultimately take a subservient position to it, the latter asserts the opposite: that the brand must fit into consumers' lives. Expressed differently, brands need to bring value to the table that *exceeds* the utility associated with simply purchasing and consuming the said good or service.

Fred Reichheld—author of "The Ultimate Question"—devised the Net Promoter Score (I'm a big fan) to answer one simple question: *How likely are you to recommend company X to someone else?* On a scale of 0 to 10, only a score of 9 or 10 would be classified as a "promoter" and termed good enough. Using the same succinct methodology as a muse, consider the reasons you would recommend (or not recommend) a company:

- Admiration
- Trust
- Respect
- Authority
- Credibility
- Likability
- Affection
- Charisma

## VOLUNTARY TIME SPENT (VTS)

As I'll discuss in more detail later, not all conversation is good conversation, especially when it comes from a blabbermouth, an ignoramus, an arrogant SOB, or a disreputable source.

If there's one anecdotal common thread that runs through the entire marketing ether, it's "time spent." A central hypothesis of mine is that the more time consumers *voluntarily* elect to spend with a "brand," the more likely they are to be favorably predisposed toward that brand, and hence the more likely they are to purchase that brand, recommend that brand, or both.

Marketing has a very real role to play in the ability to engage consumers, be engaged by consumers, be discovered by consumers, surprise consumers, and participate in consumers' lives—even make their lives better. Toward the middle of 2007, Delta emerged from Chapter 11 and quickly fell into the obvious trap of crowing at the top of its lungs about how it was changing. Its 30-second spot showed video units at the back of each seat, and yet when I flew back from Orlando a few months after this spot broke (in business class, no less), I found myself staring into nothingness.

My challenge to Delta was simple: Instead of talking about changing, how about proving it?

*On the same day of my post*, a Delta "Twitter" account mysteriously appeared updating people on some of the changes being made at Delta.

But what made this so surreal was that the voice was not in brand-speak or corporatese. It was distinctively human.

Here are some examples:

- *playing around with this twitter thing 12:43 AM May 10, 2007 from web*

The voice was certainly informed:

- *@Blephen—been trying to make the employees happier, too. Gave out bonuses and part-ownership in the company: http://tinyurl.com/28ddae about 18 hours ago from web*
- *revamped the award ticket system for you SkyMiles members recently: http://www.delta.com/awardt . . . —you can shop around, calendar-style about 18 hours ago from web*

It even responded to other people:

- *@stevegarfield—enjoy your flight! about 18 hours ago from web in reply to stevegarfield*

- *@arielwaldman — sorry about your troubles with United. The industry is broken. We're working hard to fix it — better employee training, etc. about 21 hours ago from web in reply to arielwaldman*

It had charm:

- *@bloggersblog — a busy airline never sleeps ;) about 22 hours ago from web in reply to bloggersblog*
- *@chrispirillo: what makes you so surprised? :) 01:55 AM May 10, 2007 from web in reply to chrispirillo*

It cared:

- *Reading ideas at http://delta.com/change (been working hard on the next version of the site) 12:38 AM May 10, 2007 from web*
- *thinking about how to reduce your time spent at JFK: http://tinyurl .com/ywr3o5 about 20 hours ago from web*

Here was the thing. It was not an official voice. How could it be? Which faceless corporations or brands would ever show such humanity? If anything, this was 100 percent rogue.

So now the real questions:

1. Who did the voice belong to?
2. Did its unofficial status make it a *fake* voice or anything but?
3. Was it sanctioned by Delta? It could very well be a purposeful unofficial voice. After all, humans can say many things corporations (or brands, for that matter) can't.
4. Was this (or should this be considered as) the voice of the brand? Was it speaking as an official agent of the company? And if not, did it even matter?
5. What would become of the voice?

I have some hunches as to answers 1, 2, 3, and 5 — after all, I had been in confidential e-mail conversation with the voice — but I think the real conversation was in question 4.

This was one of those very clear — even seminal — moments in marketing that reflected a clear departure from the norm and status quo. It was a *big* story, with even *bigger* implications for all of marketing and its future.

Marketing and conversation might be oil and water *today*, but soon they could become very willing bedfellows . . . with ground rules, parameters, and terms of engagement that govern, respect, and manage the expectations of both parties.

# 4

# The Birth of Generation i

The consumer is in control. The consumer is in control. The consumer is in control. It's like a broken record. Worse still, it's like a broken record being used as slow and painful torture.

Here's a thought. Marketers are not in control. Consumers are not in control. No one is in control.

That's the whole point.

In a new marketing world, where *conversation trumps communication*, there is no hegemony, only partnership.

Take the so-called empowered consumer (and for purposes of this exercise, why don't you think of yourself as one of those targets who purchase on-command). I don't know about you, but I'm not sure I remember the last time I returned home from a long day at the office and flexed my empowerment muscles, stared at my in-control self in the mirror, and roared in triumph. (Okay, it was last week, but for an entirely different reason.)

Actually, what we tend to do is flop onto the couch and watch a bit of television—a DVD or a prerecorded show—visit a few entertainment-based web sites, play a game or hop into Second Life, or just read a book.

Other than the fact that we have freedom of choice, more choice than ever before, and more opportunities to skip ads, are we really "in control"? Are we really "empowered"?

Make no mistake: Consumers have changed irrevocably, and one of the major and most significant symptoms of this change is the zero tolerance that consumers have for bad advertising, subversive PR plots, manipulative marketing, and unforgivably bad customer service.

Even if it were true, ceding control from one extreme (us) to the other (them) is not only unrealistic but also a cop-out and a big fat lie. In fact, the next time you hear someone utter the phrase "the consumer's in control," I want you to stand up and shout out, "Joseph Jaffe told me to tell you that you're a big fat liar"—and you won't be far wrong, since this person is most likely uttering this phrase as a buzzword du jour and has no plans for any follow-through whatsoever on the back end.

## CONTROLLING THE CONVERSATION IS JUST A FANCY WAY OF DISGUISING A MONOLOGUE

The problem is that we may concede that consumers are in control, and yet we continue to send them messages in a controlled, detached, and disconnected fashion.

## THE BIRTH OF GENERATION i

That's just not going to work with Generation i—as in "I," as in "me." This is the generation that actually has nothing to do with age but is all about mind-set. With a hat tip to Apple's i-suite—iPhoto, iPod, iTunes, iMovie, iLife, iPhone®—for inspiration, Generation i is all about "what have you done for me lately?"

Generation i is not who you think. It's not just the youngsters anymore, the geeks, the game-playing kids ... actually it *is* the game-playing kids, but "game-playing" refers to the virtual world, Second Life, where the average age is 33,[1] and "kids" refers to anyone young at heart, any person with a zest and zeal for life (after the 30-second spot), any human who gets the social side of media.

Generation i is not defined by a demographic or by a psychographic. Members of this group are not square pegs who fit neatly into square holes. They are not easily understood and classified by generalization, oversimplification, or averaging.

Let me emphasize this point in different words: If you attempt to "reach, connect, and effect" Generation i through conventional de-

---

[1]According to Linden Labs, the maker of Second Life (January 2007).

mographic, psychographic, or other syndicated tools designed to make your life easier, you will surely fail.

Witness the composite face of Generation i, a magnificent mash-up of fragmented passions unified by shared ideals that you'll never understand unless you are a part of the mosaic yourselves. (See Figure 4.1.) Generation i is a way of life, an attitude, an outward

Figure 4.1    A Mosaic Mash-Up of Me with a Close-Up of My Most Important Organ

face to the inner workings of the many-to-many model in flawless action.

Even though this makes me look like a Vulcan, for illustration purposes I decided to enlarge the most important part of the picture—my ear (which even sized normally is larger than most).

## THERE IS AN "I" IN NEW MEDIA

George Orwell warned against media as early as 1946 with a criticism of radio: "The music prevents the conversation from becoming serious or even coherent."[2] The same backlash was leveled at television when it began its crusade at converting every last one of us into an accomplished couch potato. Fast-forward to the American essayist Stephen Miller, who published a book in 2006, entitled *Conversation: A History of a Declining Art*, in which he lamented the role of computers and MP3 players in preventing real conversation.

If Orwell were alive today, my feeling is that he'd take Miller to task and challenge him on the assertion that the digital revolution is not a profoundly interconnected labyrinth of networked relationships. I believe that Orwell would have been a prolific blogger and podcaster and, at the very minimum, would have had a Twitter account, a Facebook Profile, and a Second Life avatar.

I'll concede that I might be a tad liberal here in toying with George's legacy, but my point is this: There is a world of difference between media and new media. Whereas the former continue to push the boundaries of solitary confinement, the latter shrink and flatten the world and make it a global village inhabited by myriad i-individuals who function as a coherent and like-minded community.

---

[2]Quoted in "Chattering Classes," *The Economist*, December 19, 2006.

## "I" AS IN INCREDIBLE

Generation i is less about control and empowerment and more about communal connectedness and consciousness. It is about extraordinary collective achievement by virtue of the contributions of ordinary individuals (the "wisdom of crowds"). And its corollary is equally true: The ordinary individual is able to realize extraordinary aspirations by virtue of the collective (the "long tail").

Take Jeff Jarvis, for example. An ordinary man by normal standards, today Jarvis is an influential and highly respected authority. The primary reason for this influence is his blog, Buzz Machine (www.buzzmachine.com), which has over 3,285 other blogs linking to it, many of which have hundreds (and some thousands) of *other* blogs linking to them. Don't get me wrong—I'm not diminishing or marginalizing Jarvis's talent in any way. All I'm saying is that without the 3,285 odd blogs linking to him, Jarvis is nothing more than a hothead—all ranted up and nowhere to rave.

## YOU ARE THE COMMUNITY YOU KEEP

Jarvis is only as strong as his weakest link. However, unlike a chain, he is most certainly not an equal link but rather a central cog, around which a rather intricate and beautiful conversation is occurring.

Jarvis is a type of "prosumer"—a "producing consumer" and proof that today's "empowered and in control" consumer is really nothing new. All we need to do is go back to 1980, when futurist Alvin Toffler, envisioning a time when ordinary consumers would become producers themselves, coined the term. Little did he know that this particular prediction would not only come true but indeed shake the very foundations of business and brand building, communications, creativity, control, and trust.

Jarvis is a conversation starter, a conversation catalyst, a conversation moderator, and a conversation conduit. Why the hell can't brands do and be the same? Is it because Jarvis is a human being and brands are inanimate/inhuman? (A heresy or hypocrisy, if true, given all the investment in babies, bunnies, and puppies designed to personify brands and bring them to life.) Is it because Jarvis is honest and brands are not? Is it because Jarvis is about as politically correct as Michael Richards, Don Imus, and Mel Gibson at a UNICEF convention?

Generation i and its subset, the prosumers, are rewriting the rules of persuasion, and the marketing communication business—if anything—is *all* about persuasion. Generation i is also helping us understand more about what it will require to connect and resonate with a new creative class who, for the most part, are disinterested in the wares we're peddling. They're still eating, sleeping, flying, renting, driving, investing, cleaning, hosting, medicating, and entertaining . . . only the way they get to the point where they're armed with the goods and services they need to go on their merry way is fundamentally different compared to 50, 20, 10, or even 5 years ago.

The prosumers help us understand phenomena like consumer-generated content, blogs, podcasting, social networking, wikis, and so on. And it is *only* by understanding both generation i and its prosumer class that we will ever be able to figure out what to do next.

## CGC DOES NOT EQUAL DMJ4M

When I typed "Chevy Tahoe" into Google recently, the third result was the following: "Chevy's 'Make Your Own Tahoe Commercial' idea not exactly going as planned." I clicked and arrived at a post dated March 31, 2006.

> As part of a creative new ad campaign for the new Tahoe, General Motors has teamed up with Donald Trump's "The Apprentice" franchise to create a website that allows prospectives to make their own commercials online. The website allows readers to select backgrounds, video shots, and input text in an attempt to win prizes ranging from a Jackson Hole Getaway to a trip to the Major League Baseball All-Star Game.

Rather predictably, certain surfers had been using the spot-building web site for purposes that didn't exactly put Chevrolet's newest vehicle in the best light. Unfortunately, GM's webmeisters appeared to be asleep at the wheel, in terms of reorganizing and responding to this glut of consumer-generated content.

This was the product of Chevy Tahoe's infamous Do My Job For Me (DMJ4M) campaign, which clunkily attempted to justify the alleged seven-figure overinvestment in the glorified product placementalooza that was *The Apprentice*. Instead of truly partnering with its consumer/customer base, Chevy created an artificial and forced environment where it hoped people would create tens of thousands of Chevy ads that reflected the typical suburban soccer mom returning from her grocery shopping while driving on some snowy arctic tundra.

The consumer-generated content (CGC) they got instead was hundreds of neutral to negative ads that ran along the lines of:

Forget Iraq's missing weapons—here's the real weapon of mass destruction, killing an extra 1,000 smaller-vehicle occupants bicyclists and pedestrians annually. Way to go, Chevrolet.

This SUV gets 12 miles to the gallon, releases tons of carbon every year that'll stay in the atmosphere for 100 years. Temperatures are rising, polar icecaps are melting, growing food is getting harder, violent storms are increasing, global warming is happening now. What will you tell your kids you drove?

Okay, the second one was created by Al Gore, but don't tell me that one commercial by *one* prosumer doesn't hold a lot more sway than any 30-second spot you've ever seen.

Ironically, the prosumer-created commercials were everything that modern-day communications are not: honest. Perhaps that is why they resonated so strongly.

Chevy was really powerless to do anything about the sea of negative commercials. The carmaker was damned either way, and whether it wielded the long arm of the law, talked to the hand, or gave its customers the middle finger, it was in somewhat of a

helpless situation. Some people believe that Chevy was still insulated by the fact that the people who are aggressively anti-SUV and
the people who are most likely to buy or lease an SUV are mutually
exclusive. I believe that ignoring the conversation (see Chapter 13)
is an incredibly risky strategy.

But let's take a step back and do some clear context-setting: Exactly what are prosumers, and how do they differ from consumers?
While we're at it, how do they and the overarching Generation i
help us understand the changing landscape? And how can conversation help us understand, cope with, and ultimately partner with
that changing world . . . to win?

# 5

# The Rise of the Prosumer

The root "-sumer" by itself means nothing in particular (with apologies to the Uniform Medical Expense Reporting System and Uma Thurman), and yet it got a bad rap when it acquired a big "cons" in front of it. Silliness aside, I feel compelled to acknowledge the trees that were felled in order for me to spend a few pages on a debate that may seem trivial to some but I assure you is not.

There are those who feel it is time to retire the term "consumer," which means little more to most people than a person who consumes — or as Jerry Michalski put it (as quoted in *The Cluetrain Manifesto*), "a gullet whose only purpose in life is to gulp products and crap cash."[1] They say it is decidedly one-sided; lop-sided in the favor of the supplier; the manufacturer; the marketer. They say it zeros in on only a small fraction of the equation — the consumption of goods and services — completely overlooking the producing element.

After all, as eloquently penned in an *Economist* article, the Web was designed completely counterintuitively — thanks largely to the big greedy corporations who took a bet on things like pipelines, bandwidth, server capacity, and access charges. In their business model calculations, they placed a large bet on the act of downloading and in doing so played right into the hands of mass marketing. The Web was groomed way back when to be another television set, capable of pushing, forcing, ramming, and streaming tons and tons of mainstream content across the cyberwaves.

Something funny happened, though, along the way to cable and telco dominance. Human beings realized that there was a seat at the table for them, and not just an ordinary seat but a pretty major seat,

---

[1] See C. Locke, R. Levine, D. Searls, and D. Weinberger, *The Cluetrain Manifesto: The End of Business as Usual* (New York: Perseus Book Group, 2000), 78.

which allowed them to participate on an equal footing. The blogosphere, podosphere, YouTube phenomenon (and the list goes on) pays tribute to a new world order, one hallmarked by the mighty "upload."

You see, the Web was designed and built all wrong. It is only now that we scratch our heads and wonder why it takes five times as long to upload a file as it does to download the same file.[2] Gee, I wonder if it has anything to do with greed.

> The Web has been hard-wired for one-sided communication and not for two-sided conversation.

Consumers are not one-way paths to summer houses in the Hamptons and winter getaways in Vale. It is downright negligent to downplay, ignore, or minimize the consumer's *pro*active involvement in a business that is all about disposable time—with its most priceless, precious, and scarce commodity: attention.

## Is "Consumer" the Right Word?

So should we replace the term "consumer" with "prosumer"? Perhaps. To understand my bias and position on the subject, I wanted to call this book "The Prosumers." I even contacted Alvin Toffler's office to get his buy-in on the subject.

I'll come back to this in a moment, but before I do, I wanted to put a number of popular alternate terms on the table.

### User

The only profession that calls its customers "users" is the drug trade. I feel nauseous every time I hear people refer to consumers as users.

---

[2]See PC Pitstop, http://www.pcpitstop.com/internet/bandwidth_about.asp.

The worst offenders are those who should know best—the tech industry. I don't buy for a minute the ridiculous excuse that people "use" the Web or that the Web is addictive and so why should we push back on any analogies to addiction. Riiiiiiight.

The descriptor "user" has a very limited scope when it comes to a utilitarian or product-centric function—a technology application, for example. Microsoft Word has users, but Office has consumers.

I wholeheartedly reject calling humans "users" in any frame of reference.

## Customers

I understand and empathize with drawing a distinction between customers and consumers and absolutely feel a little more affection for a customer—someone who has an established affinity for and history with a product, good, service, or brand.

The problem with the word "customer" is that it too is rather limiting—for the simple reason that not everyone is your customer (although you'd love them to be, wouldn't you?). And with at least 256 shades of customers, from loyalists to haters, the term is so general as to be too vague and even misleading.

## Citizens

Citizens of the world, unite! It sounds great on paper and even out loud. To be honest, I kind of love the idea of thinking of the human race as a band of brothers and sisters, united by common goals and single causes and focused on common agendas.

I truly believe the world is flat and getting flatter (and smaller) by the day. That said, we also need to recognize the tremendous diversity and voluntary fragmentation that divide us as quickly as they unite us.

"Citizen" is a lofty but overly ambitious term. I sure wish we all behaved like true citizens, but in the context of marketing the term falls a little short of any actionable and tangible state.

## Humans

Kumbaya. Get over yourself. Even weaker than the "citizen" angle.

## WHERE DOES THAT LEAVE US?

There aren't many times I differ from the sages who wrote *The Cluetrain Manifesto*, but this is one of them. If the word "consumer" is the gun, then bad marketers are the ones who pull the trigger. At the risk of being compared to Charlton Heston (for the record, I'm about as National Rifle Association as the Dalai Lama), I'm just saying that until we arrive at a *better* term for consumer, I'm just going to stick with it. Personally, I don't feel that there's anything wrong with the term per se, but rather with those who *use* and *abuse* the term. I absolutely concede that there are technical and semantic problems with the word and what it stands for, but I just don't see any improvements from the laundry list of possibilities I've just enumerated.

In addition, I want to reiterate that I am a proud, card-carrying member of the marketing union. So what if 99 percent of my fellow members are dimwits? That doesn't make the mission statement any less valid. While I deplore advertising in most forms and marketing in many forms, I remain resolute that marketing is as critical a part of our economy, society, and corporate ecosystem as any other function.

Consumers are an inextricable part of this ecosystem, and just because they consume the products they buy or buy into certain brands doesn't make them any less empowered or important. In fact, we are arguably being quite patronizing by insinuating or implying that they are helpless or hapless in the process.

Consumers are ultimately what make the world go round. They vote with their wallets; they exchange their hard-earned dollars, pounds, euros, pesos, and yens for value, and the lower you go on the socioeconomic totem pole, the more important and valuable these decisions become. So don't think for a second that consumers are the lame ducks that mass marketers would like to believe they are.

The second distinction or nuance is that consumption is pretty much like the air we breathe or the blood that pumps through our veins: Every second of every day we are consuming . . . consuming

time, consuming content, consuming media, consuming love, consuming conversation. Even when we're producing the content that
Toffler warned us we would be, we're simultaneously consuming
(time, background music, alcohol). So what's the big whoop with
the idea that consuming is a bad thing?

For a full recap, take a look at Figure 5.1, a chart from fellow
blogger David Armano.

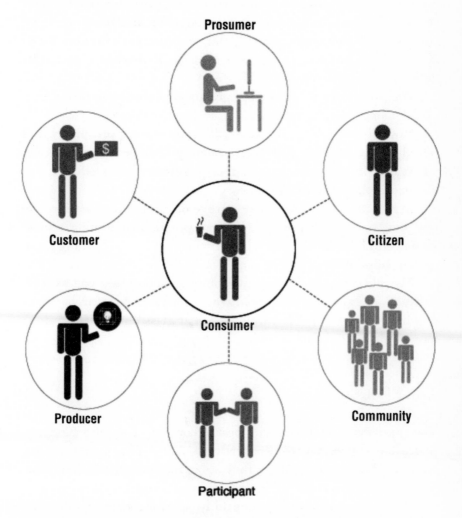

Figure 5.1   The Many Faces and Interpretations of the Consumer

---

**Production is the new consumption.**

---

## CASE CLOSED: THE NEW WORD IS PROSUMER, RIGHT?

Wrong. Prosumers are just one part of the new equation. They don't replace the out-of-vogue consumers, but they are different—a subset that deserves recognition and respect. We also have one more category: the producers, starring not just Matthew Broderick and Nathan Lane but *you* (at least according to *Time* when it picked its 2006 Person of the Year).

The producers are a subset of prosumers, who are in turn a fraction of Consumer Nation.

How do you tell them apart? All producers are prosumers, but not all prosumers are producers. Some prosumers are producers, whereas most consumers are neither prosumers nor producers. It's like one of those MENSA riddles.

Research needs to be done to prove or refute this assertion. I'm not going to do it right now, as I'm indisposed, busy writing a book. However, I'll back this research, participate in it, find funding for it, or help run it if you'd like to help.

My role is to postulate the question, not spoon-feed you with security blanket answers and tidal waves of warped research. That's punditry for you. I get to throw stones at glass houses, and I don't have to clean up the mess (unless it's mine).


## THE PRODUCERS

The producers are those who create content. They are bloggers, podcasters, LonelyGirl15, RocketBoom, Ask-A-Ninja, your mother, Arianna Huffington. In short, they are in the content creation game, but really they're in the business of conversation.

The producers are not constantly sparking conversation, but they are *always* accelerants. Producers are not journalists. They're just people with passion—and people who have been given the ability to express themselves in new and exciting ways and in so doing have built the next generation of media, the new celebrity.

Amanda Congdon, host of one of the most popular video blogs, RocketBoom, parted ways with Andrew Baron in July 2006. Today she is represented by Endeavor Agency and appears on www.starringamandacongdon.com and www.abcnews.com.

Producers are still consumers—literally and figuratively. They buy, purchase, digest, utilize, and "consume" products, goods, services, and brands. They also consume *other* producers' content (both mainstream and grassroots). They add to it. They riff on it. They evolve it. Sometimes they even disagree with it. Most of the time they acknowledge it and pay tribute or track back to it.

This is the Producer's Honor Code.

Producers are *by default* influencers. For example, a blog that has 500 other blogs linking to it, has a network of incremental subscribers and thus an army of exponential readers a mouse click or RSS feed away.

Is trust earned? Is influence earned? Yes and no. Yes, for all the obvious reasons, and no, in that trust and influence can be manifested in today's new marketing world in the blink of an eye through the random discovery of a new blog, web site, podcast, or newsletter.

Trust and influence can also be broken down and destroyed just as quickly (if not more quickly). Take many of the mainstream media outlets, newspapers in particular. They've taken decades upon decades to build up the all-important trust and mystical affinity, only to find out that (a) trust and influence are earned and re-earned on a daily basis, (b) trust and influence are not the same thing, and (c) people will look elsewhere for new sources of news, information, and commentary based on relevance and also based on . . . yes . . . the ability to join in the dialogue.

This is why traditional media companies, like Viacom, are out to sea right now.

Hope you brought a lifejacket.

## THE PROSUMERS

Prosumers are absolutely in the content business, but rather than create it, they're more like content harvesters—curators perhaps, even content moderators.

They're merchants of conversation.

Take Mack Collier. He keeps a blog called The Viral Garden. One day he decided to list the top 25 marketing blogs, using the ranking and popularity analytical tools of Google, Alexa, and Technorati. Every week Mack updates the list, and in doing so he has built a bridge to more than 25 other blogs and more importantly is on their—and their readers'—radars.

Mack actually lives with one foot in the producer camp, one in the prosumer camp, and one in the consumer camp. (Math was never my strong suit and don't even go there with the third leg joke.) He also is a fine example of the *trichotomy* of today's "consumer"—the shape-shifting diversity that makes us humans pretty damn tricky to pin down, compartmentalize, and fit into any neat and convenient boxes.

Toffler referred to prosumers as producing consumers, or consumers who produce as much as they consume (or at least enough to be recognized as such). Luminaries like Doc Searls have called for the elimination of the term "consumer" largely for the same reason: the rise of Upload Nation.

I've been on board the upload train for a while. Consumers who produce have an entirely different set of expectations, standards, rules, and terms of engagement. They have a lopsided active-to-passive state of being, and joining and participating in conversation are their terms and conditions of sale. When they purchase a new MP3 (yes, some do) on iTunes, buy a ticket to a movie on Fandango.com, or one-click their way to a new book on Amazon.com, they are most definitely going to tell you about it—whether you asked to be told or not.

### Pro = Proactive

Said prosumers are demonstrating a new behavior trait that extends beyond the production benefit. It is the second distinction between pro-sumers and con-sumers—namely, being proactive, volunteering information, value, ideas, help, support and the like.

They display an acute awareness of and connectedness with their colleagues, cohorts, and community. They implicitly acknowledge a "pay-it-forward" ethos with no quid-pro-quo expectation in exchange.

If you think about it, isn't this one of the deepest quandaries of the current state of marketing and advertising? *We are stuck in limbo between giving and getting back.* The latter governs and warps the former under shrinking operating windows and time frames.

It is this almost altruistic character trait that makes prosumers incredibly valuable and yet elusive. They're not waiting around for you to "make their day." They're creating a great day every day. And if you play your cards perfectly, you'll be helping them by giving them tools, techniques, ideas, inspiration, content, and brand-assisted opportunities to make the world a better place in the process.

Take Kyle McDonald. Kyle is a proactive consumer who started with a dream. Well, actually, he started with one red paper clip and a dream (or delusion) of trading in and trading up his one paper clip for a house of his own. (See Figure 5.2.)

Figure 5.2   One Paper Clip: The Improbable Story of Communal Exchange

To get from A to B, he followed steps C, D, E, F, G, H, I, J, K, L, M, and N.

Kyle discovered that the actor Corbin Bernsen (formerly of *L.A. Law*) was an avid snow globe collector, and it was the exchange of a snow globe for a walk-on role in an upcoming movie produced by Corbin's production company, Public Media Works, that finally resulted in Kyle's home.

---

You can listen to my podcast interview with Corbin Bernsen at www .jointheconversation.us/oneredpaperclip

---

The house in question was in a place called Kipling, Saskatchewan, in Canada. Now, before Kyle came along, I had never even heard of Canada! What a PR coup for the country.

Relax already, I'm just kidding. I had really never heard of Kipling, Saskatchewan, before. How is it that the smart townsfolk of Kipling, Saskatchewan, could pull off a conversational coup that all the corporations in the world could not? Where was Staples? Where was Office Depot? Where was Home Depot? Where was WH Smith? Where was OfficeWorks? I recall seeing Kyle on CNN inviting everyone to a housewarming party that the town of Kipling was throwing in his honor. I'll bet the bed-and-breakfasts were bursting at the seams!

## THE CONSUMERS

Today's consumer is not yesterday's consumer. As I outlined in my book, *Life After the 30-Second Spot*, today's consumers are:

1. Intelligent
2. Empowered
3. Skeptical
4. Connected
5. Time-pressed
6. Demanding

7. Loyaless (the word is made up, the meaning isn't)
8. Always on
9. Ahead of the curve
10. Vengeful

Hell, there's even a new term: "mouse potato" was added to *Merriam-Webster's Dictionary* in 2006. I don't know about you, but I would imagine that mouse potatoes could whip couch potatoes' butts on any given Sunday. (It takes a lot of calories to navigate deftly through YouTube videos.)

Today's consumer is your best friend and your worst enemy. As Ben McConnell and Jackie Huba wrote in *Citizen Marketers* (Kaplan Business, 2006), *people* are the message. Forget mediums and that fogy Marshall McLuhan: The real context is in the hearts, minds and *hands* of those who keep us in business—our customers—and those who keep us honest—consumers (not necessarily ours).

# 6

# The New Consumerism

The new consumerism is marked by three primary insights that shed light on the motivations behind the need and desire to help and befriend perfect strangers and hint at the real reasons for the rise of consumer-generated content, social media, and social networking:

1. Building connections
2. Beating the system
3. Making a difference

## BUILDING CONNECTIONS

Building connections—meaningful bonds between like-minded people—acts as both the currency and the language of conversation. Like a powerful electrical circuit, each link helps complete the chain and convey the current.

The new consumerism thrives and feeds on the pay-it-forward mentality in which fleeting moments of clarity unite and celebrate the truth and commonality we all share. This is the Linked In age of the new "rolodex" that can be endlessly sliced, diced, sorted, sifted, filtered, and categorized and that may resurface either within a week or never again.

These connections often lead to personal experiences, feelings, and reflections being shared within a sea of anonymity.

Each string of communication is a conversation in the making, and each conversation is a seed capable of sprouting a relationship. The problem, of course, is that marketers today are hoping for one-hit-wonders—those magic beans capable of producing a beanstalkon-demand. That's a fairy tale, and like all fairy tales, it ain't gonna happen.

The digital world is full of these connection opportunities—from Facebook to MySpace, from LinkedIn to Second Life, from track-backs to podcast audio comment lines. The ability to link to and with one another, extend or request friendship, add oneself to a community map, or acknowledge a list of preferred or recommended sources (blogrolls, playlists, and so on) points to the connectedness that makes the wisdom of consumers so profoundly important and unprecedented.

Of course, connectedness is also available "offline," in the analog, traditional, or real world, although there I would refer to them not as connection opportunities but as connection challenges. The reality is that a world without digital is fragmented, dispersed, isolated, and thus challenged. Events that are geographically constrained are extremely limited by an acute scalability conundrum. And just in case you're about to blow your top, simmer down and chill out. . . . I am in no way undermining or understating the power of human contact, personal face-to-face encounters, or traditional connectivity, which remains without question paramount. . . .

Put the two worlds together, however, and you have magic. Call it *connection integration* or call it anything else you like . . . just make the call. The ability to execute against a truly fluid mash-up of the nontraditional and the traditional presents unprecedented moments through which to qualify, unite, convert, and, yes, converse.

People naturally want to connect. Originating in our DNA, it's a gravitational force that we are just now beginning to exercise with clout, conviction, and commitment. Connection is our life force, our calling, the ultimate actualization.

Weight loss has always worked best in numbers (preferably less than more). The entire Weight Watchers movement is built around conversation. Communal activism and activation translate into motivation and willpower when a team is cheering (or jeering) you on.

At the beginning of 2007, I decided that enough was enough: It was time to lose some weight. Ahead of the birth of my third child, I wanted to make sure I was healthier, fitter, and happier.

Figure 6.1    Consumer-Generated Fatblogging Logo

Even at six-foot-one, tipping the scales at 224 pounds was not impressive. (Unlike my cut Second Life avatar, Divo Dapto!)

When I came back from vacation on January 2, I decided to do a few things . . . call them resolutions if you like:

- Attempt to lose 40 pounds
- Go back to the *awesome* Weight Watchers regimen
- Not shave until I broke 200
- Share the experience with others as a way of forcing myself to lose the weight or risk the humiliation of failing my community

I had no idea there was a "Fatblogging" movement a-brewing.[1] (See Figure 6.1.) Thanks to fellow blogger and friend Jason Calacanis, I decided to try weight-loss-by-community and join the

---

[1]See sample posts at http://www.technorati.com/search/fatblogging.

movement, which is one part support group, one part education network, and one part cathartic and masochistic motivation.

Every Friday I post to Jaffe Juice a journal entry of my previous week. I begin each post with my weight in pounds. (See Figure
6.2.) When this book went to print, I was 193.5 pounds. By exposing myself and experiencing this degree of vulnerability, I've taken
on a powerfully motivating weight loss regime and with the release
of this book, one hell of a maintenance program. Moreover, I'm
making new connections and friendships.

Here is one of my Fatblogging posts:

> My first Fatblogging weigh-in and it's been a good week, considering I
> was on the road Sunday thru Thursday (with a brief pit stop back in
> Westport) in Orlando and beautiful Montreal.

> One of the biggest changes I've made in my diet is related to the
> travel. Before, I used to check into a hotel at 11 P.M. and *then* order
> room-service. Likewise, when I got home at 11.30 P.M., I would heat
> up pizza or the like. Now I eat nothing or have an apple.

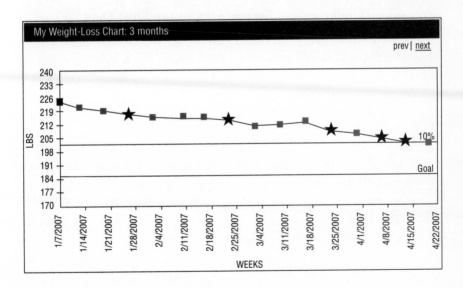

Figure 6.2   My Weight-Loss Progress Chart

And where was Weight Watchers in all of this? There are conversational elements within the online application that encourage conversation between consumer and consumer, but what about between brand and consumer? What about the WeightWatchers brand communicating directly with the Fatbloggers? What a great opportunity to join the conversation.

My Fatblogging efforts even got me featured in the *Los Angeles Times*. Who knew that being fat could get you into the newspaper!

## BEATING THE SYSTEM

It sure feels good to beat the man. Especially when the man is a dunce, bully, egocentric, or greedy doofus. The new consumerism plays to the innate feeling of accomplishment that comes from solving a riddle, finding a dollar bill in the street, or discovering a new web site that allows price comparison shopping. Increasingly, the new consumerism is also manifested in the creation by consumers of their own web sites to share the love and pricing discoveries.

Take Paul English, who couldn't take it anymore when it came to trying to get a human being on the other end of the telephone line. You know the pain, right? We're talking fingernails-on-a-chalkboard effect every time you call a toll-free number or a company customer service line and you're thrust into a torturous maze of touch football (and you're the football).

> Touch 1 to continue in English.
>
> Touch 2 if you're a business.
>
> Touch 3 if you're a single mom with your baby in one hand, pasta boiling over on the stove, bills waiting to be paid, and a second kid waiting to be picked up from school. Your wait time is approximately one hour, owing to the unusually high call volume we're currently experiencing because *our product is so damn complicated and flawed*, but please be patient (as in funny farm), customer @#@$#%^$&, because you are *reaaaaaaaally* important to us.

Touch 0 to speak to a representative.

0000000000000000000000000000000000000000000000000000000
00000000000000000000000000000.

I'm sorry, you pressed an incorrect key. Please resubmit your Social Security number, weight, and deepest and darkest secrets.

Your wait time is now less than one minute.

Click (either the sound of you being disconnected or the trigger of a gun).

If this sounds like an experience you've ever been through, you wouldn't be alone. And so Paul did something about it: He noted the exact sequence of digits that would expedite the process of getting a human being on the other end of the line. (See Figure 6.3.)

And Paul was not alone either . . . other prosumers joined in and contributed to an exhaustive list of "cheat" codes. So successful was Paul that he received his 15 streams of fame in the *Wall Street Journal*, on ABC, in *Oprah* magazine, and in countless other media outlets.[2] He also forced the Interactive Voice Response (IVR) industry to issue a defensive (and pathetic) statement about the value of the automated industry.

Yeah, right. Let's be clear about something here. The entire IVR industry is an inward-facing shrine to corporate greed and laziness. When Home Depot's incompetent CEO Bob Nardelli receives $210 million for his failure, there's something fishy in the brew.[3] I wonder how much it would have cost HD to invest some of Nardelli's money into a few more outsourced call centers or stay-at-home moms (à la JetBlue) to further tip the scales of humanity in their favor?

Then there's the wonderful BugMeNot, which allows consumers to bypass those pesky registration procedures that every web site seems to enjoy so much. So the next time you need to

---

[2]For a list of English's appearances, see http://www.gethuman.com/press/.
[3]See *USA Today*'s editorial of January 8, 2007, at http://blogs.usatoday.com/oped/2007/01/our_view_on_ceo.html.

| Company Name | Toll-free Number | "Cheat Codes" |
|---|---|---|
| GEICO | 800-841-3000 | Press 2; at prompt press 6; at prompt press 1; at prompt press 5; at prompt press #; at prompt press #; at prompt press 2. |
| Sony / Playstation | 800-222-7669 | Say "agent"; at prompt say "agent"; at prompt press 1; at prompt press 1. |
| OfficeMax Rebates | 866-765-5702 | Press 2; at prompt press 2; at prompt press 2; enter fake phone #; press 1 to confirm; press 1 to confirm. |
| United | 800-864-8331 | Press 0; say "agent," say "yes"; say "domestic" or "international" as appropriate. |

Figure 6.3    Sample "Cheat" Codes

visit the *New York Times* and don't have a user name and password, just bookmark www.bugmenot.com, save time, and get on with your life.

Beating the system is part of the new consumer's cultural makeup. It is the response to all those years of one-sided control and limited engagement opportunities. It is the antidote to IVR technology, user registration, and all the other clunky ideas companies come up with when they'd rather save a buck than earn a smile.

And it's here to stay.

There's just no limit to beating the system when common sense is enlisted in the cause. And as long as establishments continue to patronize their patrons, they will be distrusted, boarded, and forced to walk the plank.

## MAKING A DIFFERENCE

Last and most definitely not least (and not as sinister) in the new consumer arsenal is the simple and succinct desire to make a difference, to change the world, to have an impact on the life of another person (one of the million closest strangers).

Before my iPhone, I had an iPod nano (PRODUCT)[RED]. In fact, the second I heard about it, I bought it. It says something, I would hope, about how I spend my money and who I choose to spend it with. Admittedly I could have just given this money directly to the UNITE charity. I know this. The point is that sales of (iPod)[Red] enable consumers to align themselves with like-minded brands and companies that think good and do good.

We are about to witness an extraordinary age of social awareness and activism. Al Gore might not have invented the Internet, but he certainly has played a role (not *the* role) when it comes to catalyzing the conversation of environmental responsibility and ownership.

*An Inconvenient Truth* asks hard-hitting questions, and if you think about it, every single screening becomes a default town meeting, albeit a fragmented one. More importantly, the conversation started by the movie has not only endured but gathered commitment and conviction. In addition, it utilizes a suite of new marketing approaches, including personal and custom content, online pledges (to see the movie), and advocacy calls-to-action to sites such as www.stopglobalwarming.org and www.climatecrisis.net—all designed to evoke communal conversation.[4]

This powerful craving to effect change is not solely *green*. It is a multicolored and multifaceted prism of diversity and expression that ladders up to the relentless pursuit of meaning and accomplishment on a grand scale.

We've already seen the effects of MoveOn.org, a group of "connected," like-minded individuals who attempt to beat the system and make a difference. Whereas their efforts in the 2004 U.S. presidential election might not have produced their ultimate ROI— namely, a Democratic victory (largely owing to an inferior "product")—their impact was seismic in establishing and accelerating a long-lasting momentum that resonated strongly in the double-barreled Democratic victories in the House and the Senate races in the 2006 midterms.

Or how about http://www.ihumpedyourhummer.com or www.fuh2.com, which contain a collection of communal multimedia with a very singular focus. Here is one description of a submission:

I am in this video humping a hummer. I did this because I believe that hummers and their owners/drivers should be disgraced for their actions, especially those who use their vehicles in an urban context. The pollution generated by hummers is as outrageous as the unnecessary

[4]See Rohit Bhargava's blog Influential Marketing, http://rohitbhargava.typepad.com/weblog/2006/06/lessons_in_mark.html.

noise they create and the unnecessary space they take up. They are wasteful monsters hulking over pedestrians, cyclists, and even people driving reasonable useful cars. As I see it hummers are constantly violating the city and environment whenever they are used for non-vital non-offroad reasons. As such I have chosen to violate this H2 sexually, raping the car as it rapes the social and ecological environment around it.

Also I think it's funny. We should work towards mass hummer-humpings where packs of people gang-bang hummers that are in use. Stalling the owners and ridiculing them at the same time.

> I think therefore I am.
> I am because we think.
> We think and so we act.

Besides these illustrations, this book is peppered with tributes and testaments to the new consumerism—the wisdom of crowds with a fresh can of whoopass to boot. You'll see how liberated conversation has an incredibly empowering effect on ordinary consumers, who by themselves are generally passive but when connected with one another become an unstoppable, mean machine that takes no prisoners as it rolls through the 256 shades of corporate mediocrity.

At times you'll see anomalies rise and fade in the blink of an eye. Steve Rubel, publisher of MicroPersuasion—might refer to these people as "shooting stars." McConnell and Huba would call them "firecrackers." I'd call them "sir" and "ma'am" if I were you. A while back when I wrote a blog post citing Andy Warhol's famous comment about 15 minutes of fame, I noted that today *ordinary* people are capable of achieving 15 *posts* or 15 *streams* of fame.[5] They rise meteorically and then seem to fade away. But they never quite go away, do they? As long as they are written, posted, and spoken about in books, blogs, podcasts, message boards, and the like, "ordinary" people are in fact immortalized.

---

[5]See "Your 15-Posts of Fame" at JaffeJuice, http://www.jaffejuice.com/2006/02/your_15posts_of.html (February 14, 2006).

## SHAPE-SHIFTERS

To make your life even tougher, don't think for a second that a producer is only a producer, a prosumer only a prosumer, and a consumer only a consumer. Au contraire. We humans are complex beasts, capable of transforming ourselves, disguising ourselves, and reinventing ourselves at warp speed. As mentioned earlier, all producers are prosumers and consumers, all prosumers are consumers, and for the most part consumers are "new" consumers and yet capable of making fleeting transitions to the center of the earth and back again.

Think of a classic vinyl record (you know, those outdated things your parents listened to that preceded those smaller shiny outmoded things called CDs—you can purchase them all in eBay's antique section). Each track is clearly demarcated as a concentric circle. If each track represents another demographic or segmented bucket of likely buyers, then today's scenario could be represented as a worn, scratched-to-bits record, and the effect of the interconnected nature of the different consumer groups would be equivalent to the sound experienced by aggressively forcing the needle from side to side. That screeching sound is heinous and jarring, isn't it? Only today they call it hip-hop, and it's music to the ears of the many (just not to yours).

## THE AHA MOMENT

To put this all together, I'll offer *this* segmentation methodology, which outlines the three groups against a content differentiator. According to Jakob Nielsen—there is a 90:9:1 rule, which breaks down as content consumers (90), light content creators (9), and heavy content creators (1).[6]

Take everyone's favorite community-powered melting pot, Wikipedia. Fifty percent of all Wikipedia edits are conducted by

---

[6]See "Lurker:Contributor 9:1," an October 11, 2006, post at Jaffe Juice, http://www.jaffe juice.com/2006/10/lurkercontribut.html.

0.7 percent of its users, and 1.8 percent of users have written more than 72 percent of all articles.

I've given these groups distinct names: consumers, prosumers, producers. (See Figure 6.4.)

This illustration takes the 90:9:1 rule and neatly overlays it on a familiar rock of marketing principles: Roger's Diffusion of Innovations Curve. The theory (by which I mean *my* theory) makes three claims:

1. Producers, followed by prosumers, are more likely to be innovators and early adopters of new products or offerings.
2. The "long tail" wags wildly when it comes to content *creation* by the pro-sumer versus the con-sumer. Its corollary, content *distribution*, holds true in the reverse (via the mouse potato).
3. The success of a new product introduction or launch is influenced by the ability to engage and be embraced by the "pro"-camp.

In all three cases, the "how" is through conversation.

Implication? Simple. *It's worth thinking about the 1 percent as a means to reach, connect with, and affect the 99 percent*, as opposed to

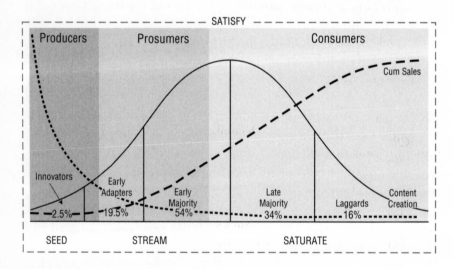

Figure 6.4   A New Way of Conceptualizing Influencers

throwing all that good money after bad attempting to engage the followers or the masses.

## THE OFFICE SUCKS: AN A–Z DEMONSTRATION OF PROSUMER NATION

After the first episode of the U.S. version of Ricky Gervais's wild British series *The Office*, I posted a blog entry entitled "The Office Sucks." I was appalled by the incredibly unoriginal and literally 100 percent imitation of the original British series. From the casting to the actual lines, the American show was an insult to originality—a painful reminder of the state of creativity today. Our lives are littered with autopilot clones of once bright sparks—bastardized versions of the real thing. It's like watching the results of last night's lottery and then playing the same numbers every week after that. Pathetic.

Anyway, I posted my feelings about *The Office* and then went on my merry way. Turns out that the series has blossomed, matured, and taken on a life and identity of its own. Terrific. I'm still not watching, though.

Adam sent in this comment:

> I agree completely. The original BBC [show] was funny mainly because Gervais is a genius. His supposed carbon copy in Steve Carell is not funny at all. The new office is people trying to be funny. They only succeed with the mostly slow witted viewers.

Adam's post was dated December 9, 2006, but the thing is, I wrote the post in *March 2005*!

Many of these comments weren't coming from regular or loyal readers of Jaffe Juice. They came from window-shoppers, passersby, consumers who happened to do a search for *The Office* or, most likely, "The Office Sucks" on Google, only to find my blog entry as the *number-one search result* for the latter phrase. They clicked, they read, they joined the conversation. They added to the consensus.

If you're NBC (and you might be), every year you gather in a bunker to theorize, strategize, and conceptualize new ways of convincing consumers to watch your programs. I'll give credit where credit's due: You're getting smarter at reengaging lapsed viewers and helping later-comers to the party lower the dissonance associated with missing too many prior episodes or seasons. Putting your content online helps tons.

But to what extent are you joining the conversation already in progress? Do you know how many people are talking about you—good, bad, or ugly? Here's some help: According to Technorati, as of August 27, 2007, over 23,000 blog posts included *The Office* and NBC.

So here's a thought. Why not send the publisher of Jaffe Juice (that would be me) a box set of the first two seasons of *The Office*? Why not prepare a special road show and invite highly influential producers, prosumers, and consumers to an advance screening, along with the obligatory token stars? You prostrate yourselves every year to the least important group of people—advertisers and marketers—who are nothing but leeches that suck the life out of your real life force and lifeblood: your viewers. So why not call on the people who really count?

This so-called conversation (between me and readers of Jaffe Juice) was really a lopsided one between a producer and his prosumers and consumers. The space that could or should have been filled by NBC was conspicuously void.

# 7

# The Six Cs:
# Three Phases of Conversation

In *Life after the 30-Second Spot*, I pooh-poohed the four Ps (which continue to be taught in colleges and universities around the world to unsuspecting students who will no doubt encounter a rude awakening when they realize that marketing is not a formula, and certainly not one that deals in the commoditized and oversimplified Product, Place, Price, and Promotion).

Here's a recap:

*Product* — Is Volvo the only safe car on the market? Not a chance. Is Volvo the safest car in the market? I know that a lot of Volvo owners would like to believe this is the case, but increasingly safety has lost its differentiated competitive edge as an overarching product attribute and benefit. It's six of the reality that safety features are now standard in most cars (even the airbags have airbags) and half a dozen of the consumer awareness that advertising does nothing more than attempt to cloud and distort an otherwise obvious reality.

*Price* — Perfect information and transparency have all but obliterated the short-term gains from psychological pricing gimmicks and misdirection. Take the General Motors employee-pricing discount promotion, which neatly telegraphed any and all margins to Consumer Nation and was so successful that it dragged the dregs of Detroit (DaimlerChrysler and Ford) into the bottomless and endless (the temporary promotion lasted for months) quagmire of deep-discounting.[1] Toyota is still laughing all the way to the dealership.

---

[1] See "General Moaners" at Jaffe Juice, http://www.jaffejuice.com/2005/06/general_moaners .html (June 23, 2005).

*Place* — Multichannel distribution is not a luxury anymore, but a necessity. The only superstore today is the Web, and the consumer expects nothing less than 24/7/365 as standard operating procedure. Deploying an exhaustive distribution strategy is nothing more than the way to ante up, and anything less may severely impede a brand's ability to compete. Wal-Mart's bricks-and-mortar stores are a liability as long as shelves are bare, inventory is unbalanced, customer service is nonexistent, and ambience is about as welcoming as open-heart surgery. Walmart.com is only slightly better. U.S. television networks devour each other's lunch and themselves in the process when each pits its content against the others' content. Only through liberating content to travel the hallways of the Web and the corridors of iTunes have they finally learned that human beings have only one set of eyes and an attention span that registers only a fraction of what that one set of eyes can take in.

*Promotion* — Mass marketing, communication, and media are now located on a continuum ranging from Muzak to white noise to wallpaper. (I'm even giving you a choice, which is more than you give your consumers.) Promotion has become so bland, boring, benign, and ineffective that you would hardy know it's there. It is the ultimate irony that a business that was historically all about disruption and intrusiveness has now been relegated to an afterthought. Promotion — and by promotion I mean *communication* — without a solid foundation of Relevance, Utility, and Entertainment (RUE), *combined* with a commensurate consumer response of Experience, Permission, Involvement, and Conversation (EPIC), is but a grain of salt in a wilderness of nothingness. (That sound you hear is the sound of silence. Hello, job insecurity darkness, my old friend. . . .)

## INTRODUCING THE SIX CS

If the four Ps are being commoditized, what comes next? Say hello to the six Cs (which used to be the five Cs before a series of good conversations helped me revise and evolve the thinking). (See Figure 7.1.)

To understand the six Cs, take a journey back, however reluc-

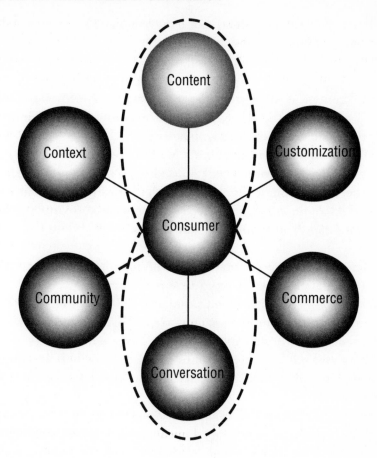

Figure 7.1    The Six Cs

tantly, to the first wave of Internet-mania, the fuzzy period between 1999 and 2001. Back then the thought leaders in the space (all two of them) proclaimed that the new marketing model was based on three Cs: Content, Commerce, and Community. They were right about all three, although it is interesting to see how right they were given the addition of the fourth C—Context.

*Content*—I continuously toy with the familiar adage "Content is king." I ended *Life After the 30-Second Spot* with the line, "Content is King. Now, more than ever." Absolutely. Whether it's called branded entertainment, long-form content, original content, or consumer-generated content, content remains the great catalyst from which anything is possible.

That said, I've also said the following:

- "If content is king, when did it become the court jester?" This is a reference to the explosion of gratuitous "brand integration" and abuse of product placement.
- "Content might be king, but what if there is no monarchy anymore?" This more recent spin alludes to a new democracy (derived through peaceful or violent means) in which command-and-control is replaced with engage-and-enrich, where drag-and-drop is now care-and-share.[2]

Content is still very much a foundational ingredient or variable in a rather elaborate recipe or equation.

*Commerce*—Three points on Commerce 2.0. First, money makes the world go round, but it shouldn't rule it. Yes, of course, return on investment is a critical component of any campaign, initiative, or undertaking and not an optional extra anymore, but there is so much more in play and at stake. Short-term planning and thinking is just plain shortsighted.

Second, the major difference between 1.0 and 2.0 is the insight that a Web presence is not just a cheaper place to sell stuff. Sadly, this pithy proclamation is not widely held—or should I say practiced. The reality is that way too many corporations still look at the Web as an inherited stepchild next to their favorite son, the bricks-and-mortar stores. (And the same applies to messaging, relationship, and service with respect to television, experience, and customer service, respectively.)

Third, the C of Commerce reminds us why the word "consumer" is still most definitely valid. It is the counterbalance to the previous assertion about ROI obsession, which restates that we're still in the building business (building a brand, building sales, build-

---

[2]On engage-and-enrich, see David Brazeal's comment on Jaffe Juice www.jaffejuice .com/2006/12/drag_and_drop.html. On care-and-share, see Brian Keith's comment on JaffeJuice.

ing equity, and so on). I reject the altruistic notion that marketing is the devil and our budgets are nothing more than bottomless charity coffers. At the same time, I reject any viewpoint that fails to recognize that everything we do has some kind of lasting impact on society, humanity, morality, and community (see next point). The C of Commerce is the ultimate equilibrium (or at least it should be).

*Community* — Can you hear me now? Can you hear *us* now? Do you believe in the wisdom of crowds? Do you believe that the collective consciousness of ordinary human beings will outsmart you every time (unless you're Steve Jobs, I suppose)? Can you imagine how powerful AOL would have been had it from the start focused on community and nothing else? Dial-up versus broadband, fee versus free, walled versus fenced — these would have been nothing more than minor irritations if being a member of AOL had become a movement, a cult(ure), the source of a sense of belonging and ownership. Oh well, time to move to the next television campaign.

Community remains the gravitational force that links us all together and connects the dots between passions and shared visions, between ideals and commonality. More on that later. . . .


## ENTER THE REMAINING CS

*Context* — This chapter is a context setter: It offers a conceptual framework and directional map for where marketing is heading, where conversation fits in, and thus how to approach marketing from a revolutionary (and investment) standpoint. Context is all about the moment — the where and the when — which often means the difference between *spam* and *bam!* (hat tip to Emeril).

It is no coincidence that the digital revolution has become inextricably tied to context, and indeed has been an integral contributor to the rise of context as a brand necessity. Context is also closely linked to another C — Control — in an environment that is no longer based on a lopsided power structure. Any insights we might gain from walking a mile in our consumers' shoes is short-lived if we hop in a cab at the one-mile mark and leave our consumers stranded. We need to focus on every mile, the extra mile, the last mile. We need to become a part of our consumers' lives, walking with them[3] and with our community. We need to be a part of their conversations (provided, of course, they invite us).

A rather esoteric illustration of context was the incredibly twisted yet sublime promotion for the film *The Ring Two*. (10-second premise: People watch a strange video; their phone rings and a sinister voice announces certain death within 7 days.)

It's that simple. Just as simple as keying in a few friends' (about to be ex-friends) e-mail addresses and cell phone numbers. I tried this on my sister, who received an e-mail from me (just like one of those viral thingies) telling her she just *had* to watch this really cool movie trailer. She clicked on the link and noticed that she was watching the actual video from the original movie. (The assumption is that the recipient has seen the first movie, as many people had.) Just then she was jolted by the sound of her cell phone ringing. Nervous laughter. What a weird coincidence. She answered, only to hear the same voice hissing at her that in seven days. . . .

The next phone to ring was mine, and a transcript of that conversation would have to be rated R!

*Customization* — Customization is the culture of the world we live in. No two human beings are created the same. No two consumers have the same specific needs, wants, motivations, fears, hopes, and dreams. Customization is obvious in some industries, such as the automotive industry. But what about entertainment? Or financial services? Customization is the universal exchange rate between goods and services and consumers' hard-earned dollars. It is the language of Generation i, which rhymes with "my," as in, "I want *my* mortgage (or *my* movie) *my* way." It's bigger than burgers (Burger King says "Have it your way," but if they mean that, why can't I have fat-free fries?) and more important than selecting which quilt pattern you'd prefer to be wiping your bum with.

*Conversation* — Conversation is the sixth C, and arguably the most important of the lot. A reader on my blog asked a really inter-

[3]An idea attributed to Mack Collier from the blog The Viral Garden and Beyond Madison Avenue.

esting question: "Why not consider the entire 'consumer segment' as a defined medium [messaging distribution channel]?" To give some additional context, this person was responding to a memo about whether it's accurate to refer to Consumer Nation as "Agency of the Year," which the advertising trade publication *Ad Age* had earlier proclaimed. If anything, it is *the producers* that deserved the compliment, but it got me to thinking . . . why *not* carve out and dedicate a chunk of dollars for consumers and plan against this? Sure, we'd gravitate toward incorporating word of mouth and "viral" into this bucket, but that's not what I'm talking about. What I'm talking about is the ability to invest media dollars in actual conversation, which we can think of as the gift that keeps on giving.

## THE SEVENTH C: CONSUMER

Just as the fifth P was People, we need to acknowledge that no model is complete or representative if the consumer is not front and center — or in this case, the cog that binds the construct. No matter what happens, anyone who is worth anything (except Steve Jobs again) subscribes to a timeless fundamental: Consumer- or customer-centricity is paramount to any meaningful brand longevity, health, and prosperity. Now if only they would start putting this into practice!

# 8

# The Content-Conversation Relationship

In the six Cs model, content and conversation are joined at the hip but are not equal. They are linked and need each other to survive, and yet one is more evolved than the other.

The fact is that *entire* industries (we're talking music, Hollywood, and, yes, marketing communications) have been built on a lopsided content model built on five beliefs or assumptions so firmly held that many people think of them as solid facts:

1. Content is created by corporations ("professionals") . . .
2. Content is consumed by consumers . . .
3. . . . And never the two shall meet.
4. Consumers will pay for content. (That's not a belief—it's an order!)
5. Content is an end unto itself.

This book is here to tell you that all five of these "facts" are fiction.

Content is *not solely* created by corporations. The new "professionals" are you and me. What the establishment still doesn't quite get is that all the so-called crap out there (the "poorly produced consumer work with subpar production values," and so on) is only crap to a small group of elitists who are losing power and credibility by the day. Beauty truly is in the eye of the beholder, and in this case content creation has become a free-for-all. The ultimate arbiter of what is termed a rose and what is termed a thorn will be a set of eyes, a corresponding set of ears, and one incredibly coveted, scarce, and manic attention span. YouTube's bowiechick or CBS's Andy Rooney? When 60 seconds (not 60 minutes) are at stake, it's open season on attention.

Content *isn't only* consumed by consumers. It is repurposed, mashed, tagged, forwarded, edited, commented on, and so on and so on. In addition, corporations (they're still few and far between, but if my company, *crayon*, has anything to do with it, the number will grow exponentially) are becoming the new "consumers" as they turn to all the consumer-generated content and the resultant conversations and defer to these natural and authentic stories for insights, inspiration, and ideas.

You can run but you can't hide in your ivory towers anymore. Consumers are no longer content (pun not intended) to sit back and take it in the rear from you. Conversation is a contact sport, and if you choose not to participate, you will be hunted down like the dog you are . . . or worse still, ignored and forgotten.

Sorry, but paying for content is not a fait accompli. That ship has sailed, my friends. There are just too many nonpaid media alternatives for it to be possible to bully them into submission. Consumers will, however, pay in time or money for value. And they will choose how they perceive and measure that value. So if you're talking about content as a conduit to further, richer, and more meaningful conversation, then perhaps we have a deal.

All of this leads to busting the fifth myth. It's the single most important revelation that the music, television, and movie industries need to learn quickly: Either you learn to facilitate the conversation that naturally flows out of content or it will come back to haunt you. The fact remains that consumers own you. Plain and simple. Give them a sucky movie and you *will* feel their wrath. Cancel a television show midseason and you *will* hear from-ironically-your most "engaged" consumers. Is this how you repay them for the precious time they invested in your brand? Shame on you.

Today the Web is littered with case after case of consumers expressing their communal consensus. Take "Save Friday Night Lights, which helped toward securing a second season for the show."[1] In rare cases, the networks are learning slowly; for example, NBC's Brilliant But Cancelled web site (www.brilliantbut

---

[1] See http://www.savefridaynightlights.com/official-petition-thread-save-friday-night-lights.

cancelled.com) gives "cancelled" content a new lease on life with its most loyal, fervent, and thus engaged audiences.

## THE THREE PHASES OF CONTENT

Marketing as a conversation is not to be taken lightly. It is neither an overnight hit nor a one-hit wonder. It is not fabricated, nor can it be manufactured. If it looks too good to be true, then usually it is. Don't be fooled by false promises of community, dialogue, or partnership, as they are temporary, fleeting, and almost always unscalable.

---

**Authentic conversation scales organically.**

---

The first step in joining the conversation is understanding how conversations come to be—how producers, prosumers, and consumers are all interwoven in an elaborate tapestry of passion . . . a hypnotizing mating ritual between like-minded linkers . . . a viral web of extraordinary clarity.

At the risk of extending a metaphor too far, content's causal role in the conversation can be recognized in three distinct branches, each with offshoots of its own.

### The Three Phases of Content Production

| *Creation* | *Contextualization* | *Propagation* |
|---|---|---|
| Initiating | Commenting | Sharing |
| Extending | Trackbacking | "Digging" |
| Mashing or Repurposing | Tagging | Listing |

## CREATION

The creators of content are no longer the chosen few. Sure, there are chronic creators out there (I am one), just as there are those who flirt with their short-lived moments in the sun, but at the end of the day everyone is a content creator, and as long as another person is around to read, listen, hear, digest, watch, or view, there is the potential for a response, a reaction, feedback, or a conversation.

Consumers are slowly but surely recognizing that they are entitled to participate, express themselves, and realize the sense of accomplishment that comes with the ride. Traditional marketing and media execs still can't quite figure out *why* consumers are so willing to create rather than sit back and be spoon-fed the middle-of-the-road swill that has been diluted, compromised, and bloated with artificial contaminants. Here are four reasons why consumers are becoming the new "mass media" in terms of the aggregate content they produce:

1. *Because they can.* This is probably the most basic reason and yet the most difficult to comprehend (much like the metaphor that is about to follow). We can stick the frog with as many pins as we like, then slice, dice, and dissect it until the cows (or is it toads) come home, but we'll never figure out why when we kiss the frog it becomes a prince. Nobody said that human beings are supposed to be rational, logical, or linear. A carefree attitude permeates the content revolution, and for the most part content creators participate for no particular rhyme or reason.

   Whereas most "consumers" engage sporadically in one-off content contributions, on aggregate they make up (or will soon) the bulk of the content out there. In fact, according to *Screen Digest*, by the end of 2006 CGC videos made up 47 percent of the total online video market in the United States, and by 2010 more than half (55 percent) of all the video content *consumed online* in the United States will be consumer-generated, representing 44 billion video streams.[2]

   Next comes the double-barreled premeditated aspiration I call F&F: fame and fortune.
2. *Fame (I want my 15 streams of fame).* Nothing complicated or new here. People want to be noticed and acknowledged. Now they have the means, motive and opportunity.

[2]See the January 15, 2007, press release at http://www.screendigest.com/press/releases/press_releases_15_1_2007/view.html.

3. *Fortune.* Kudos to Doritos, which was essentially the first brand to take the CGC phenomenon to the max (reach). Doritos asked "consumers" to make their own submissions for consideration as the official Doritos commercial for Super Bowl XLI (2007). While I am not a big fan of cramming new marketing into old marketing, I'd be the first to concede that this is one idea I wish I had come up with myself. Anyway, it turned out that three of the five finalists were professionals, and I don't mean "pro-fessionals" as in "pro-sumers," but small advertising agencies taking their shot at being hired (fortune) in addition to being noticed (fame).

   Personally, I believe Doritos should have offered up two categories: man-in-the-street and man-in-the-cube, if you get my drift. That said, I was reasonably comfortable with the blurring (or relaxing) of what are normally incredibly anal rules and regulations, provided that consumers didn't cry foul about not being given a fair shot.

4. *The Third F: Self-Actualization.* The "f" is silent, but if it stood for something it would probably be a four-letter word synonymous with "bugger off and leave me be." The rise of the new, democratized creative class has been intense, and to celebrate their newfound muscle they're throwing a giant global party to which you have not been invited. In some respects, it is Maslow's top of the heap need for self-actualization that makes me quite content to defend the descriptor "consumer." In this case, there's a whole lot of consumption going on—the consumption of passion, voluntary time, and creative juices. Put differently, consumers are quickly realizing that producing content is as fulfilling as consuming it.

The creation phase of content is split into three categories:

- Initiating original content
- Extending existing content
- Mashing or repurposing content

## Initiating

No shocker here. We're talking about consumers, prosumers, or producers having something to say and saying it. It could be George Masters expressing his love for his iPod mini or the wildly popular "Ask a Ninja" video podcast series. Original content should be like the word suggests . . . original. Now there's a lesson for a series like *The Office* and the 99.9 percent of television that pounces on any idea (great or otherwise) and then dilutes it to the point of unrecognizable numbness. Perhaps that's why an obscure weekly installment of a ninja answering normal questions in a highly abnormal manner (except of course if you're a ninja) now brings in around 500,000 downloads per episode.[3]

## Extending

As much as we'd like to believe we're all highly original entities, we often need a source of inspiration (as a content or conversation catalyst . . . can you see a role for brands emerging yet?) in order to get in the game. In this case, think of the layers of an onion, except that instead of peeling away layers we're adding them. At the core is the original idea, the spark—the Converse Gallery Creative Brief per- haps-and over time the single serving of inspiration becomes a collection of brand passion and creativity.

*Snakes on a Plane*, the New Line Cinema movie starring Samuel L. Jackson, became an Internet legend, with an unprecedented amount of consumer-generated content emerging in the form of posters, trailers, T-shirts, musical scores and tracks, bumper stickers, and so on.

## Mashing or Repurposing

We are living in a mash-up world. You've probably heard the term many times (and if not, please see me after class for a crash—mash— course in new marketing), but have you completely grasped the

---

[3]Within two weeks, not factoring in long tail, according to "Ask a Ninja."

enormity of its pervasiveness and the implications for our culture and, a little closer to home, for your capacity to build affinity, bonds, and relationships between your brands and the consumers you serve? (See Figure 8.1.)

You might think that the three most important letters in the world are CRM (customer relationship management), but you could end up finding out that the all-important acronym is in fact, DRM (digital rights management). Once again, the music, enter- tainment, and movie business is front and center . . . but so too is the *brand world*.

## Signs of Life

The whole mash-up concept is a "sign of life." It's a clear and pres- ent indication that consumers want to participate and play. They're a playful bunch at heart, and in their daily search for meaning, rele- vance, purpose, satisfaction, exhilaration, peace, and frivolity, they have stumbled upon little old you—often because you've been jump- ing in front of them at every twist and turn their whole lives and now they're pausing, reflecting, and responding (as opposed to ig- noring you or pushing you out of the way).

This is your open invitation to figure out how to find the delicate balance between control and camaraderie. When I deliver my vari- ous presentations around the world to eager beaver brand mar- keters, I often tell them to go back to their offices and burn their brand guidelines books—if not literally, then at the very minimum conceptually. Your consumers are color-blind. They don't know the difference between Pantone 155 and 156. Moreover, they don't care! You might really think that it makes a material difference whether the car is always shown with one door open or never pho- tographed from the bottom up; you might really believe that it is mandatory to have the ray of light appearing from a cloud or that the can of soda should never be rotated beyond 75 degrees. But at the end of the day these are just irrelevant checks and balances de- signed to make you feel secure and help you justify your reason for being. Sorry about that.

When consumers choose your brand for their "experiments,"

Figure 8.1    Logo 2.0: Mash-Up Style

*they're choosing your brand.* How else would you like me to explain this to you? When Jose Avila III chose FedEx boxes for his interior decorating and furnishing needs, he chose FedEx. Not DHL. Not UPS. He wasn't interested in what "Brown" could do for him.

For those of you who don't know the story of Jose, here it is. Jose Avila III (see Figure 8.2) is a software programmer who de-

Figure 8.2    Jose Avila III

cided to leave the great state of California for the great state of Arizona. His motivations were financial. California was too expensive. Arizona was not. Jose was looking to furnish his new apartment and by his own account wanted to go to IKEA but could not afford to do so at the present time. So instead he furnished the entire apartment with FedEx boxes. He made a bed out of FedEx boxes. He made a dining room table, a desk, a coffee table, even a sofa—all out of FedEx boxes. (See Figure 8.3.)

You can imagine what happened next, right? FedEx served up a fresh cease-and-desist (which these days is tantamount to a sue-and-rue), accusing Jose of trying to profit off FedEx's intellectual property. Forget the arrogance of this for a moment and think a minute about the cluelessness of slapping a consumer on the wrist for reaching out and "voting" in favor of a brand. Think about the irony of "intellectual property" for a moment. We spend hundreds of millions of dollars to invest in brand equity so that our consumers will notice, consider, choose, and prefer us . . . but when they do end up making that elusive choice, we curb, curtail, and repress them.

This, by the way, is a classic sales mentality. We focus on making the sale and forget about after-sales service.

Yes, I know that this wasn't a direct or straight purchase per se, but Jose was a customer, and a loyal one at that.

Anyway, the story continues. A civil rights attorney at UC Berkeley defended Jose pro bono, Jose ended up on the *Today Show*, *Countdown with Keith Olbermann*, CNN, and so on, and FedEx got annihilated by the blogosphere and anyone with half a brain.

FedEx missed out on a moment of truth, and one it may never get back. The tragedy was not what it did, but what it *didn't* do. Jose could have been FedEx's spokesperson. (I bet he'd have come dirt cheap, too.) FedEx should have called a "pull-out-all-stops" with its media and creative efforts and figured out how to embrace Jose . . . because at the end of the day Jose embodies everything that we're trying to achieve.

This response sums it up best (worst): "The FedEx brand is one of our most valuable assets," says Howard Clabo, a FedEx spokesman. "In this particular instance, we simply asked that the violator stop using our brand for their personal benefit."

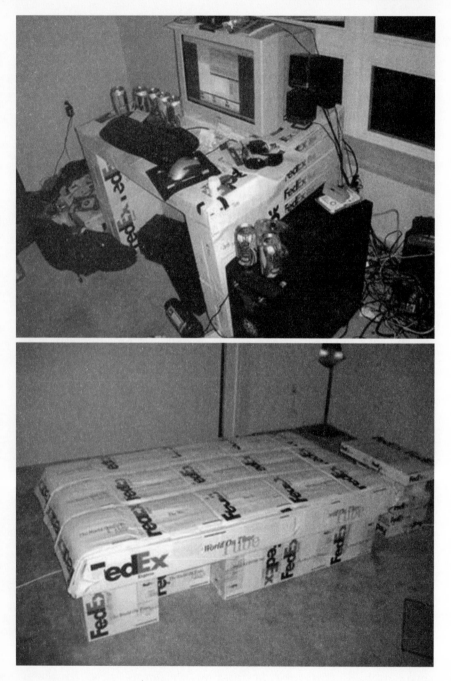

Figure 8.3    FedEx Furniture

Ladies and gentlemen, when you start referring to your customers as violators, you are most certainly not a creator of brand life but rather a prophet of brand death.

## It's Time to Play "What Would You Have Done?"

That's right, ladies and gentlemen, it's time for the game that armchair critics love to love and brand managers hate to hate. So what should FedEx have done? For starters, it could have called in Dakota Jackson or Bruno Mattsson to rework Jose's apartment—using the boxes—but with a professional's help. They could also have invited consumers to submit their furniture designs and possibly even have put the best of them on display in some kind of gallery. Jose Avila was the spokesperson of their dreams (and subsequent nightmares) and would have been so much cheaper than Burt Reynolds, Tom Hanks, or the cast and crew of *The Office*. (FedEx has invested extensively in "bland integration" in this series.)

But let's not heap all the blame on FedEx. The culpability for losing a conversation was not theirs alone. What about UPS and DHL? Why not come to Jose's rescue with a lifetime supply of boxes, accompanied by a message to the effect of "Ours are stronger than theirs"? And what about IKEA? How much would it have cost them to furnish Jose's apartment free of charge versus what they would have gained in goodwill, PR, and free advertising?

The only conversation that did ensue took place independently on the blogs—bloggers talking to other bloggers, which is sweet in an ineffective sort of way, but not very productive for the brand. In this case, and many others like it, the brand was somewhere on the continuum of detached, arrogant, gagged, and hopelessly out of touch. Arguably, any quadrant that did not represent a "present and reporting for duty" outcome was tantamount to AWOL. (See Figure 8.4.)

It's as simple as that. If we don't engage in our consumers' lives, how can we ever expect our consumers to do the same?

Producers are most likely to be content creators, but as we've seen, anybody and everybody has moments when they create conversation via content generation.

**Classifying Engagement**

| | Not Present | Present |
|---|---|---|
| Interested/ Involved | Gagged | Engaged |
| Not Interested/ Not Involved | Out of Touch | Detached/Arrogant |

Figure 8.4    Classifying Engagement

> If engagement is an active state we strive for our consumers to exhibit, then we need to do likewise.

## CONTEXTUALIZATION

Content alone, with no contextualization, is like being all dressed up with nowhere to go. There are three primary means of adding layers of meaning, labels of relevance, and filters of specificity to content in its purest form.

### Commenting

Earlier I offered up some ideas (motivations) as to why consumers create. What about commenting? Commenting is the quintessential embodiment of joining the conversation, and there are obvious benefits. Here are ten offered up by the blogger Chris Garrett.

1. It's the right thing to do. People complain about not having enough comments on their own blog but don't take enough time to comment on others.
2. Comments help you make friends and influence people. Blogging is partly a networking activity. People are more likely to link to you (or do more than that) if they have heard of you.
3. When you comment, people click your link to see what other interesting stuff you write about.
4. By commenting, you develop a blogger's eye for the point of interest in a story and train your brain to think of something interesting.
5. Create commentable content. By observing which posts you commented on and which you did not (or couldn't no matter how hard you tried!), you develop an awareness of what works to attract comments.
6. Comments = ideas. You managed to comment. Could your comment be expanded into a post?
7. You never know who is reading.
8. What you give you get more of back.
9. Comments should be short, fast, and to the point, and they should make an impact. Commenting gives you an excellent chance to sharpen your writing skills.
10. Comment on fresh blogs for fresh perspectives. If you comment on new blogs every day, you're exposed to new ideas and different ways of looking at things, and that may show you a way out of the echo chamber.

Not surprisingly, this post produced a comment factory of its own, with over 95 comments on it by the time this book went to print.[4]

I would add one more item to this list: Commenting is addictive. Not only will you experience the conversation firsthand, as opposed to being lectured about it or reading about it in a book, but more importantly, you'll discover firsthand the power of engagement and

[4]See http://www.chrisg.com/10-reasons-commenting-is-good-for-bloggers/.

the gratification that comes with stepping out of "lurker" mode and making a tangible and valuable contribution. As geeky as this sounds, you'll be exhilarated by the comments of the blogger-in-residence and/or other readers on *your* comment.

In an early algorithm designed to evaluate a blog's talkability, a very simple formula was applied. Take the total number of comments and trackbacks associated with any given blog as a percentage of total posts. This ratio gives a pretty good idea of a blog's resonance and engagement with its readers.

Peeling this back a few layers reveals a simple premise: A post without a comment is like a dog without a bone. Pretty sad and lonely. To this day, I gauge my blog's relative health with a subjective and unscientific assessment of how many consecutive posts earn comments (note that I said "earn") and how many comments they receive. There was a time when I would hit double-digit comments every 25 posts or so. Now this happens a lot more frequently. Earning a healthy number of comments is a clear indication that I'm on the right path and resonating with my audience.

Included in the comment trail is a very familiar recurring name: my own. My propensity to join in my own conversation is critical — perhaps even more important than creating the conversation in the first place. Talking and then walking away is simply another form of one-way communication — nothing better and nothing worse than a newspaper or magazine article.

Speaking of which, newspapers — and to a lesser extent magazines — are doing a great job learning this lesson. These days it is not uncommon to find a comment section or blog or some other kind of conversation catalyst next to the original articles.

This is why I contend that blogs without comments turned on are in fact not blogs at all. My position is that comments are mandatory. I'm more extreme than most in that I also believe that comments should not be moderated. It just seems a little too convenient to be able to keep the neutral or positive comments and throw out the critical or negative ones (whether they're justified or not). That said, in many cases moderation is not just desirable but necessary. As they say, everything in moderation, right?

So what are the lessons for brands? For starters, it is time to move from a culture of "no comment" to one where comments are seen as signs of life. According to the Keller Fay Group, the average American has more than 100 conversations a week about products and services and more than 70 brands are mentioned per week in those conversations. If this is the case, pray tell, where are the brands in these conversations? Obviously, there's not much (legally) that can be done when one person is talking to another, but when the same conversation arises and develops on a blog or a podcast or a discussion group or a message board, why shouldn't and why couldn't a brand be a part of the dialogue?

## Trackbacking

We are living in a climate and a culture where links have become powerful instruments of social currency. There are plenty of "hat tips" that occur constantly in the blogosphere whereby one participant gives credit (more often than not graciously) to another for his or her part in the thread, either as initiator (creator) or facilitator (contextualizer).

The trackback is a terrific mechanism that creates a visible trail (call it a "long trail" if you like) all the way back to the beginning of a particular conversation, idea, revelation, or bitch. Every ripple outwards is another layer of context, meaning, and interpretation on top of the original core message. With every additional interpretation, there is, of course, the risk of broken telephone syndrome, but at least there is a default checks-and-balances system designed to *backtrack* to the inflection points representing truth, honesty, emotion, subjectivity, exaggeration, misrepresentation, and delusion (all our willing participants around the table of conversation).

The trackback runs on an honor system: People supply a link to acknowledge the source or inspiration behind a post. The same honor system is used by the Podsafe Music Network, a thriving repository of rights-cleared music from singers, songwriters, and bands from which podcasters can select and play to their heart's content without any fear of recrimination or compensation. (Music industry take note!) All the podcaster has to do in return is to acknowledge having played the track. Indeed, trust is the new social glue that connects the dots.

## Tagging

The ability to tag or label a piece of content such as a CGC video, blog post, or photograph with keywords such as "FedEx," "furniture," "clueless," "dumb," "DHL," "IKEA," or "Jose Avila" does a few very powerful things. For starters, it associates a brand, say FedEx, with certain descriptors such as "clueless" and "dumb" (hey, if the shoe fits . . .). Now anyone searching for examples of cluelessness or stupidity is most likely going to encounter Jose Avila. Remember "The Office Sucks"? In that case, Google did all the heavy lifting, but with tagging that process is accelerated because content is compartmentalized right from the get-go.

Tagging could just as easily be "tagged" into the creation category, but for the most part it is less a product of the content and more associated with where that content is stored and set up to be consumed at a later point in time.

## PROPAGATION

So you got your content, dressed up nicely in a beautiful shrink-wrapping of context. Now what? In many respects, your job is essentially done. The content-context one-two punch is prime for the final C—Community—or at least for "going viral."

On November 15, 2001 (not too long after the infamous happenings of 9/11), Tom Farmer and Shane Atchison arrived at a DoubleTree Club in Houston, Texas, around 2:00 A.M. Despite the fact that Tom was a member of Hilton's honors program (he was a gold VIP no less), they were refused rooms. Worse still, they encountered a hapless clerk named Mike who showed them ambivalence and disdain. "I have nothing to apologize to you for," said Mike, who seemed to be having difficulty understanding the word "guaranteed."

Long story short, Tom and Shane ended up elsewhere but didn't let this incident go unnoticed or unpunished. Being the road warriors they were, they created a PowerPoint presentation (I guess Keynote wasn't available at the time) and sent it to a bunch of friends who in turn sent it to a bunch of *their* friends.

The presentation included consulting gems like a perceptual map indicating where DoubleTree fitted into the pecking order of desirability, as well as an estimate of future revenue lost owing to the severed relationship.

DoubleTree ended up losing way more than just $18,000 in 2002. (Although I do hear that their Kabul branch is doing swimmingly. Mike is the night clerk there, in case you were wondering.)

Tom and Shane turned to e-mail to actualize themselves and exorcise their demons. Today Tom and Shane might take a video using their Motorola Razr phones or an audio recording using their iRivers. They might post the video to YouTube or submit it to a few podcasts; it would be a good candidate, for instance, for the "Loser of the Week" segment on my podcast. Today the damage would be so much more intense, which is not to say that their original mode of distribution didn't hit the spot. Case in point: Six years later an author is writing all about it and it is new all over again.

## Sharing

Sharing is caring, or so that lovable purple dinosaur named Barney says. Then again, he's a dinosaur and so he's extinct. Sharing is not always the same as caring—or at least not for everyone. Tom and Shane certainly cared about alerting others to the shoddy service offered by DoubleTree.

Sharing itself is a natural behavior. From declaring undying love by shouting it from the highest rooftops to writing a letter to the editor, when we feel strongly about something-good, bad, or ugly—it is natural to want to talk about it to others. I stress the word "natural." Forcing or manipulating others to spread the word—especially when they might not feel comfortable or strongly about it—is decidedly *un*natural. This is another lesson to guide you on your viral ventures.

## "Digging"

As a verb synonymous with searching for someone or something, "Google" will become an official word in *Webster's* someday, but I hope the word "Digging" makes it into the dictionary first. When somebody likes something — or rather, when someone feels strongly about something — colloquially we say that they "dig it." "Digging it," on the other hand, refers today to a web site that uses consensus and the wisdom of crowds to determine who's who in the zoo — namely, which articles deserve to be on the front page and above the fold rather than buried on page 2 and beyond.

News aggregators like Digg represent a sea change in how old-school communication is progressing to a two-sided conversation. Digg also highlights the welcome liberation of news from hidden agenda, subjective filtering, and bad old control.

If only Digg had been around during many of the previous presidential elections. That way, all the candidates' propaganda might have taken a backseat to the issues that the voting public really cares about.

Speaking of Fox News, they — along with several of the 24-hour cable news networks — have been quite progressive in allowing their viewers to vote on which news stories should make the broadcast. This probably has more to do with the fact that there are just so many times the same news can be repeated the same way over a slow news period, as opposed to raw innovation. Digging is a popularity contest with radical propagation consequences. The mash-up between human power and technology power is an unbeatable combination, and we can expect more sophisticated means of spreading to become pervasive in our lives.

As an aside, there are growing concerns about abuse and manipulation of this methodology, especially when technology is involved. We need new solutions to quickly weed out these elements, using the same combination of technology checks and self-policing human balances.

## Digg Revolt

Around May 2007, *users* of the popular human-curated news site Digg began posting links to web pages that revealed the copyright encryption key for HD-DVDs. By midday on May 1, Advanced Access Content Systems (AACS), the consortium that manages HD-DVD licensing and controls the intellectual property for the encryption code, had notified Digg (along with other news sites) of the breach and requested that Digg remove all stories referencing the crack code. Digg complied.

Within hours, in a movement that came to be called "the Digg revolt," community members flooded Digg's "Popular Stories" pages with links to stories containing the HD-DVD hack, as well as numerous stories criticizing Digg for submitting to corporate pressures and removing the original set of stories. Although it was still debatable whether submissions containing the code violate the site's terms of use, it was clear that the Digg community did not take lightly the site's decision to exert control over the community-driven news-filtering process. The site's management decided to change their position and squarely back their user base, against AACS.

At 9:00 P.M. that same evening, Digg founder Kevin Rose published a blog post (referencing the actual crack code in its header) in which he wrote that, based on the community's swift negative reaction to Digg's decision to comply and take down the offending posts, Digg would in fact allow stories and comments containing the code. Rose wrote, "You've made it clear. You'd rather see Digg go down fighting than bow down to a bigger company. We hear you, and effective immediately we won't delete stories or comments containing the code and will deal with whatever the consequences might be. If we lose, then what the hell, at least we died trying."

Link to complete Digg blog post: http://blog.digg.com/?p=74.

As of this writing, Digg is still up and running, and continues to defer to its community for the curation of online news, including links to stories that contain hack codes that will allow users to run iPhones on non-ATT wireless networks (as an interesting side note, the iPhone was cracked by the same hacker who released the HD-DVD code.)

## Listing

Everybody loves a list, which is a different type of aggregator — certainly not as sophisticated as Digg, but effective nonetheless. In the blogosphere, lists are synonymous with link bait, and in many cases this is tolerated by our predictable egos. When Jaffe Juice was voted 11th in Todd And's "Power 150" list of top marketing blogs, I immediately crowed about it and naturally linked back to Todd And so that I could direct my readers to see for themselves how utterly important I was.

PS: *Who the hell is Todd And???*

I have no idea, but he has great taste in blogs.

Todd actually and possibly unwittingly started another conversation in setting up his Power 150 list. In his extensive workings, which included Alexa and Google rankings, he included the "Todd And Score," which was a completely subjective rating he assigned to blogs based on what he perceived to be quality content, creative approach, and relevancy. Todd did assign a low weighting to his score, relative to the other complex and intricate algorithms; as he explained it to me, by taking out his score, the overall rankings were almost completely unaffected. But in doing so, he added a human lens to his list and branded it in a way that differentiated him and his list from the rest of the pack.

PS: Todd's Power 150 has since been picked up by Advertising Age (www.adage.com/power150)

## COME ON IN, THE WATER'S FINE

At every possible point on the creation-contextualization-propagation path, there exists an opportunity for brands to participate in the dialogue—to join the conversation already in progress. Sometimes their role can be active and integral to determining where the conversation heads and what transpires as a result. Other times they can begin the conversation—providing the spark, the bellows, the accelerant, the altar, or the marshmallows. (It doesn't always have to be about life and death.)

## A PIXEL FOR YOUR THOUGHTS

Alex Tew, a British university student, came up with a bizarre and yet brilliant concept—the first one-million-pixel homepage. He then set out to get all one million pixels sponsored. Alex was profiled across the gamut, including in the *Wall Street Journal*. He certainly could be described as an entrepreneur, even an opportunist, but he was primarily a member of generation i — a guy like you and me, with a good heart and an even better brain!

While Alex may have milked a million-dollar cash cow, what he really was doing was unveiling a million different conversations, a million opportunities for small companies and brands to get noticed, and a million ideas for future copycats, including:

- www.worldofpersia.com
- www.nickelsforkatrina.org
- www.monpremiermillion.com

What struck me as I read about Alex was that his efforts represented a very interesting consumer behavior trend — namely, the democratization of experience itself. In many of these cases, consumers were giving others the opportunity to buy into (literally) a cause, experience, action, idea, and so on. Some were frivolous and others not.

# 9

# What Conversations
# Are in Your Future?

What does all of this mean for brand marketers? Here are the figures, courtesy of a landmark survey piloted in early 2007 by yours truly and TWI Surveys on behalf of the Society for New Communications Research (SNCR).

The survey was conducted via online survey among 260 marketing communications professionals during February 2007. Among these respondents, 65.8 percent were U.S.-based, 11.9 percent were from Europe, 8.8 percent were from Canada, and 44.3 percent reported to either the CEO/COO/president or a senior marketing executive.

The topline results were revealing, to say the least, but before revealing the key takeaways, here are a handful of verbatims from the respondents answering the question, "What is your definition of conversational marketing?" (See Figure 9.1.)

## CAPABILITY LAGS COMMITMENT

As the following chart on beliefs and understandings illustrates, 57.3 percent of the sample either agreed or strongly agreed that monitoring conversations is important to overall success, but only 45.8 percent and 39.6 percent either agreed or strongly agreed that their organization had a good understanding of where conversations were taking place, as well as what was being said in these conversations. (See Figure 9.2.)

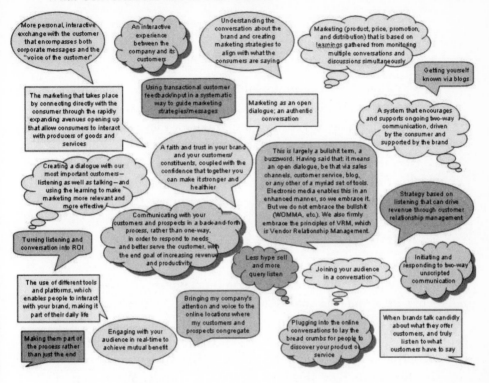

Figure 9.1 Definitions of Conversational Marketing

The SNCR-Jaffe survey revealed an overwhelming consensus in favor of the correlation between customer conversations and brand reputation (98.5 percent), bottom line (83 percent), and loyalty (94.6 percent), and yet when asked the question about the extent to which these customers own the brand, only 38.5 percent

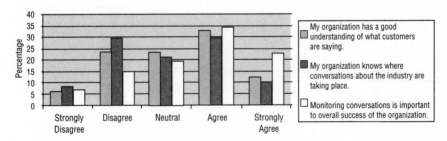

Figure 9.2 Beliefs and Understandings

were in agreement. (See Figure 9.3.) There are a few explanations (some more obvious than not) for this disconnect:

1. The first three questions address the individual respondent and the fourth refers to the organization. It thus might not be surprising that anyone willing to take a survey on conversational marketing would have a different perspective than the organization.
2. The disconnect illustrates the massive cultural and organizational shifts that need to take place within companies in order to make the journey from communication to conversation.
3. Honesty.

Asked whether their organization incorporates conversational elements into ongoing marketing strategies, 29.4 percent of the sample replied that this happened "often" or "very often." On the other end of the spectrum, one in ten respondents indicated that their company "never" includes conversational elements, whereas one in three indicated that this happened "rarely" or "never." In other words, conversational marketing is still incorporated into ongoing plans only sporadically or on an ad-hoc basis. This is probably true of larger organizations, particularly those with larger brand portfolios. In these companies, conversational

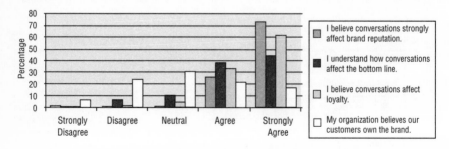

Figure 9.3   Leave Branding to the Professionals!

marketing is adopted on a case-by-case basis and is usually the work of a handful of individuals who are a little more adept with or open to experimentation than their colleagues. In these cases, adoption follows the COST—Cultural, Organizational, Strategic, and Tactical—analogy (Chapter 18). (See Figure 9.4.)

Drilling down a little deeper into the types of approaches being deployed over a 12-month time frame, we see blogs and RSS leading the way, with one out of every two respondents currently deploying some form. Next come social networking and conversational/customer service, with four out of ten currently using them. I have to admit that I'm a little troubled with the customer service numbers; I can only surmise that they reflect siloed organizations—where marketing or advertising or PR is not connected to

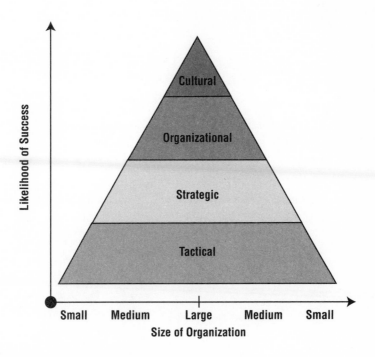

Figure 9.4   The COST Challenge

customer service—or the fact that customer service is not being deployed as a proactive conversational strategy. Next come CGC and podcasts, with one out of three respondents saying that they use these forms. (See Figure 9.5.)

When categorizing these approaches into community-versus-dialogue-versus-partnership, partnership is the one area that seems to lag in adoption behind community and dialogue. Wikis, co-creation, and open-source marketing are being used in only 1 out of every 10 respondents' organizations.

Bringing up the tail are virtual worlds like Second Life.

On the flip side, over 50 percent of the sample indicated that they would *not* be deploying wikis, co-creation, open-source, or virtual worlds within the next 12 months. In light of planning and budgeting cycles, the speed at which corporations tend to move, and the vast array of approaches that may be higher up the prioritization list, this is somewhat understandable.

That said, let their loss be your gain.

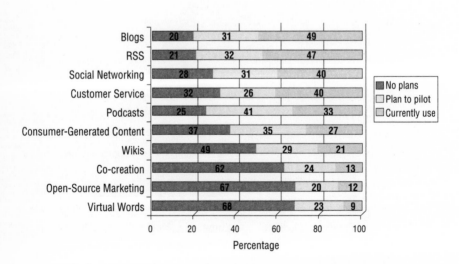

Figure 9.5   Adoption of Conversational Approaches (12 Months)

## Marketing Communications: Funneling Its Way toward Conversational Marketing

In perhaps the most shocking finding, a full 56.9 percent of respondents contended that in five years' time they would spend more on conversational marketing than on traditional marketing. Another 23.8 percent believed they would spend the same amount. In other words, 81 percent of all respondents believed that in five years they would be spending as much if not more on conversational marketing than on traditional marketing.

I won't lie to you. I am a big believer in the axiom of lies, damn lies, and statistics, but when I see data like this, it's hard to ignore. Even a number that was 50 percent lower would still translate into massive budget reallocations, strategic and cultural realignments, and, no doubt, tremendous organizational shifts.

Looking a little deeper at these numbers, a few things become evident:

1. The majority of the market is still at square one. A majority (55.1 percent) of respondents are spending 1 percent or less of their marketing communications budgets on conversational marketing, and 70 percent are spending 2.5 percent or less.

2. In five years, however, 16.4 percent expect to be spending 25 percent or more on conversation, and a full 42 percent expect to be investing 10 percent or more. This expectation seems to be inconsistent with the earlier prediction against traditional marketing; however, one very plausible explanation could be the continued meteoric rise and growth of interactive marketing (including its very popular subspecialties of video and search) and digitalization of all media at the expense of so-called traditional media. This inference is further validated by a 2007 report by Veronis Suhler Stevenson, which projects internet advertising to become the leading ad medium in the US by 2011.

3. How about one year's time? Two-thirds of respondents (67.7 percent) will be increasing their investment in conversation

within the next 12 months. Three out of four of this subset will be increasing their budget only marginally versus substantially. This could indicate an overall climate of cautious experimentation, using a classic test-learn-evolve methodology.

## SUCCESS METRICS ARE BROADER THAN SALES ALONE

Just under one-quarter (23.5 percent) of respondents felt that boosts in sales were the primary determinant of success, compared to 28.8 percent who felt that a more intimate knowledge of customers was the key driver. Almost one out of five (19.2 percent) associated buzz or PR with conversational success, which would be consistent with a growing interest in word-of-mouth marketing and, specifically, connecting with influencers and opinion leaders as a way of spreading "viral" goodwill. Rounding up the leading indicators of success, 18.5 percent said it was attributable to improved brand health.

In this era of accountability and scrutiny of ROI, it is time for a new acronym to emerge—namely, ROC (Return on Conversation, of course). Even though the last thing the industry needs is a new acronym, the consensus does seem to indicate that best practices in conversational marketing are not just focused on longer-term indicators of success but permeate the organization across multiple levels—insights, word of mouth, brand equity—converging on a powerful and profound common thread or theme: the consumer.

That said, all of these indicators can and arguably should be converted and translated into a harder and more tangible metric of success—be it placing a value on total customer and media impressions or a multiplier that bridges brand health and stock price.

## ORGANIZATIONS ARE ABOUT TO GO THROUGH TURBULENT UPHEAVAL

Just who will be responsible for conversation? Twenty-one percent held that PR or corporate communications will hold the key. Closely behind was the marketing department, with 18 percent of the vote. Lagging way behind was customer service, with 4 percent, and both general management and advertising brought up the rear. The majority of respondents held that "some combination of the various departments" would hold primary responsibility over conversation. (See Figure 9.6.)

I'm pretty sneaky in that I offered up "all of the above" as an obvious choice. If you think about it at the end of the day, conversation *should* permeate the entire organization; it is way too important to be a silo or vertical function of expertise. True enough, except that I don't have to tell you how difficult it is to break down the silos of corporate organizations.

Look within your own company if you need any convincing. Just how exactly do you think you're going to be able to pull off this mammoth exercise in conversation, collaboration, and integration?

This is one of those times when I would actually advocate for a horizontal silo—one that would oversee and connect the entire organization, as opposed to a vertical department-by-department responsibility.

I'm calling for the establishment of a conversation department, led by a chief conversation officer. Said CCO would report to the very top and thus bypass any blinkered or biased silos. The conversation department would be populated by true generalists with expertise across marketing, advertising, internal communications, corporate communications, customer service, government, analysis,

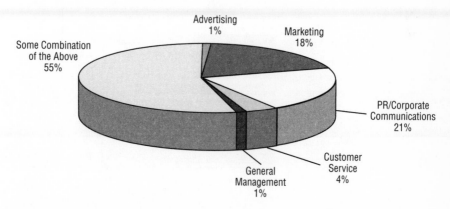

Figure 9.6   Who Should Be in Charge of Conversation?

and press relations. They would be responsible for monitoring and listening to conversations, understanding and contextualizing them, responding to and catalyzing existing conversations, and, ultimately, joining them. The only remaining part of the mix would be starting conversations, and to this end they would serve in an advisory capacity or support role to the necessary constituents. As to whether they should have sign-off or veto authority to ensure a certain quality control, I could argue either way.

What do you think? Do organizations need another department and C-type? How far would you take this? Weigh in at www.jointheconversation.us/chief

## CHALLENGES AHEAD: TALENT, CULTURE, METRICS

When asked about the primary challenges that prevent companies from investing more in conversation, just over half the sample (51.5 percent) reported that "manpower restraints" were an impediment, followed by fear of loss of control (46.9 percent), inadequate metrics (45.4 percent), the culture of the organization (43.5 percent), and difficulty with internal sell-through (35.8 percent). (See Figure 9.7.)

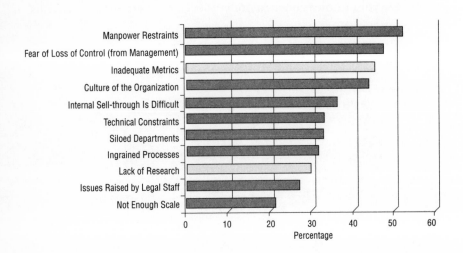

Figure 9.7    Business Challenges Impeding Investment in Conversation

Other barriers included ingrained processes, siloed departments, technical constraints, and lack of research.

Put them all together and four distinct clusters emerge:

1. *Talent and capabilities.* The data seems to suggest that companies are prepared to explore a reality in which conversation plays a core role, but that they are constrained by the lack of ready, willing, or able team members who are fully conversant in community, dialogue, and partnership. Since most companies have more money than brains, the ability to invest in people, processes, and technology should—as the chart suggests—be high on priority lists.

2. *The need for change management.* Such investments will not happen, however, until there is a deep-seated belief in and commitment to a culture and environment of open, honest, and direct conversation—not just between the company and its customers (and vice versa) but also between employee and customer, and between employee and employee. The shift from command-and-control to care-and-share is a gargantuan leap of faith, and its implications for how the company conducts business should not be underestimated.

3. *Research and metrics.* One way to help seed and sell through the idea is by proof of concept. Like it or not, the world still functions on precedents and best practices, even when there are few of these to go around. In this case, new metrics will need to be defined and benchmarked in order to reveal new insights.

4. *Organizational dynamics.* If you get this far, trust the rot of lethargy and paranoia to inhibit any sweeping reforms. Companies are going to need to be able to overhaul many of their ingrained processes in order to refresh the ways in which they react and *proact* to the lively and unpredictable passion, opinion, creativity, and attitude of conversation.

# 10

# Why Are You So
# Afraid of Conversation?

The following chapter has been written in full by anyone who cares
enough to answer the question posed in the chapter title. In true communal fashion, I opened up this chapter to my readers, to my community . . . to you! Through a wiki (a community-powered and
completely editable collaborative tool), people not only contributed to
this chapter but edited other people's contributions as well. The chapter is reprinted here with only length-related edits. You can view the
chapter in its entirety, as well as the historical and chronological evolution and development, on *www.jointheconversation.us/wiki*

I kick off the chapter and then *you* take over!

You've just seen the figures . . . the stats suggesting that organizations (yours) are not equipped to deliver against the promise and
potential of conversation. You certainly feel it is important, and yet
you are hamstrung by inactivity, indifference, and insecurity.

If you think about it, all our professional lives have been spent
trying to understand our consumer, trying to get closer to our consumer, trying to connect with our consumers. In many respects,
these efforts have been a series of guesstimates, combined with artificial techniques such as focus groups, syndicated research, and various number-crunching exercises. After all of this, what do we really
know about our consumers?

We are so afraid of our consumers that we feel the need to place
them behind a one-way mirror as we nervously stuff our faces with
M&Ms, hoping that the group doesn't become unruly and decide to
"storm the castle." We've treated our consumers like caged animals

and taken unprecedented steps to ensure that any communication between us and them is controlled, contrived, and largely one-way.

Only now consumers have awakened from their slumbers; rising from their artificial cocoons, they are reaching out to us to make first contact.

And yet here we are—petrified, paralyzed, beside ourselves with indecision and angst, fearing the wrath of legal affairs and the paranoia of actually responding to the "gullets whose only purpose in life is to gulp products and crap cash." Perhaps it's time to face our fears.

Perhaps it's time to come out of hiding.

Perhaps it's time to deal with the realities of "first contact"—the good, the bad, and the ugly.

Perhaps it's time for us all to realize that consumers do have power. They control their own decisions and are not afraid to turn on us at any moment.

So let me ask you: Why are you so afraid of conversation?

## John Wall (Ronin Marketeer) on Taking the First Step

People fear the conversation because it is new. It is different. It's like the trepidation of a new golfer facing the country club for the first time. You've been practicing your skills (marketing, your swing, whatever), and here's this place where the pros live, play, and chat. They have their own language, customs, procedures, rituals, and inside jokes. You scare yourself: *Will I get kicked out if I put my golf shoes on in the parking lot?* Or *What if someone comments that my posts and opinions are ridiculous and stupid?*

The irony of it all is that once you have made it past the first step you find that it's much easier than you feared. Most people are astonished at how many crappy golfers are at the country club (and others will argue that it's not even about the golf). But you won't know who they are and who the next billionaires are unless you get inside and look around the club.

If that carrot doesn't get you, remember the stick: If you are a professional, it's your duty to learn about how to do your job more proficiently. If not, your business will eventually go to those who do.

There are only three kinds of people: bus drivers, bus riders, and pedestrian targets. Who do you want to be?

Seek out the experts. Unlike the 100-year-old country club, these groups tend to be 20 minutes old or less. There's always a person willing to explain the secret handshake and give you the tour.

## Kevin Behringer (Fly-Over Marketing) on Walking the Talk

There are two main reasons that people are scared of conversation. One very real fear is summarized by John Wall: People are scared of looking stupid. It's the old "don't raise your hand in class" concept of not being confident enough in your ideas, your beliefs, or your opinion to put it out there for others to read/view/critique/criticize. Letting people possibly criticize you is a scary thing because they're not just criticizing your idea, they're criticizing *you*. This often becomes a reason not to join the conversation.

The second reason is the concept of the "digital memory." With the advent of social media and the shift from traditional "control you by talking at you" media, when you put an idea out there—when you join the conversation—you not only lose control, but that loss of control is there for everyone to see . . . forever. For many people, it's a fearful thing to go "on the record" and potentially embarrass themselves, their family, their company, you name it. With the unfailing memory of the Internet, these fears are even more real because the record of your failure (or idiocy) is there for good. It's nearly impossible to take it back.

That said, it's important to move beyond these fears. It's very obvious when talking to "old marketers" (not age old, but philosophy old) that the concept of giving up control by joining the conversation scares them. The old way of putting out a sterilized message that really doesn't say anything only works if you don't look out into the world to see if it's working! What really happens is that these marketers put out this message that they want people to believe and then go on with their lives or business, not living out that message. Then every customer who sees the dissonance between their words and actions says to themselves, "That company doesn't walk its talk." This has gone on forever, but companies used to be blissfully ignorant because no one heard the opinions of those customers. Now the customers are talking, and if you don't "walk the talk" down to every last period and comma . . . they're gone.

It's time to treat people as people. If you treat your customers like numbers, they'll act like numbers. Numbers without loyalty. Numbers who don't care about you or your company. Numbers who base their decisions on the things you have no control over.

And they'll become someone else's numbers.

### Roman Mandrick (KsanLab) on Risk and Inertia

First of all, marketing VPs are afraid of conversation because they don't want to risk. They play not to lose because their career is at stake. Why do I have to be worried about conversation with my customers if all I have to do is to fulfill plans and achieve goals that are being set by top managers? What if our product is not good enough? What if the customers tell the truth and it's not very nice to hear and report to my bosses?

The point is that there is no choice. You have to start a conversation; otherwise, it will eventually be started by your consumers and you will be out of the room. If your product is not ideal and has significant flaws, don't lie please. You better tell the truth to your customers. You have to be honest, or you have to be very, very afraid of any conversation with your customers.

The second reason why even CEOs are afraid to start a conversation is inertia. It's inertia that kills new mind-sets, new approaches to get your customers happy. It kills your future incomes, growth, and development. It can't be seen right away. Today you're paralyzed by inertia; in one or two years, you'll find yourself and your company trying hard to sell your product.

### Lee Hopkins (Better Communication Results) on the Insights of the Internal Market

Of course, the conversation is both external to the company as well as internal. Marketers traditionally focus on the external market (naturally, because it is far larger in size than the number of company and key supplier/partner employees), but the conversation paradigm/philosophy that now governs how the Internet works (and has always governed how people relate to each other) means that both in front of and behind the corporate firewall there are conversations occurring that marketers need to be paying attention to and contributing to.

However, most medium-large companies are not able to quickly reengineer their internal IT structures to help marketers facilitate these conversations. And even if the various departments (IT, marketing, finance, and so on) *were* able to work seamlessly together, many marketers would be highly apprehensive about contributing—because they can meet the person they are electronically conversing with down at the water cooler or in the parking lot. If the online conversation becomes heated or there is disagreement, it can be easier to hide behind a monitor than behind the water cooler.

But it is the internal conversation that may turn out to be the most important to marketers, and the one they should be focusing on first. Employees have a vested interest in ensuring that the business does well, and thus they often have ideas about a product's marketing, packaging, design, build, or usability that are crucial to hear before the world at large says the same things but perhaps not so politely.

At the end of the day, marketers may eventually have no choice but to join the conversation with the external market, but they may also choose to miss out on the richness of the long-term face-saving insight that comes from the internal market. Which would be totally understandable and very sad.

## Sivaraman Swaminathan on Why Conversations Are Never Assembly-Line

Perhaps it is a good idea to trace this to the history and growth of organizations in the industrial age. This was the age when efficiency was the focus. Organizations were built around driving productivity. People were trained to do things over and over again—faster and quicker. For over a century, people worked in an era of mass production. Hence, they forgot the ability to develop conversations.

They worked in large organizations that told them what to do rather than get them to explore what to do.

We therefore moved from:

- An era of the "inventory of goods" to an era of the "inventory of ideas"
- An era of "scarcity" to an era of "insatiable choices"
- An era of "information poverty" to an era of "information overload"

Imagine the kind of shift they would have to make for this new ecosystem. Companies were not ready for a conversation era and an environment where one has to express, empathize, engage, enable, and empower. The mind-set a marketer must have is not to "inform at any cost" but to "spread at no cost." This is a new marketing paradigm that demands new thinking, new rules, and new ideas.

Conversation at the end of the day is two-way. Conversations require:

- A capability to accept reality, as it were, because that's how consumers talk among themselves
- The ability to listen and respond in an unbiased manner
- Skills to experiment, learn, and develop
- The ability to change the course of one's action swiftly, even if the decision was wrong

Most marketers are used to the good old one-way communication where a message is sent and lots of fingers are kept crossed, hoping that the message sticks. In a conversation, it won't. It will bounce right back, and it won't look anything like what you originally sent; it will be a breathing human being's response to your initial action.

## Sean Ammirati (Profitable Signals) on the Corporate Disconnect

In my interactions with senior VPs of marketing at organizations of all sizes, there seems to be a bigger disconnect. That disconnect is that most aren't actively monitoring or "reading" the things being written about them on the Web.

Marketing executives need to listen to the conversation and act on what they hear before they can join the conversation. So why aren't they listening?

Listening to the online conversation is much easier than focus groups and phone surveys ever were! There are literally dozens of online tools to monitor the conversation for mentions of a company's executives, name, and industry.

Acting on what you hear becomes *essential*! The suggestions, complaints, and new product ideas will be so compelling, and if you care at all you'll have to act. Blog posts and comments become natural opportunities to "write" into this emerging conversation. You don't need a blog or social network to do it! You can just comment on other people's posts and join the conversation. As that becomes more comfortable, it gets easier and easier to participate.

### John C. Havens (PodCamp NYC) on Misuses of Conversation

I actually don't fear conversations. I fear the unwelcome stepchildren of true conversation, including:

- Small talk
- Demeaning language
- Corporatese

We all converse. But we shade it according to our needs and desires. Sometimes we hide—hence the small talk. We parry any genuine jabs at connection and stick to "safe" subjects while waiting for our drinks at the bar. At best, these pleasantries can fill gaps in time much like a stint at Tetris brought to life. At worst, the vacuum of gray matter and lack of effort made at conversation can tarnish the soul and wound the artist within.

Demeaning language can be the bailiwick of the boardroom, with barbed jibes intended for levity cutting at the core of one's character. Veiling their tongue-poison with phrases like, "Don't take it personally," or "Just kidding," purveyors of negativity galvanize the erosion of true conversation by instilling fear instead of fellowship.

Corporatese contradicts the reality that all humans and their institutions are fallible. While branding can be an opportunity to creatively present your vision to the marketplace, corporatese condescendingly spins where it wants for buzz. This hyperbolic language replaces reality with rhetoric and alienates the audience it should embrace.

I used to fear certain conversations until I learned that there's valor in speaking truth with a purpose. It's a risk to speak your heart/mind when your sole purpose is to improve the life of your listener; they may not like what you say no matter your intention. But if they're willing to take critique and transform rather than retreat, they'll welcome your counsel.

*The true wisdom of a conversation lies in listening.*

Ironically, we tend to fear silence in a conversation, but we all seek out the people who'll let us bend their ear. Perhaps to help curb our fear of genuine connection while speaking, we should treasure the communion of shared discourse not dependent on words.

## Debra R. Murphy (Vista Consulting) on Learning New Tools for Conversation

It is not fear that is keeping corporate marketers from joining the conversation. It is lack of knowledge.

The evolution of the Internet into a medium that encourages interaction and socialization has placed more burdens on marketing. It's a new game once again, and marketers are now faced with the challenge of applying the second-generation technologies to their marketing mix. They have an enormous learning curve and are bombarded with an overwhelming amount of information that needs to be absorbed before they can feel comfortable employing this new media as a marketing tool. Change has happened at such a rapid pace that those who are not early adopters have to totally immerse themselves to figure out what to do. To find the time and energy to learn about the technology, experiment with the tools, learn the etiquette and culture, comment, socialize, and become part of the new social networking world is massive.

It takes the new media visionaries to apply these technologies in ways that make them more relevant to all types of businesses. Now many will be trying to figure out how to take advantage of this channel, quickly, in order not to be left behind. More will enter the conversation; it is just a matter of time.

### Peter Stephenson and Fred Madderom (On Communications) on Having Something Interesting to Say

Why be afraid of conversation when it can lead to genuine engagement?

We've all been at the client working session where the facilitator "rabbits on" about "who would your brand be if it were a person." You can't stop thinking about a boring and mind-numbing conversation with your tedious uncle, who you always get caught with at the obligatory family barbecue.

To engage in conversation you need a story to tell. One that is engaging. Now ask yourself: How many multinational brands could hold an interesting conversation with their customers today at a barbecue?

Consumers are moving on from brands that are unable to engage with them. With increasing consumer control and the growing importance of brand authenticity, it's inevitable that marketers will need to join the conversation or, quite frankly, consumers will move on without them.

> *The more in control we are, the more out of touch we become. But the more willing we are to let go a little, the more we're finding we get in touch [with consumers].*
> —A. G. Lafley, Chief Executive Officer, Procter & Gamble, ANA conference.

Good conversations are surprising. They are engaging, intriguing, and about opinions and ideas. They challenge and inspire you.

But above all they are a natural part of life. In most conversations, you only need to introduce yourself, have a point of view, and be a good listener to achieve a meaningful relationship.

Marketers, agencies, and media need to think differently. They need to become inclusive. The language of conversation needs to be reinvented as well.

The funny thing is that we often find that our tedious uncle actually did have something interesting to say. It's just that people need to have the patience to dig hard to find it, a quality not all consumers have in this fast-paced world today.

### Frans Jan Boon on Being in Control

*Old habits die hard.* For years and years, marketers have been used to communicating one-way. The rare online response in the early days of the Internet was handled by the online agency or, worse, by the internal IT department.

*Afraid of losing control.* Marketers used to be in control, to a certain level, of the communication process. Marketers who want to maintain a certain level of control have to join the conversation. But above all, marketers need to realize that they will never have total control anymore.

*Attitude and experience.* Many marketers have heard of MySpace, Facebook, YouTube, and others but have never really experienced any of them. This leaves them unaware of both the positive and negative influence these can have on their company, brands, products, or themselves. To be fully aware of that, they have to join this networked society and gain experience. Get to know the online etiquette, culture, and common phrases. Know how to interpret online conversations and how to (re)act. Only then will they be able to decrease their fear of conversations and start one or participate in one.

## David Levy on Being Human

It's ironic that anyone would be afraid of conversation, since human beings as a species are hard-wired for it. Our ability to communicate and to tell stories is one of the handful of tiny incremental differences in our DNA vis-à-vis other mammals that makes us human.

That said, one of the reasons we are so afraid of conversation is that these roles we play as marketers, whether on the agency side or the client side, get in the way of our essential humanity.

Ultimately we are all *human*, but when you attach titles like "VP of Marketing" or "Account Executive" to our humanity, sometimes our good sense goes out the window. We start thinking about "measures of success," "risk," "making our numbers," minimizing our "burn rate," and other sundry worries that attach to us like barnacles in the workplace. Not to diminish such concerns—most of us have to put the pork chops on the table.

But we often go too far in our method acting. We get too into playing these roles, and we find ourselves intermediated, disjointed. Our various roles jockey for position and fight for our own attention. We lose site of the basics: talking, listening, writing, narrative. That is us.

So joining the conversation might be another way of describing a pathway back to our essential selves. To reintegrate them. The "joining" is the key. The more we can participate and experiment, the more we can forget about the roles we play and remember that "the conversation" should come naturally.

## Elizabeth Harrin on Why Size Matters

I think it is interesting to look at the characteristics of organizations that appear afraid to start a dialogue with their consumers. Utility companies are good examples: You get an automated phone line, a bill, and maybe a newsletter and no hint that the company wants to hear what its customers think. Small companies, on the other hand, appear to be more open to conversation.

So if there are companies that are conversing, what makes it so hard for the others? Larger companies have their own specific challenges:

- The larger the company, the larger the pool of clients. Where can you possibly start? Listening in to the online conversations already taking place about your company (or competitors) is a toe in the water. But when you want to dive in, commenting on other people's blog posts really isn't enough.
- Large organizations are unwilling to put their reputations in the hands of low-level employees. Blogosphere conversations are etched in society's electronic memory, and blogging has the potential to make every employee a journalist. In companies where only the top directors are allowed to comment to the press, and only then through the curtain of their PR department, it's a very large leap to blog posting, online forums, and podcasting.
- Marketers in large organizations move slowly. It's not their fault. Large organizations move slowly—it's just how they work. The time it takes to research, present, have approved, and implement a conversational marketing strategy means that large organizations are by their nature less agile than their smaller counterparts.

## Mitch Joel (Twist Image) on the New Power of the Individual

I don't think marketers are afraid to join the conversation. I think they're afraid of the new reality. The new reality is simply that an individual—someone like you and me—can have real power. Marketers spend their days worrying about losing control of their brand. They should be much more focused on the fact that they never had control of their brand. They were simply able to scream louder than the individual.

All of these social media tools have democratized the media and given rise not just to citizen marketers but to the core truth that if you do indeed have voice, then you have control. When one individual can create a blog posting called "Dell Hell," that forces a major corporation to look at its customer service, because said individual is now able to scream as loudly as the corporation by leveraging simple Web-based tools that gave him access to voice, access to a community, and, more importantly, access to the collective wisdom of people who share a similar point of view.

Marketers should stop interrupting the conversation with their benign messages and should start getting involved in the conversations by providing unique content, care, and authenticity through transparency. You know, start acting like human beings.

In the end, maybe that's what they are truly afraid of: being transparent, authentic, and human. The days of hiding behind a strategic public relations campaign or a multimillion-dollar ad campaign may be coming to an end, and that end may be evaporating faster because the average person is commanding real power through social media and simple online tools to harness the voice and the community.

### Austin Kronig (Fresh + Squeezed) on the Demands of Conversation

When it comes to Web 2.0 and joining the conversation, marketers are too concerned over the amount of responsibility and maintenance required to initiate and monitor consumer dialogue. Call it complacency, but marketers worry that by joining the conversation they have eternally wedded themselves to their consumer. In a space eminent for immediate outbursts and widespread consumer havoc, marketers worry about the representation of their brands and don't want to deal with the myriad of consumer sensibilities.

Today marketers can more effectively persuade through two-way conversation. However, this form of communication requires marketers to have something important to say on a regular basis. Meanwhile, two-way conversation tests a marketer's ability to listen. If attention isn't placed on the consumer, all conversation and ideas are thereby lost. Under this new model, then, marketers must become facilitators of new ideas with the understanding that "the consumer always knows best."

## Michael Seaton on the Client Side

Who's afraid of the big bad conversation? Not me.

I believe that the fear of conversation ultimately stems from being frightened of hearing "You failed" or "You made a mistake" from one's peers and superiors. Perhaps chances are not taken because no one else has previously taken chances within your environment. No one has witnessed any radical departure from the conventional wisdom or challenge to the status quo. Why? Because the prevailing perception is that support on these types of initiatives will not be there. Anything out of the ordinary, or beyond the tried, tested, and tired, will be frowned upon. *Unfortunately, the phrase "think outside the box" applies only to thinking, not to actually doing.*

The real problem is that fearless leaders are far and few between. Most individuals never even try. So the game for many becomes one of sitting on the sidelines, waiting for other brave souls to take the leap. Some other "sucker" whose mistakes we can point a finger at. Begs the question: Why is it that way?

Sir Ken Robinson has brilliantly spoken about how children are born with vast creative talents that are then systematically squashed from the earliest opportunity. Through the education system and through negative reinforcement from parents, mistakes are made out to be very bad things. However, mistakes are fundamental building blocks in the learning and growing process. Robinson points out that creativity in education is as important as literacy and should be treated as such. Yet it is not made a priority. Kids in school are taught to be average, to regurgitate and not deviate—to suppress the urge to be creative.

He has said that "to take chances is to not be frightened of being wrong." In other words, those who are not prepared to be wrong will never come up with anything original or be creative. Wrong has bad consequences. And unfortunately, this is the model of many organizations—where the stigma of making a mistake looms large.

So there you have it. That is the basis of the fear of conversation. Blame it on the system and don't worry about it any further. Whether you believe that consumers are not able to handle the truth of conversation or not does not really matter. The system has made your mind up for you. There is no fear of making a mistake as long as you let someone else get into the conversation and you remain silent. Protect yourself from ever hearing anything bad and don't change, just do what you are used to. Being insulated is good.

But wait a minute. What if not joining the conversation is really the mistake?

## Duane Brown (Creative Traction) on Looking at Conversation from the Consumer's Perspective

The enemy of both business and creativity is fear. People are afraid of messing up and having it become public knowledge. Fear is what stops people from following their heart and passion. Fear is what kills off a good idea because it's different. Fear is the one thing we shouldn't be using as to why we don't join the conversation. However, there are four other reasons why people don't join the conversation:

*People are lazy*. My generation is lazy; yeah, there I said it. Sure we do MySpace and Facebook, but they don't require real work or brains to have a conversation. Society is lazy as a whole, and this needs to change.

*Respect of your peers*. We don't feel like we are respected at times. I know I've felt this way recently from people older than me. Say what you will about my generation, but respect and speaking to me as a person and not a kid goes a long way. I think the ad agency Crispin Porter + Bogusky said it best for their truth campaign: "Teenagers can't stand being manipulated; they do not like being 'played.'"

*Standing out from the crowd*. No one wants to be different — so says the majority of people in the world. Having a viewpoint that is different from the vast majority of people is a frightening thought, but it's a thought that needs to be embraced. When I look online and see that I'm the only one who thinks or feels a certain way, it's hard to hit Publish and let my thoughts out in the open, because more times than not I will get flamed for speaking out. The online world has made being different wrong, and this needs to stop.

People seem to start just saying what the majority has already said even if they don't feel that way. We need to embrace radical ideas and opinions because that's how the Internet has gotten to where it is, and that's only going to push it forward.

*No one is out there and listening.* When I don't feel like I'm being listened to, it gets under my skin. Even if you open the channels of communication and don't walk the talk, your community is going to know and be insulted. Now that we have the Internet, that has changed, because I can gather with the collective and voice our concerns as one. It's one thing to be out there, and it's another to actually listen. Listen to what we have to say, and we'll guide you to the promised land.

There was a reason I wrote this from the perspective of the consumer. Regardless of whether you are a communication expert by day, we are all consumers by night, and we need to keep that in mind. They can smell lies from a mile away, and if you don't write with passion, honesty, and integrity, we will know. Never underestimate the intelligence of the consumer—it's insulting. Some would say my thoughts are nothing new, but it's a reality for more than some people.

# 11

## The Ten Tenets
## of Good Conversation

An article published in the *Economist* in December 2006 entitled "Chattering Classes" brilliantly outlined the origins and nature of good conversation. The implications for this book, for marketing as a conversation, and for the future of your brand as a conversation catalyst are sublime.

### Do's:

- We trace back to an eighteenth-century French Enlightenment philosopher by the name of Denis Diderot, whose conversations were "enlivened by *absolute sincerity.*"
- The characteristics of other famous conversationalists — including the likes of Gore Vidal — include great brilliance, *fantastic powers of recall*, quick wit, and charm.
- Cicero in 44 B.C. declared that good conversation requires *"alternation"* among participants; he also advocated dealing seriously with serious matters and gracefully with lighter ones.
- Remember people's names (attributed to Plato).

### Don'ts:

- Winston Churchill was known as one of the best talkers of the 20th century but a poor listener.
- Do not speak too much; do not interrupt; never criticize people behind their backs; do not talk about yourself; never lose your temper (Cicero).

Here are my 10 tenets of what I think constitutes good conversation. The rest of this chapter discusses specifically how they apply to marketing as a conversation.

1. Good conversation is natural (not forced).
2. Good conversation is honest.
3. Good conversation is balanced.
4. Good conversation is open.
5. Good conversation is organic.
6. Good conversation is timeless.
7. Good conversation is valuable.
8. Good conversation is heated.
9. Good conversation is viral.
10. Good conversation is productive.

## GOOD CONVERSATION IS NATURAL (NOT FORCED)

Just as you shouldn't be setting out to "do a viral," neither should you be going out to converse for the sake of conversing. Conversation is inherently permission-based. You wouldn't go up to a stranger and just start talking or expecting them to listen and/or talk back for the sake of it. Why, then, would you try to pollute conversation the same way you did with all of your marketing communications to date?

Moments of truth present opportunities for natural conversation. Take the EepyBird duo, who embarked on a famous set of experiments using two-liter bottles of Diet Coke and tubes of Mentos candy. Their exploits are well documented along the halls of YouTube. They certainly weren't the first set of people to do silly things with everyday items; that kind of behavior has made the people behind *Jackass* quite rich, while others have had their fleeting moments of guffaws and sniggers on late-night or reality television. And yet, something caught on with these two guys. Perhaps it was the subplot of the mighty Coca-Cola company sitting on the sidelines, watching as a spectator instead of participating as an active driver. Or perhaps it was just the fact that it was so damn cool.

Coca-Cola could have entered the conversation at any point. But would its participation have been natural? Timing is everything, and the implication here is straightforward: Don't talk just because you can. You've been doing that for far too long, and now is the time to acknowledge the fact that you were given two ears and one mouth for a reason.

On the flip side, there are many ways in which you can absolutely become part of a conversation without necessarily forcing it. Take the basic act of coming out of "lurker" mode and leaving a comment on someone else's blog.

Hypothetical post by a blogger (let's call him Joseph): "I hate Apple. They're a bunch of egotistical bastards who keep forcing me to exchange my iPod for a better one which I can ill afford. I purchased the original one (the battery died). I purchased the Mini. I purchased the nano. I just purchased the (iPod)$^{Red}$ because I wanted to be a part of Bono's Unite movement. But I'm done now. I'll never buy their product again."

Hypothetical comment response: "Hey, Joe. We really appreciate your passion and that you've been such a loyal customer. The reason we keep on spitting out new products is because we, at Apple, Inc., are obsessed with innovation, creativity, and moving forward. Tell you what, if you send in any three of your older iPods, we'll send you a 60-gig iPod Video on the house." Signed: Steve Jobs.

Okay, that scenario has about as much chance of happening as me falling pregnant, but what if? And before you say it, let me preempt your very narrow-minded first reaction: If we do it for him, we'd have to do it for everybody. Translation: We expect our customers to fork out their hard-earned cash to buy into our valuable brand, and what we give them in return is the ability to own a teensie-weensie part of the uber-experience. Give me a break, I beg of you.

## GOOD CONVERSATION IS HONEST

Advertising (communication) is a business in which people lie for a living. And we don't even do *that* well anymore. We are constantly going to market with deficient products, and the only way we can do them justice is to make up lies about them, which after a while we begin to believe ourselves.

Instead of opening up healthy, honest dialogue about how to fix what is clearly broken, we continue to spin our webs of deceit and misdirection around what was once pure and real.

Take the Bentonville, Arkansas, upstart Wal-Mart. The late Sam Walton surely knew what he was doing when he built an organization that thrived on honest conversation. In fact, it was Sam himself who used to walk up and down the aisles of his stores and not just talk, or even listen, but rather engage with his employees and customers. Something went horribly wrong along the way. Today Wal-Mart cannot pass wind without being accused of contributing to global warming or destroying the environment. Besieged with labor relations woes, you would think the company would be the quintessential candidate for staying quiet. Not likely. Instead of engaging in honest conversation, Wal-Mart plunged itself into fake conversation.

Jim and Laura were two ordinary people who decided to trek across America in their RV. Now, for those of you who don't know this, Wal-Mart lets all RV owners park their vehicles in its parking lots as they rack up the miles on their journeys. It makes total sense. Free parking that comes bundled with a Wal-Mart store only walking distance away. So it should be no surprise that the happy couple decided to blog about their travels and adventures on a blog called "Wal-Marting Across America." What a terrific idea-except for the fact that Jim and Laura were not really Jim and Laura at all, but instead paid journalists fronted by an organization called Working Families for Wal-Mart and conceived by the PR firm Edelman. What could have been a super idea—Wal-Mart providing all RV families with their own blog, blogging tools, training, and so on—quickly became a minefield when the impersonation was exposed.

Making matters worse was that one of the many anti-Wal-Mart watchdogs quickly realized that www.workingfamiliesforwalmart.com was available, registered it, and put up an anti-Wal-Mart site! (See Figure 11.1.)

Figure 11.1    Working Families for Wal-Mart

How is it that brands become pathological liars and, as in the case of Wal-Mart, forget their heritage, their purpose, and their life force along the way? It's not a size thing. Complaining that they're just too big to care or use common sense is a cop-out. Big can be small. Small can be the new big, as author Seth Godin points out.

## GOOD CONVERSATION IS BALANCED

This is like asking you what color Napoleon's white horse was. Hint: It wasn't black. Conversation is two-sided, but it's more than that. It's also balanced. Both parties are equal participants, and as such, they are heard and have time to vocalize their contributions on a level playing field.

Viral nirvana was achieved with the phenomenon that was *Snakes on a Plane*. People went nutso, created CGC trailers, posters, soundtracks, *SoaP* T-shirts, and blog posts. (See Figure 11.2.)

Figure 11.2     CGC *SoaP* T-Shirt

> What is the sound of one hand clapping?

But where was the conversation? People were talking among themselves, and the studio got out of the way—out of its own way and out of the way of the movie's fans-and let the conversation take place unimpeded. Could the studio have done more, though? Could it have offered up the stars of the movie to engage directly with the most passionate fans? (The parallel here would be engaging a company's employees with its prospects and customers.) Could the studio have played a more direct and overt role in helping convert prospects through the final mile, i.e., ticket sales?

Although some felt the box office receipts were underwhelming or disappointing (more on that in Chapter 19), given the hoopla around the movie, it did still open in first place in the United States and outsold the number-one movie during the same time period in the previous year (2005). *Snakes on a Plane* was less about "what they did wrong" and more about the one that slithered away. In years to come, marketers will reference this movie (much like the landmark BMW Films) as the first time sheer, unmitigated passion and excitement gushed across the social mediasphere. It is a clear indication that marketers need to show up to the party (see Chapter 12). It's not enough to sponsor the party and supply all the snacks, booze, and music. When you're the host, you and your brand need to be in the huddle with sleeves rolled up, prepared to get dirty in the raw realities of balanced conversation.

## You Can Always Do More When It Comes to Conversation

Jim Nail, Cymfony's chief strategic and marketing officer, wrote a terrific post on his blog, Influence 2.0, about *Snakes on a Plane*. He essentially provided a marketing strategy on a silver platter to the folks over at New Line Cinema, instructing them to do three things:

- Stay the course. Don't revert back to traditional marketing efforts.
- Don't treat this as a campaign but as a momentum continuity effort.
- Continue using new marketing approaches to extend the *SoaP* experience via community, dialogue, and partnership conversation.

Jim proposed several ideas to New Line for *SoaP* experience (as opposed to giving up on it), including "exploiting this campy B-movie with special fan showings, spicing up the DVD with an audience participation track, packaging 'how to throw a home *SoaP* viewing' kits, and stocking official Snakes Gear in the online store like official *SoaP* rubber snakes, masks, and snake puppets."

His advice—forget the movie, the fun is in the social experience—

was fairly shocking for a movie studio. Jim was recommending that New Line move from amplifying an exposure (the movie or DVD) to extending an event (from rubber snakes to audience participation tracks) to ultimately enhancing an experience, making it a social experience as enduring and invaluable as the *Rocky Horror Picture Show* franchise. More on this in Chapter 14.

## GOOD CONVERSATION IS OPEN

Spare a thought for General Motors. The carmaker has not exactly enjoyed a good time lately, and by lately I refer to the last 20 years (give or take a month).

GM has been ravaged in the press, savaged in the blogosphere, ripped apart by the unions, and spanked by the Japanese auto manufacturers. But who cares — GM has billions of dollars to spend on traditional advertising to rectify the situation. Ha!

I've posted way too often about GM and offered up my two cents countless times. One of my pearls of wisdom was that GM should stop advertising completely. Instead of flushing zeros down the toilet, the beleaguered company might want to consider passing on this "saving" to its employees, or perhaps reinvesting the money in R&D or, better yet, a collaborative/consumer-driven effort to help drive innovation and a value proposition that could be embraced and internalized by the masses of consumers who are buying Toyota and Honda instead of Pontiac and Chevrolet.

To its credit, GM has not been shy about experimenting and launching new efforts (necessity is the mother of invention). Nothing has come of most of them, but one effort has certainly been successful.

Over the past few years, GM joined the conversation through a variety of blogs, including the GM FYI Blog, and through the efforts of Bob Lutz, GM Vice Chairman for Product Development and Chairman of GM North America. While GM has been dragged through the ringer for its failed experiences dabbling in anything with a pulse, it is through dialogue, community, and partnership that real resonance has been felt.

In June 2007, the *New York Times* columnist Thomas Friedman penned a column that labeled GM the most evil company in the world based on its incentives for the purchase of a HumVee. GM's attempt to submit a letter to the editor in response ended in frustration. The company was first told to shorten the letter, then to eliminate an objectionable word: "rubbish." The letters editor told GM that the word was inconsistent with the tone of the *Times* op-ed pages. Finally, the company's communicators decided to post the company's response in its FYI blog. They published both versions of their letter to the editor and also the e-mail exchange with the letters editor.

Again, the community of readers and commenters supported GM. Of course, not all the comments were supportive, but most were, like this one: "Rubbish has also been used in letters plenty of times. And this one: "Now that's some ballsy corporate blogging! Kudos to GM for leveraging the power of the blog to overcome the power of the pen."

The response led to an article in the *Washington Post*, to which Friedman responded in his next column. There he conceded that traditional journalists had not yet come to terms with the power of blogs. What Friedman meant to say was that traditional journalists had not yet come to terms with the power of conversation.

Indeed. Not only do community, dialogue, and partnership provide organizations with an effective means of bypassing the press as a conduit for getting messages to the public—as illustrated in the GM case—but they build communities of supporters that can overcome the power of the press when it is misused.

## GOOD CONVERSATION IS ORGANIC

Good conversation typically does not have a start date, and it most definitely should not have a hard and fast end date, either. This is why I place conversation higher on the totem pole of engagement—or whatever it is that you're choosing to rank-than media or communication. Conversation isn't a line item on your media flowchart (shudder)—a fairly shocking idea for a movie studio—and along these same lines, conversation should not be sporadic, intermittent, or lopsided in terms of stimuli, momentum, and effort.

There is a difference between natural and organic. The former is the opposite of forced, manipulated, or premeditated, whereas the latter characterizes dialogue that is productive and healthy, and it is these qualities that will dictate its length, intensity, direction, and momentum. Great conversations may last for the duration of a cross-country flight, a chance shared ride in a taxicab, or a lifetime. Most of the time (with or without being stoked or otherwise maintained), conversations will die out and fade away (although their embers remain); some of the time they will linger and take on a life of their own far beyond any expectations.

Take my own "viral" video? Entitled *Tiger Did It*, this video takes you to the 2005 Masters tournament and a titanic struggle to the finish line between Tiger Woods and Chris DiMarco. Segue to the 16th hole, where Tiger Woods chips off the fringe of the green and pulls off—inarguably—one of the most miraculous and unforgettable clutch shots in golfing history. Even more remarkable is how the ball comes to a stop inches from the hole, with the Nike swoosh front and center (upside down, which upset the brand purists, but consumers didn't give a hoot), followed by a piece of brand nirvana: The camera pans and zooms into the shot. Time stands still. The Nike swoosh seems to will the ball into the hole.

And the rest is history.

Well, almost. I fall off my couch, screaming like a blithering idiot. My wife dumps all over me for scaring the living daylights out of my kids. I collect myself, TiVo the moment, and within 30 minutes I have downloaded it to my Sony camcorder, uploaded it to my PC, remixed it into a 30-second spot (yeah, yeah), and uploaded it to my blog.

The rest is a blur. The post gets "Scobelized" (the term given to recognition by the renowned blogger Robert Scoble), and within moments my lowly blog has gone from hundreds of views to hundreds of thousands. I may revisit this later in terms of Nike's reaction (or the lack thereof), but for now I want to comment on the organic nature of the comments on my original post.

There were comments from marketing people (my blog is, after all, a marketing blog). Some lauded my brilliant viral efforts (huh? I was *"just doing it"* myself and not really thinking about the consequences, which could have included Hootie Johnson's legal vultures swooping down on me with a cease-and-desist), while others berated me as a snake-oil salesman (you can be the judge).

And then something interesting happened. The conversation was joined by people who had no interest in marketing whatsoever. Some thanked me for capturing—and immortalizing—the shot. One person had been flying, another had been out with the family, and both had missed the moment, but because of Jaffe Juice they were given a second chance to view this once-in-a-lifetime event. Still others were golfing enthusiasts and chose to talk about Chris DiMarco and how his two short misses on the final few holes could have made all the difference.

Jaffe Juice became a mosh pit (mash pit) of diverse opinion, perspective, and passion. I did not control it. I did not scold the golfers for their lack of marketing input. I let the conversation do what it was supposed to do. Happen.

You can view the video at www.jointheconversation.us/tigerdidit

## GOOD CONVERSATION IS TIMELESS

If good conversation is organic, capable of being joined at any time by anybody for any reason, then great conversation should be equally capable of standing the test of time—enduring for the length of the passion the participants bring to it (and sometimes beyond). This is perhaps one of the most tangible differences between communication and conversation—the former being subjected to and constrained by arbitrary parameters and boundaries that are almost always one-sided and *not* customer-centric. The latter, on the other hand, continues as long as the fumes of connectivity necessitate connections.

There's no doubt that the simple text link (and you thought Google had a monopoly on this) is the silent catalyst and that together with Google (strike the earlier comment) the link makes it incredibly easy for a conversation's potential to expand and endure.

An innocuous comment on a nondescript blog today could (and most likely will) be around long after you exit this world.

## GOOD CONVERSATION IS VALUABLE

Another substantial difference between communication (PR, advertising, direct marketing, and the like) and conversation is the ability to add value, which extends far beyond selling stuff. Chuck Porter, chairman of Crispin Porter + Bogusky, said it best: "Nobody wants to talk to a salesman" (especially when one is not looking to buy). All things being equal, if brands are supposed to fit into our lives, make a difference, and essentially add value, they're going to have to be part of something bigger . . . something that extends beyond the bare-bones and lifeless transaction . . . something that has more depth and substance than "emotion" (whatever the hell that means).

I give you Exhibit A. On the right is a human being—a normal, blemished female who, let's face it, wouldn't exactly turn heads on a ramp or catwalk. On the left is a supermodel, a goddess, the object of every man's fantasy and every woman's desire. (See Figure 11.3.) Would you believe me if I told you they're the same person?

The before and after is part of the continuing conversation of the Dove brand, the Campaign for Real Beauty, which, in a short film titled *Evolution*, makes a statement: "No wonder our perception of beauty is distorted. Every girl deserves to feel beautiful just the way she is. Get involved at www.campaignforrealbeauty.com." *Wow*. Talk about setting the cat among the pigeons. No seriously, talk about it! Dove's Campaign for Real Beauty is a rare example of what happens when communication and conversation intersect. This is truly transformational. Powerful. Valuable. Needed. Timely (as in about time).

Indeed, *Evolution* scooped the highest honor—the coveted Grand Prix—at the 2007 Cannes Advertising Festival. It was the first time a "viral" entry had won in the film (i.e., "30-second-spot") category and certainly demonstrated the power of an idea with an accompanying conversational offshoot.

Figure 11.3    Dove's Evolution

Personally I believe Dove (Unilever) and its agency, Ogilvy, had no clue how powerful this campaign could and would become. I believe they entered into this as just another campaign, without any intention of it becoming a movement, a call to action, an idea whose time had come. (After all, this is the same company that came up with all the Axe and Lynx frivolity.) That said, they had the good (no, great) sense to get out of the way of *a conversation whose time had come* and let it snowball from there.

Can Dove ever go back to the old way of doing business—communication? I don't believe it's possible. This is like biting into the forbidden fruit in the Garden of Eden. No more frolicking around naked, unaware, and oblivious. Besides, you're not as well endowed as you thought you were. Like the movie *Constantine* with Keanu Reeves (I realize I'm zero-for-two with that obscure reference), where Keanu's character transforms Rachel Weisz's character to a point where she is explicitly aware of every angel or demon presence around her that was previously invisible to her, this is the situation Dove finds itself in. No more hiding. No more pretending. No more disconnected (siloed?) communication. Only "reality advertising." Only conversation. Only truth. The brand is reborn. Hallelujah.

## Good Conversation Is Heated

Can't shake the devil metaphor. Oh well.

This assertion is somewhat controversial, but I wholeheartedly back and stand behind it. Conversation between two or more parties that occurs within a community of like-minded thinkers who are in total agreement is pretty benign and bland. It's arguably not even conversation but just consensus. It's like that painful conference panel you attended where all the participants were like a chorus of bleating sheep, pandering and nodding heads in synchronous agreement. Makes you want to puke, don't it?

Great conversation is heated. The heat of passion, mixed with diversity of opinion, makes for an original exchange of viewpoints, attitudes, and perspectives. This is probably the hardest tenet for marketers to come to terms with (kind of like letting go of control).

AOL banked on this when it launched the Discuss Campaign in the United Kingdom. (See Figure 11.4.) Similar to the HSBC example cited earlier, AOL took a conversation starter and exploded it into a full-blown conversation. The 30-second spots were terrific; however, as the blog entry below explains, the activation was a little subdued:

> The aol/discuss campaign would seem on the surface to be a great idea, that highlights important issues, aims to get people involved in the brand and plays to aol's strengths in security online, especially parental concern. The campaign has been running since the start of 2006, has generated 83 "articles" by 39 authors, in 14 categories on the aol/discuss site. Yesterday I counted there were 4,468 comments, total. The most in response to any one article was 740 comments (the article was "Is the internet a good or a bad thing"). The average number of comments on an article is 54. That doesn't really seem a great response from a major advertising campaign. I'm sure the advertising has moved tracking measures on things like "aol is the leader in ensuring my children's safety online" and so on, but it's hardly set the online community alight.[1]

[1]See herebenotions, http://herebenotions.typepad.com/herebenotions/ (October 19, 2006).

Figure 11.4    AOL's Discuss Campaign

As I see it, the *problem* here was two-fold:

1.  AOL viewed this as a campaign instead of the kind of idea that could easily snowball into a movement. Case in point: Type in www.aol.co.uk/discuss and you'll default to www.aol.co.uk.
2.  The conversation wasn't heated *enough*.

As one blogger pointed out, "I can't help thinking that the aol/discuss format would've worked better as a true-blog rather than the message-board/blog hybrid that it is at the moment."

Heat is a vital ingredient in any conversation worth its salt in passion. Receiving 740 comments is a substantial response (my record is 113, but then again, I am one and AOL is many), and it reflects not only responsiveness but that magic word "engagement." We spend our whole professional lives trying so very desperately to get our consumers to respond. In kind. In cash. And when they do respond, we have the gall to temper and nitpick the kind of response they give us. Preposterous.

I once blogged about Crocs, those ridiculously ugly shoes that everyone (including myself) wears. The post was inspired by an article I read by Mike Wagner about the polarizing appeal (or lack thereof) of Crocs and why 'tis better to hate than not to feel at all.[2]

Actually it's not about hate at all, but allowing for and respecting a difference of opinion . . . or just an opinion-one that produces results like this:

> They've seen Crocs go from selling 1,500 pairs of shoes and a revenue of $24,000 in 2002 to last year's sales of 6 million pairs with total revenues (including shoes, accessories, and clothing) hitting $108.6 million. In May, the financial gurus at Crocs projected 2006 sales to reach over $200 million.

When I was in South Africa, one of my best mates—let's call him Grant (actually that is his real name)—came to visit. He was wearing *the* most butt-ugly shoes I had ever seen in my life. I told him that I wouldn't be seen dead in shoes like that. The next day I purchased a pair for myself and my two kids. I love these shoes and talk about them to everyone.

The shoes in question? You guessed it . . . Nikes. Just kidding, they were Crocs.

You see, the problem with the world that we live in today is that we've all become a little numb, haven't we? We take a middle-of-the-road break-even position, avoiding the big loss but avoiding the big win as well. We live in a world of artificially inseminated and falsely perpetuated reality, and when we hear even the smallest whisper of dissension, we put our fingers in our waxed ears, scream

---

[2]See "Hate My Brand . . . Please!" at Mike Wagner, Marketing Profs: Daily Fix, http://www.mpdailyfix.com/2006/07/hate_my_brand_please.html.

at the top of our lungs, and hope to hell that the CEO doesn't find out about our butt-ugly plastic shoes (which might as well be a metaphor for our brand or our marketing communications).

Mike offers these words of wisdom:

- Embrace the hate to find your love.
- One person's object of desire can be another person's object of disdain.
- People unite around ugly as much as beauty.
- Ugly can be temporary, while people adjust to "your kind of beauty."

## GOOD CONVERSATION IS VIRAL

Here's a profound thought: If you want people to talk about you and your brand, why not give them something to talk about?

The industry has a systematic and chronic problem: Most of the time when we open our mouths, nothing but hot air comes out. We are typically nothing more than oxygen invaders, attention parasites, purveyors of spam (which is not limited to unsolicited messaging but encompasses irrelevant, distasteful, mindless, and insulting communication as well—at least in my book), and then we have the utter gall to attempt to transfer this burden onto the shoulders of our consumers, expecting *them* to be messengers and willing accomplices to our fruitless mission.

Good conversation, like good content, wants to be free and strives to soar to limitless heights. It just so happens that "good" conversation can be both positive (healthy, constructive, thoughtful, and so on) and negative (juicy, meaty, heated, critical, and so on), and it is the latter type that is a lot more noticeable and "sticky" as far as the naked eye can see. This is a red herring, however, and it distracts us from the real truth, namely, that our consumers are not going to talk about us or anything we have to say if we are bland, mediocre, middle of the road, unnoticeable, on the fence . . . you get the picture. If we have nothing to say, our consumers are most undoubtedly not going to continue a nonexistent conversation on our behalf.

As mentioned earlier, anything that is naturally good enough will be shared—even virally if you like. Absolutely you can—and should—grease the wheels and give your consumers tools, means, and the freedom to be talked about, commented on, and ultimately shared without necessarily overstepping your invitation to participate in their daily lives (because, let's face it, that's what we often do best . . . interfere in our consumers' lives).

## PROOF OF LIFE

How do you know when you've arrived in the conversational marketing space? There are many ways of gauging the extent to which your ideas are resonating and your brand is becoming an enabler and your marketing is becoming part of the conversation.

One way is getting spoofed.

Even the seemingly untouchable Dove *Evolution* was spoofed in the form of "Slob Evolution" for www.campaignagainstreal life.com. (See Figure 11.5.)

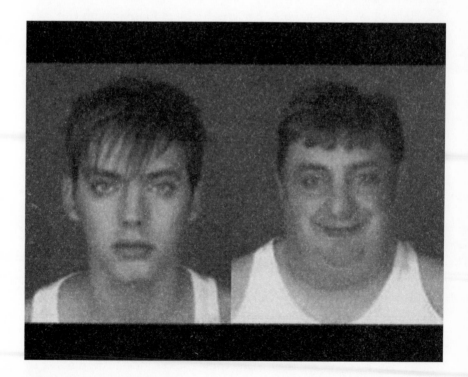

Figure 11.5    Slob Evolution

Who said viral (much like the shift to the one-from-one model) had to be unidirectional and initiated by you?

Sometimes they're going to laugh with you; sometimes they're going to laugh at you; but as long as they're laughing, they're alive — and so are you.


## GOOD CONVERSATION IS PRODUCTIVE

Heated-up Crocs sales aren't the only thing that can come out of heated conversation.

Need more substantiation? How about a South African wine you normally would never have heard of called Stormhoek? In tandem with the United Kingdom's most popular blogger, Hugh Macleod, *blogging doubled Stormhoek's sales in less than 12 months*. And before you wine (get it?) about a small base, we're talking about tens of thousands of cases.

Here's how it played out, per Hugh's blog, Gaping Void:

> Earlier this year I sent out a hundred or so complimentary bottles of Stormhoek wine to bloggers, just to see what would happen.
>
> **Three Provisos:**
> 1. The bloggers had to live in the U.K., Ireland, or France. They needed to have regularly kept up a blog for at least three months previously. Their blog could have a readership of three or three thousand — size or status didn't matter, just so long as they were genuine bloggers.
> 2. They had to be of legal drinking age.
> 3. They were under no obligation to say anything about the wine, good or bad. If they just wanted to snarf the wine and say nothing, or say something negative, that was fine. It was their call.
>
> As it turned out, a lot of them ended up writing about it. A meme of sorts was created, and it spread.
>
> I have been saying this for years, and still not everybody believes me: *"Blogs are a good way of making things happen indirectly."*
>
> No, bloggers and their friends didn't start suddenly descending on

supermarkets, buying the wine in large numbers. That's not how it works.

What happened is that *by interfacing with the blogosphere, it fundamentally changed how Stormhoek looked at treating their primary customers* (the supermarket chains) and the end-users (the supermarkets' customers), *i.e., it caused an internal disruption, both within the company and the actual trade.* Wine drinkers' basic purchasing habits didn't change because of the meme, but the meme allowed Stormhoek to align itself more closely with said habits.

What matters is the internal disruption.

You have to remember: There are hundreds of thousands of vineyards in the world, all trying to sell to the 12 or so mass-market wine buyers in the United Kingdom. So you need a story that cuts through the clutter.

And the best stories have market disruption baked in.

With the disruption came a new and different story that the supermarket buyers and the importers wanted to hear. Telling the story made the sales process easier. With easier sales, the curve was raised.

So my advice with business blogs is to think of them not as sales channels but as disruption channels. Much more effective.

# 12

# The Five Ways You Can
# Join the Conversation

Your brand—bless it—is itching to make a difference. Now you get
the chance to let it loose to run amok among the chaotic and unpredictable mortals of the human race.

Relax, I was just kidding. Sort of. Before you throw caution to
the wind or throw yourself off a very tall building (perhaps that
ivory tower you've been working from for so many years), here are
five primary ways in which your brand can become a part of the
conversation without giving away the kitchen sink (although that's
quite possible, too).

1. Listen to a conversation.
2. Respond to a conversation.
3. Join—or be invited to join—a conversation already in
   progress.
4. Catalyze a conversation.
5. Start a conversation.

You'll note that these five approaches are not necessarily in logical or chronological order, or not at least in the way you would have
expected. They are, however, arranged in a systematic way. Think
of them as an itemized, step-by-step guide to your future.

## LISTENING TO A CONVERSATION

A while ago, I participated in an interesting conversation, one in
which I listened (observed) and one to which I later contributed

(participated). The thread concerned various "items" that every company should be monitoring.

This thread was started by Cameron Olthuis, expanded by Steve Rubel, further enhanced by Jeremiah Owyang, and supplemented by both Joseph Jaffe (yours truly) and Omar Ha-Redeye.

The list is maintained and updated by Shel Holtz at the New PR wiki. Here is the list (with my contribution in italics):

1. Company name
2. Company URL
3. Public facing figures
4. Product names
5. Product URLs
6. The industry "hangouts"
7. Employee activity/blogs
8. Conversations
9. Brand image
10. Competitors
11. Images/video like YouTube, Flickr, TVEyes, Google Video, and Yahoo Video
12. Tags and social search tools like del.icio.us
13. Social voting tools like digg.com
14. Meme-trackers like Techmeme.com
15. "Advanced Listening"
16. Feedback URL and link threads
17. Use "Voice of the Customer" log to track sentiment, instance, and/or voice
18. Develop new roles, such as "brand monitor" or "blogosphere watcher"
19. Use self-clipping services like Google or Yahoo alerts for keyword mentions, but also audio and video hits as well . . . services like Podzinger, for example, to ascertain conversational audio levels
20. Media mentions by news features in search engines such as Google or Yahoo

21. Relevant media news wires, such as Reuters (international), AP News (U.S.), U.S. Newswire, CCN Matthews (U.K., Canada, international), CNW Group (Canada), Mercopress (South Africa), allAfrica (Africa, general), and HR Net (eastern Europe)

22. Utilize RSS and aggregators like Bloglines in order to aggregate, integrate, and assimilate all relevant incoming and outgoing moments of truth (perceived truth perhaps, or even "truthiness," the term coined by Steven Colbert, according to Rob Stevens)

23. Use wikis like PmWiki to discuss and debate pretty much everything from 1 to 19 and most importantly attempt to turn all the talk/conversation into walk/action

24. *Repeat 1 to 20 to look outside of your own circle; evolve the perspective from yourself, through your direct competitive set to your indirect competitive set and ultimately to your aspirational/non-endemic/noncompetitive set (this is where you want to follow the leaders, so to speak—Apples, Nikes, Googles, or whichever company you admire)*

25. *Create a proactive capability/budget in order to quickly execute against everything you're monitoring—specifically opportunities like FedEx furniture, Tiger chipping in on the 16th*

26. *Conversely, have a reactive process in place to comprehensively and compellingly respond, especially when you're on the bumpy receiving end of the stick*

27. Search term volume

28. Search term rank

29. Relevant Wikipedia entries

30. Third-party influencers

31. Key stakeholders

32. Press release pickups

33. Blog pickups using services like Technorati

Don't worry if you don't understand many of the terms in this list. Do worry, though, if you have absolutely no clue what conversations are going on *right now* about your company and brand.

Every single time somebody mentions "Joseph Jaffe," "Joe

Jaffe," "Jaffe Juice," "*crayon*," "*Life After the 30-Second Spot*," or "*Join the Conversation*" I know about it. From newspaper articles to blog posts, from podcasts to bathroom walls (if they have an RSS feed), nothing escapes my vain and watchful eyes. By setting up a simple alert through Google or the like, I am on my way to being "plugged in" to a budding conversation. People who are trying to get my attention know very well that it is just a matter of time before I find them and inevitably respond. People also note that I'll respond far quicker to criticism than praise.

Throughout this process, I've observed firsthand that anyone can be "turned around" if spoken to as a human being and given the consideration they deserve. People want to be heard, and the first step to being heard is to listen. Profound, I know, and true.

The biggest lesson perhaps has become a personal and professional mantra for me: *To understand the power, velocity, intensity, and direction of a storm, you need to fly straight into its heart.* This is exactly what the National Weather Bureau does with an incoming storm, and it is exactly what we need to do in order to come to terms with the full potential and power of social media, communal passion, and the networked effects of the crowds.

That said, there is also a fine line between a gung-ho suicide mission and a more careful and considered approach. The latter strategy relies on listening and learning. As a brand, you want to be that person in a meeting who keeps unusually quiet but has everybody hanging on every pearl of wisdom he utters when he does open his mouth. You're about as opposite to this as could possibly be imagined, right? You have no inkling whatsoever as to whether your consumers give a damn about what you have to say. And when you blurt out your falsely concocted mumbo-jumbo, you're anywhere between a hothead and a doofus.

It all begins with being aware of what is being said at any given time. There is no need to re-create the wheel here. We keep on talking about being great storytellers; dialing up and tapping into deep-seated passions and loyalties; engaging our audiences with meaningful and relevant dialogue; providing an eclectic mix of information, education, entertainment, and utility. So instead of putting your best foot forward, keep your worst foot from taking you backward. Take it out of your mouth—or perhaps I should say, put it into your mouth. Shut the hell up and say nothing. Listen. Carefully. You'll be amazed by the richness, depth, meaning, intensity, and complete submission associated with "conversations already in progress."

Rishad Tobaccowala, my good friend and fellow provocateur, talks about punching your passions into Google and then seeing what happens. Try it. Whether your passion is Honey Nut Cheerios or Pork Rinds, football or soccer, Sudoku or cooking, you'll be amazed at what you'll find. Surprisingly enough, you'll discover that the most relevant results are not coming from or through big brands, but from small communities, individuals, or informal groups of like-minded humans.

## RESPONDING TO A CONVERSATION

I have an ongoing debate with fellow social media commentator Shel Holtz about whether or not conversation is superior to communication.[1] As you'll note from this book, I believe that conversation trumps communication every time. Shel—an accredited business communicator—is a proud, card-carrying communicator. He believes that true communication, in its best and purest form, is unequivocally powerful and profound. He also believes that true communication is two-way.

Semantics aside, we both agree on one thing. Healthy and productive dialogue is just that: two-way communication a.k.a. conversation that is both healthy ("good conversation") and productive (results- or action-oriented). But there's something missing in this explanation: two-way dialogue *between whom*? Arguably, we need to evolve our thinking to move from between-two-or-more people to between-two-or-more sides in order to call a series of communications a true conversation.

---

[1] See Shel Holtz's blog, a shel of my former self, http://blog.holtz.com/.

Missed opportunities are conversations not capitalized on.

Step 1 on your brand journey to the new world is listening to the conversations already in progress—in other words, plugging yourself into the conversation. Step 2 is responding. After all, unless you act on this newfound insight, what's the point?

### Tom Locke: Brand Enthusiast and Arbiter of Cluelessness

I love the story of Tom Locke, one of the ordinary consumers like you or me. The story goes something like this (told here with a little editorial license, because that's how stories are told).

Tom had $39 to his name (or at least at his disposal), and instead of spending it all at once, he invested in as many postal stamps and envelopes as his $39 would buy and then wrote and sent out a plethora of letters to a slew of brands and corporations asking for free stuff.

Tom also decided to chronicle his exploits on a web site, where he updated his responses. As illustrated in the figure, Pfizer sent him three 50-cent coupons for Purell; however, Trader Joe's, and Kraft sent him nothing. Wrigley's told him to buy his own gum and where to buy it—in other words, what he could do with himself. Talk about loving your customers! Target, representing one of the last remaining hopes that big-brand advertising is alive and kicking, had not responded at the time I captured this screenshot. (See Figure 12.1.)

So what do you think happened? How do you think this story ends? Your mushy expectations about Target would surely lead you to hope that it found out about this experiment and sent Tom a basket of rubber bands, neatly wrapped in a red bow. Perhaps Target took this experiment to the next level by sending Tom rubber bands

| | | | |
|---|---|---|---|
| Pfizer<br><br>(#4) | Purell hand sanitizer | YES!<br><br>Three 50-cent coupons for Purell | Dear Sir or Madam:<br>I am in love with your Purell hand sanitizer. Never before have I thought that a product composed primarily of alcohol could actually moisturize my hands. Your hand sanitizer does just that. Do you have any free samples of this product that I could have? In fact, I am a free sample "addict", and I'd like free samples of any/every product you have. Thank you.<br>Tom Locke, hygiene enthusiast |
| Trader Joe's<br><br>(#5) | Unique grocery items | REJECTED!<br><br>Told me "no" — sent me nothing | Dear Sir or Madam:<br>I love your monthly product flyers (they're quite witty). I also love your products. I always turn to Trader Joe's for specialty sauces and exotic and foreign oddities. The store by my house is always giving away free samples of coffee and/or juice, and it's always good stuff! Do you have any free product samples that you could send me? Nothing easily perishable, of course. But maybe something like that good anti-Ox-idant berry and nut trail mix? Or something else? I just love surprises! Thank you.<br>Tom Locke, gourmet food enthusiast |
| Wrigley's<br><br>(#6) | Gum | REJECTED!<br><br>Told me to buy my own gum — and where to buy it! | Dear Sir or Madam:<br>I am a gum addict. I have tried every flavor of gum made, and nothing compares to your Eclipse "Cherry Ice". Did you stop making that flavor? I've heard people say that it tastes like a cough drop to them – but I love the flavor. Please send me free samples of any and every single gum flavor you have and can send me. I love gum more than I can put into words. Remember that girl from Willy Wonka, always chewing gum? I put that girl to shame. Thank you.<br>Tom Locke, gum enthusiast |
| Kraft<br><br>(#7) | Various food products | REJECTED!<br><br>Told me "no" — sent me nothing | Dear Sir or Madam:<br>Please send me a free sample of every Kraft product made. If you are hesitant to send highly perishable items like cheese, I fully understand. I'll take whatever you have. Thank you.<br>Tom Locke, food enthusiast |
| Target<br><br>(#8) | Rubber bands | No | Dear Sir or Madam:<br>I bought a bag of rubber bands from a Target store a few days back, and I must say – I'm very pleased with them. They were made by "work.org". Please send me a free bag of these rubber bands, so that I may share them with my friends. Thank you.<br>Tom Locke, life enthusiast |

Figure 12.1   The $39 Experiment

for life. After all, Tom is a *life enthusiast* and would surely have life-time value as a customer! (See Figure 12.2.)

Sadly, Target—*after taking months and months to consider Tom's request before finally responding*—rejected that request.

Are you surprised? You shouldn't be. Target's big glossy *boastvertising* has no place for conversation. Clearly, Target has no place for consumers, either.

| | | | |
|---|---|---|---|
| Target<br><br>(#8) | Rubber bands | REJECTED!<br><br>Told me "no" — sent me nothing | Dear Sir or Madam:<br>I bought a bag of rubber bands from a Target store a few days back, and I must say – I'm very pleased with them. They were made by "work.org". Please send me a free bag of these rubber bands, so that I may share them with my friends. Thank you.<br>Tom Locke, life enthusiast |

Figure 12.2   Off Target

Target, along with countless other companies on Tom Locke's enthusiast hit list, was just not in the game. These companies were not even aware of Tom—or worse still, were absolutely aware of him and just didn't care.

What a great opportunity to respond and show the outside world looking in how they think, act, and care. After all, if Target cares that much about one consumer, imagine how it must care about all of its customers. . . .

A while back, I gave a workshop on conversation to a group of educational marketers at a conference. I showed them this case study, and one woman in the audience asked: "If Target responded to this consumer, what would happen if a million more consumers sent in a million similar requests?" I smiled and said, "You just answered your own question." Think about it: In your wildest dreams, could you ever imagine one million of your consumers raising their hands and reaching out to you? What would you pay for this opportunity? Would it be worth the price of a bag of rubber bands (plus shipping and handling)?

The entire marketing communications space (like the media business and the Internet's bandwidth load times) is antiquated. It has been set up and structured to accommodate and facilitate one-way traffic, and the one-way traffic is coming from the wrong side no less. Take the average CPM (Cost Per Thousand) of a 30-second spot on TV. At a $20 CPM, you willfully part with countless shots across the bow aimed at a moving and weary target. In reality, however, only a fraction are even paying attention. A fraction of your targets watch the commercial, but only a tiny percentage of them are going to remember what they saw the next morning. A subset of these will correctly identify the brand associated with the commercial. An even smaller amount of these will form an intention to purchase the product on offer, and a final remaining quota will actually make the purchase. I'm no mathematician, but I'll bet the effective CPM at the end of the fragmented journey will be significantly more than the cost of a bag of rubber bands (plus shipping and handling).

Congratulations. You're in the rubber band distribution business. And all this time you thought you were a mass merchandiser of messages.

## Brand T&E

Everyone in sales is only too familiar with the concept of T&E (Travel and Expenses) and the importance of spending one's quota on clients, prospects, and the like. Sometimes salespeople are so intensely focused on closing deals that they neglect their T&E—and with it the importance of long-term relationship building.

So why should brands be any different? Corporations should assign aggressive "brand T&E" budgets that select employees are charged with delivering against. Their task is to make sure that the brand reaches out to loyalists, buzz-inclined influencers, and, yes of course, the blogosphere and podosphere (but it's really bigger than that) and touches them in some way, shape, or form. This effort will lead to guaranteed sampling, act as an inevitable word-of-mouth catalyst, and ensure that a conversation begins and a dialogue ensues.

Now here's the key and perhaps the catch: Their performance reviews, evaluations, and even bonus or cash compensation should be tied to their ability to spend their brand T&E allocation.

Sound like a stretch? It isn't. Just ask the Ritz-Carlton and other proactive service-based and consumer-centric organizations that have successfully empowered their employees to walk, talk, and live the brand experience with their lifeblood: their customers.

## Reaching Out to Bloggers

It is not that big a stretch to put forward the hypothesis that bloggers (and podcasters) hold the key to your conversational success. That means you're going to need to understand bloggers and what makes them tick. You're also going to need a formalized and defined blogger outreach strategy and agreed-upon rules of engagement.

So who exactly are bloggers? Is there a blogging type? What demographics make up your prototypical blogger? Sorry, conventional norms do not apply here. If you want to understand what constitutes a typical blogger, just look in the mirror. It's you. It's me. It's us.

That said, there are some pointers that help deconstruct bloggers just a smidgen.

Bloggers are naturally *snarky*.

According to Wikipedia, "snark" is derived from "snarky," from the Dutch and Low German *snorken*, which means "irritable or short-tempered; irascible." Some claim that the word is a portmanteau of the phrase "snide remark," thus characterizing a belittling or sarcastic style of speech or writing. "Snark" also connotes "backhanded" or "snidely derisive"; hence, to be "snarkish," "snarky," or "to snark at somebody." *"Snark" does not necessarily have negative connotations and can be used humorously.*

Bloggers often struggle to give a compliment without some kind of zinger. In fact, backhanded compliments are often your best-case scenario. Generally. Negativity and criticism outperform and outdraw warm and fuzzy lyrical waxing. It's just the way it is. Personally I don't see the continuum as being between love and hate, but rather between honesty and integrity on one side and everything else on the other. I believe strongly that bias and subjectivity are much more powerful and meaningful than the artificial pretense of objectivity and neutrality that plagues the mainstream media industry.

Think about it for a moment: Journalists are human beings with the same quirks, flaws, passions, and affiliations as you or me. They have political preferences and, assuming they vote at all, take an innately liberal or conservative view of how their country should be governed. So at what point do they park all of their passions at the door in order to be neutral (read: bland) and balanced (read: mediocre) in their reporting? The whole concept is absurd really. It's why Fox News is a joke in the United States; claiming to be "fair and balanced," in truth it is anything but.

The higher up the snark is in the influence pecking order, the more intolerable is the snark. A *New York* magazine article from 2006 attempted to reveal what makes the blogosphere tick so as to better understand the sinister underbelly of the elitist bourgeoisie—the A-listers.

A-listers are defined quite superficially using a metric you're only too familiar with: reach. Which is why you're probably concerned with racking up as many top-trafficked blogs as possible. Good luck with trying to win them over. (Might I suggest an Acer computer or Apple iPhone?)

The tyranny of line extension and diversification teaches us to be exceptionally good at a finite number of competencies and to avoid losing focus on that which powers us to be differentiated and coveted.

Instead, you'd do well to embrace the full extent of the conversation potential from the blogosphere. At the very minimum, you'd get less snark. Also remember that today's obscure blogger is tomorrow's A-lister and vice versa.

It's better to hone in on passion, focus, expert opinion, and, most importantly, trust and authority. Everyone's an expert on something, and once opinion is carved in cyberspace, it's there for keeps—an eternity without limitations on its growth potential and influence.

## Responding to Bloggers

I am a human. I am a podcaster. I am a resident of the virtual world Second Life. I am the President and Chief Interruptor of *crayon*. I am an entrepreneur. I am a fan of karaoke. I am a blogger. I am deeply complex and schizophrenic when it comes to the ever-fragmenting world of new marketing. In each form, likeness, avatar, profile, or persona, I have learned how to "speak conversation" and how to "write conversation." I have learned how conversation changes from medium to medium, based on what I call "authentic voice" and a commensurate set of rules of engagement.

My own personal policy with respect to conversation is simple. Every person—lover or hater, promoter or detractor—deserves a thoughtful and genuine response. What they do with that response determines whether I continue the conversation or not.

Bloggers are most certainly not fair or balanced. They take a position and often, without the facts, go off on a limb, shoot from the hip, and tear into you, your company, and your brand for "not getting it." And you roll over and play dead. What's the point?

*Respond already*, and use my rule of thumb: Everyone deserves a response, and what they do with it determines whether the conversation continues or not. People love the sound of their own voice, but they especially love the sound of their own name. Being acknowledged and recognized has an incredibly powerful effect and more often than not can completely turn someone around.

Sure there are chronic haters—contrarians and dissidents who are not, and will never be, interested in your side of the story or even in the truth. They exist in their own little world of perceptual warped reality. For everyone else, there are conversations waiting to be turned into relationships.

## DNFTT

There's a popular acronym in the social media world: DNFTT. It stands for "Do Not Feed the Trolls." In other words, do not respond to provocation or flamers.

As marketers, you'll have to make the judgment call as to when you join the conversation and when you walk away from it. Just like everyone cannot be your customer, so too is the story in the conversational sandbox.

You'll learn to deal with two kinds of anonymity—the kind that emboldens the meek and mild to speak their minds (the good kind) and the kind that gives cowards an unearned and undeserved platform to intimidate and shut you up and out of the conversation.

## JOINING—OR BEING INVITED TO JOIN— A CONVERSATION

Joining a conversation might seem like a fait accompli, but it's not. For starters, you have to be already aware of the conversation in progress before being able to join one. Duh. Second, you have to be welcome.

Let's not forget that for years upon years we've bulldozed our way through the homes and lives of consumers—and many, if not most, had no inkling of what it is we have had to say. Of course, that never stopped us in the past, and today we still struggle to learn our lessons.

To join a conversation, you have to be *invited* to join. To be invited to join, either you have to be approached (explicitly or implicitly) or you can request permission to participate and partake in the dialogue, community, and discourse.

**Houston, Wii Have a Problem!**

Nintendo kicked Sony Playstation 3's butt with its new Wii console gaming system and its killer app: Its wi-fi remote control and Nunchuk allow gamers to physically punch, swing, bat, hurl, chop, and literally get in the game. Unfortunately, when I said killer app, I was again being literal: The rogue device was constantly slipping out of hands and damaging anything that moved or didn't move, from lamp fixtures and fittings to wall hangings, fans, electrical devices, and bodies. That's when www.wiihaveaproblem.com emerged as a central repository of all the cumulative destruction being unleashed by the Wii. (See Figure 12.3.)

Figure 12.3    Wii Have a Problem

According to the web site, "'*Wii have a problem' is a blog focused on bringing you the latest trend in gaming violence, that of damage caused by 'window lickers' who should not be participating in activity of any form, yet own a Wii. Why? Because we're fanboys, that's why.*"

Perhaps that's why there are new products displayed—such as a television visor—that actually protect household appliances and furnishings from errant and airborne remotes!

The web site is a celebration of the fallibility of the Wii brand, and much like snoring or other nasty habits, it is accepted as part of the package. Rather then pretending it doesn't exist or trying to sweep the open secret of Wii's destructive tendencies, why not just join in the conversation and laugh with everyone else (except of course if you have a nunchuk imbedded in your forehead!)?

This site was not intended to beleaguer Nintendo at all. In fact, the tonality was pretty lighthearted and humorous. The postings were coming from actual Nintendo customers who were volunteering their personal photographs. Nintendo was quick to respond by upgrading the Wii remotes with safety straps to avoid freak or accidental slippage. Can I prove that Nintendo's swift response was directly in response to this web site/blog? Absolutely not. Was the presence of the site a factor in the feedback-loop and decision-making process, though? Probably.

Through www.wiihaveaproblem.com, Nintendo had a golden opportunity to reach out and join a conversation already in progress. If they had done it, I bet they'd have floored the creators of the web site, not to mention the contributors. Perhaps Nintendo could have enlisted the services of the group to act as beta testers of the new and improved remote and report back on its dependability, consistency, and reliability. Of course, the receipt of brand-spanking new consoles would have miraculously transformed the contributors into life enthusiasts.

How many times do you think you've been approached to join a conversation? The correct answer is countless times. Too many times to mention in fact. Every single time one of your customers, loyalists, promoters, or detractors raised a hand, sent in a letter to your customer service department or an e-mail to your web site, or engaged in a dialogue on a message board, you were handed an invitation to come to the party.

And?

Bueller . . . Bueller . . . Bueller . . .

## How Approachable Are You?

Ask yourself this question and then attempt to answer it. Do you know the last time a consumer reached out to you for a response?

If you asked your consumer base to rate your company and the brand itself on an approachable scale, how would you score?

What do the answers to these questions say about the kind of open lines of communication you're hoping to foster between brand and owner?

How exactly can you ever hope to build lifelong bonds with customers when there is an alligator-filled moat, impregnable walls, reinforced drawbridge, and a sign that reads something along the lines of: BRIAN DOESN'T WANT TO SEE ANYONE. NOW PISS OFF (Monty Python reference number two).

Are you a party-crasher (status quo), a party-pooper (not much fun), a party animal (too much fun), or the life of the party? Ultimately the choice is yours.

### Party-Crasher

No one likes the loser who crashes the party, right? Well, why then do you crash your consumers' parties every single waking opportunity you get your grubby impressions on? Mass marketing is constantly showing up on people's doorsteps, unannounced, uninvited, and unwelcome.

NBC acted as a *buzzkill* when it pulled down all the Lazy Sunday clips from the video-sharing web sites, thereby dampening the party already in progress.

### Party-Pooper

Party-pooping is another extension of your daily grind where you fade into obscurity, often just when things are getting interesting. Think of your typical "campaign," with its artificial start and end dates coinciding with your arbitrary provisions and considerations such as line extensions, product launches, or repositionings. Nowhere is there any consumer-centric concern, and that is because no one cares what consumers have to say, unless they're in a buying frame of mind.

Microsoft is the quintessential party-pooper, always asking questions but never sticking around long enough to wait for or respond to the answers.

*Where do you want to go today?*

I'm glad you asked. . . . Actually, I was thinking of starting a new business, and I was wondering if . . . uh, hello? Hello?

*Helloooo????!!!!!!!*

*Your imagination. Our passion. . . .*

Oh great, you're still there. . . . You raise a great point. . . . I have many dreams, and it's great to know that you feel passionately about them. Don't you? Are you there?

*Software for the people-ready business. . . .*

Oh, just get lost!


**Party Animal**

Ever heard of *Aqua Teen Hunger Force*? (See Figure 12.4.) It's a program on the Cartoon Network cable channel that until recently you most likely had not. On January 31, 2007, however, "suspicious-looking" devices depicting the Mooninites, Ignignokt, and Err prompted authorities in Boston, Massachusetts, to shut down pretty much the entire city. As it turned out, this was a guerrilla marketing stunt sanctioned by Turner Broadcasting System that went horribly wrong.

One reader on my blog suggested that even with the $2 million repayment to the city of Boston, the whole palaver still cost less than a typical Super Bowl commercial, but nevertheless, I wonder how much damage was done in the process—or perhaps how scalable this kind of imbecilic act can ever be.

The incident raised some really interesting discussion points. There was no question that the city of Boston overreacted; however, given the lasting hangover from 9/11, this is somewhat understand-

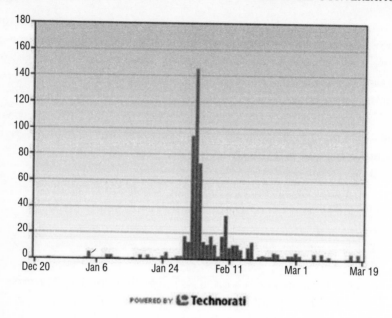

Figure 12.4    Posts by Day about *Aqua Teen Hunger Force*, December 20, 2006, to March 19, 2007

able. In fact, in participating cities like Portland passersby replaced the batteries in the devices, and some shopkeepers even put them in their stores as display units! Perhaps the biggest problem here (and this is more often than not the case) was how the various players handled the situation—a discombobulated mixture of pained silence, unfunny wit and arrogance, and helpless mea culpa instead of just direct, straightforward honesty. Back to my analogy: If you want to be a party animal, you're going to have to stick around afterwards to help clean up (as opposed to "send me a bill").

## Life of the Party

Why shouldn't (or couldn't) a brand be the center of a conversation? Coca-Cola's www.weallspeakfootball.com acts as a clearinghouse for conversation (more on this shortly). The Converse Gallery puts the brand "center and front" of a Chuck Taylor celebration. Dove's Campaign for Real Beauty galvanizes an entire community around an indelibly powerful idea.

Axe and its alter ego Lynx are terrific examples of being centers of attention without hogging the limelight unnecessarily. The mash-up of irreverence, controversy, provocation, and brand truth combined to spew out what everyone knows and believes but today doesn't really say (out loud and/or in company). Sites like Axe's clickmore.com or Lynx's lynxfeather.com and lynxblow.com are experiences within themselves that get people talking . . . and talking . . . and talking.

And for some strange reason, I find myself showering with Axe these days.

Take some time to get that horrible image out of your heads and resume reading at your leisure.

## What My Mother Could Teach Steve Jobs about Conversational Marketing

Apple has been infamously conspicuous for its lack of response to pretty much anything leveled at it by its very passionate consumer base. Of late, Apple has capitulated time after time following cracked iPod Nano screens, deficient iPod batteries, iPhone growing pains, exploding batteries . . . the list goes on. Perhaps Steve Jobs should spend some time with my mother.

I recently had a conversation with my distraught mother, who was lamenting a situation that literally had caused her sleepless nights and much angst and anxiety. My mother is a numismatist, and bless her, she is not a techie, although all three of her children are firmly entrenched in the world of the Web. Every year she conducts her coin and medal sale, and it's a very stressful time for her. As the sale comes to an end she is frantically drawing lines down ledger pages and painstakingly and meticulously reconciling, by hand, the competing and eventual winning bids before dispatching the various lots to their suitors. I've told her for years to get with it and join the information superhighway. In her defense, she's terrific at SMS-ing.

She might not pay attention to me, but she certainly paid attention to a very irate buyer in Alabama who was most peeved at the lack of response, mode of response, and series of incremental charges associated with shipping and handling, as well as tax and insurance (critical when dealing with valuable commodities in South Africa).

Here is part of the conversation.

Posted: 27 Nov 2006 16:44
MARTY
Posts       1582
Location    ALABAMASHIRE

Good Morning:

Well I received my bill from these people by e-mail this morning, and I am here to tell you they are crazy, and will not put the hose into me. Just look at the charges, which I have converted into U.S. dollars:

Lot: $558.95
Premium: $83.82
VAT on Premium: $11.77
Their Bank's Charges: $14.14
Courier: $88.91

Now, I have no problem with the first 3 items, but I'll be damned before I'll pay their bank charges or $88.91 to ship 1 medal from South Africa to the U.S.

They also allude to the fact that they want payment by "wire transfer," but if you read their "conditions" posted on their website, it reads like this:

5. PURCHASE PRICE, COMMISSION AND PAYMENT
5.1 A buyer may effect payment for the goods in one of the following ways:
5.1.1 Any valid MasterCard, Visa, American Express or Diners Club card;
5.1.2 Cheque;
5.1.3 Direct transfer; or
5.1.4 Bank draft (recommend the SWIFT TRANSFER METHOD. Kindly ask your bank for details.)
5.2 Our bank account details are as follows:

I prefer not to say any more at present, but those who know probably can figure out how this will end up.

Marty

PS: And I should not have to pay the VAT on the premium as these are being shipped out of their country.

Posted: 30 Nov 2006 15:23
MARTY
Posts     1582
Location   ALABAMASHIRE

Mates & Matesses:

This impetuous Yank learned a few things today, and that is "When in Rome, do as The Romans."

I was very disturbed and concerned about the way City Coins handled their sales, and voiced my opinions here vociferously. I also contacted these people and voiced my displeasure as to their charges and speed in getting the information out to all bidders, but all in a gentlemanly fashion.

Well, I have had a lesson the past 2 days in customer service that would be hard to beat anywhere. Mrs. Jaffe called me at home both yesterday and just now. We resolved our misunderstandings in a most amicable fashion, and now have everything under control.

So, to all of my friends in SA who may have taken my criticism of City Coins as an affront or reflection upon them I offer a full retraction of what may have been taken as harsh words.

And as for Mrs. Jaffe . . . I would not be surprised to have her as a guest in the near future, to see how us redneck country boys live.

So . . . all's well that ends well, and this ended very well for all concerned.

Marty

Now at least I know where I get my ideas from! The thread edits you just read are a classic illustration of how to respond to an online conversation already in progress. Human. Responsive. Empathetic. Genuine. Marty just wanted to be heard. He turned to his online community and support group. He absolutely could have gone straight to the source, but instead he sought advice and feedback from his peers. As it turns out, several participants were able to get the word back to my mom . . . who then promptly and decisively rectified the matter. Today Marty and my mom are in regular contact. Easy, huh?

---

*Quick tip:* Set up a series of Google alerts that will notify you immediately when anyone, anywhere, is talking about you.

## CATALYZING THE CONVERSATION

Joining a conversation implies participating as an equal partner, which is an ideal situation. However, it doesn't mean that a brand cannot step up to the plate and lead the conversation or attempt to take the conversation to the next level.

Brands have so much to offer, and even if they don't, they have tons of money to invest in amplifying, extending, and enhancing a conversation. Podcasting, for example, is one kind of conversation that is revolutionizing radio as we know it. Feedburner currently measures over 800,000 audio feeds, which is another way of saying that there are more podcasts in circulation than there are radio stations.

And where are the brands? Spamming the *free-FM*[2] waves with endless streams of write-down-this-800-number-while-you're-driving-and-try-not-to-kill-anyone-in-the-process messaging.

I've said this countless times in numerous presentations to brand marketers: "You can own this. You can build podcasting with rounding errors of your in-flux budget. Seek out the podcasters who imbue the very same brand essence, attributes, and characteristics and uplift them. Empower them. Sponsor them with new equipment . . . advanced equipment . . . hire a producer to help them put out a better product. Be a conversation catalyst or conduit—directly or indirectly."

Some are seeing the lightbulbs explode one by one with unbridled passion. Others are asking nauseating questions about demographics, adoption rates, and best practices.

I went through an incredibly painful process with an advertising agency and its "spirited" client who was all excited about sponsoring my podcast. Apparently they'd heard me mention how much I like scotch (single-malt if you're buying) on an episode and took the initiative to approach me to explore a possible partnership. Long story longer, they backed out with a pathetic litany of excuses, such as lack of budget and a corporate directive about *not* getting involved in too many smaller, local investments. To which I politely pointed out that one of their VPs of hypocrisy was speaking at a conference

---

[2]A ridiculous positioning tagline used by Infinity radio as a direct response to the departure of Howard Stern to Sirius Satellite radio.

I was keynoting about the importance and power of community and sponsoring smaller, more localized events. I won't mention the name of the brand, but suffice to say they "kept on walking."

On the flip side of the equation is Nikon. Nikon took a ground-up approach by essentially sponsoring its consumer. Nikon did what every major brand should be doing: It got out of its own way and let the real people who count do the talking—its own consumers.

Here's the frame-by-frame:

- Nikon sent a bunch of its D80 cameras to a group of Flickr users and let them snap to their heart's content.
- Nikon took a bunch of submissions and used them as part of a three-page spread that ran in places like *Business Week*.

For what seems like centuries now, I've been pleading with marketers to use the original creations from their own consumers as actual content (advertising if you must). It's great to finally see this in action. (See Figure 12.5.)

What I really loved about Nikon's approach was the following:

- It was CGC with a purpose. No "do our jobs for us," but rather, "meet us halfway."
- Speaking of which, Nikon found a great balance here in terms of working with consumers.
- Nikon's approach speaks to all three new marketing roles for advertising (which I laid out in *Life After the 30-Second Spot*): to involve, to empower, and to demonstrate.
- Nikon's campaign further speaks to the rise of product (or product as brand). In this campaign, the brand experience is all about the product in action and therefore in context.

Nikon then continued the momentum generated from the successful photographer outreach with a blogger/influencer outreach (of which I was one of the recipients of a Nikon D80 loaner camera).

Listen to my podcast conversation with "CK" and "Tangerine Toad" as we discuss the goods, bads and uglies of Nikon D80's blogger outreach program in a heated and spirited debate at jointhe conversation.us/nikond80

Figure 12.5    Nikon's Partnership with Enthusiasts. Photograph of
Penny, a French bulldog, taken by Heather Waraksa of Heather Waraksa
Photography. One of the many photographs taken by Heather Waraksa
as part of the Stunning Nikon campaign featuring the D80 during the
summer of 2006. More of her work can be seen at stunningnikon.com/d80
or heatherwaraksa.com.

## Sponsor Your Consumer

I had the pleasure of keynoting at International Events Group
(IEG)'s sponsorship conference in 2007. The theme of the conference was "Why the Next Big Thing Will Be a Million Little Things."
My message to the 1,400-plus attendees was simple: Sponsor your
consumers. Uplift them. Empower them. Save them. Celebrate them.

According to Technorati, only 8 percent of bloggers have monetized their blogs. The number is undoubtedly lower with podcasting.

In fact, Rob Walch, host of Podcast411, estimates that at least one-
fifth of podcasters never make it beyond the 10th show. The term
"podfading" has been coined to describe this premature burnout. Podfading can occur for a number of reasons, including frustration with

limited audience size and lack of growth, the time required to prepare and produce (my podcast, Jaffe Juice, formerly called. Across the Sound, barely made it past show number 13, and I can certainly vouch for the time required), and even the pressures of success.

Marketer/sponsors have *got* to step up and put their money where their consumers' loyal and passionate mouths are. There's way too much watching from the sidelines right now. The investment it would take is way less than the spare change that gets lost in the linings of marketing budget clothing (clunky metaphor, but you get the picture). Sponsorship dollars that amount to nothing but rounding errors can provide better recording equipment, assign a producer to help with editing and production in general (especially as video grows), assist with marketing and advertising (growing the audience base), and, of course, put some pocket money in the hands of the podcasting community.

The goodwill alone would offset the investment by several multiples, not to mention the tidal wave of positive word of mouth and buzz. Dewar's sponsored its consumer when it aligned with the popular podcaster Ze Frank. This sponsorship was written up in the various ad trades.

There are many reasons for Google's incredible meteoric rise and growth, which has enthralled, confounded, and frustrated most traditional media companies, middlemen, and investors. Google is certainly not the only search company. It might not even be the best one. And yet it runs rings around its nearest competitors, including Microsoft and Yahoo!

I'd like to offer up three reasons for Google's success, and as you'll see, they have a lot to do with conversational marketing:

1. *Speed to market* — This is probably the smallest contributor of the three. The fact is that if you give Google a seven-figure budget, within six days it'll not only completely implement it for you but produce bang for your buck as well. It took God six days to create the world, but unlike Google, He had to rest!

2. *Sponsoring its consumer* — Google's acquisition of Blogger helped catalyze the adoption and proliferation of blogs. Think about it . . . by giving out blogs for free, Google made it easy and painless for any consumer to become a publisher

overnight. The same might be said for applications like Gmail. And by sponsoring its consumers, Google also sponsored and catalyzed the conversation—others' conversation, that is.

3. *Distributed content*—Here's the real brilliance. By catalyzing the conversation, Google invented the impression printing-press by liberating its brand hold and control on Google.com and "exporting" its presence to the four corners of the Web, i.e., where its consumers live. Google's consumers produce brand-spanking new impressions every single time they post and someone else reads. And wherever conversation is happening, Google product is there.

### Production Is the New Consumption

One of the universal truths that has remained intact since the dawn of media through the current day and will probably endure long after the ink from these pages fades away is the fact that there are only 24 hours in the day. A lesser truth is the fact that each person has only one attention span.

Research reveals that younger consumers have become quite adept at multitasking multiple media platforms simultaneously. (Just watch your teenage son or daughter engage in multiple IM conversations, listen to blaring music, surf the Web, do his or her homework, speak on a cell phone, and, last but least, have the TV on in the background.) Now, while one might think this is a silver lining in terms of countering cannibalization, the bad news is that the one-attention-span rule still holds true in that only one form of contact remains dominant at any given time; the others become subordinate or background ambiance (or noise).

Taking us from bad to worse is the fact that consumers are choosing their dominant platform du jour with media that are advertising-light. It's a given that you need to be where your consumers are, but is that enough? You need to realize that most of your consumers are increasingly preoccupied with living their lives in a world where you are fairly inconspicuous.

In this world, your consumers are engaging in media's ultimate cannibalistic activity: *production*. When they are creating content, it is 100 percent coming out of a pool that used to be devoted to *consuming* content. This is why production is the new consumption — and why embracing the consumers playing with your content is so important.

## Starting a Conversation

I left the most common form of marketing as a conversation to the end, and I'm hoping that you'll consider the other four forms before you jump straight into the obvious alternative. Starting a conversation is one of those things that sound too good to be true . . . and usually when something is too good to be true, it is. Most of the time when brands set out to "start" a conversation, it isn't a conversation at all, but rather a communications-heavy, forced, and diluted attempt at soliciting feedback.

The networks do a particularly poor job of partnering with their audience in a rich and robust conversation. Every reality show in the United States seems to have an interruptive SMS tactic designed to "engage" otherwise passive viewers to vote with their wallets (standard rates apply) in a hit-and-hope effort to win some kind of cash prize. Deal or no deal? I'll take the latter. The strategy of connecting with already present viewers is flawed. Besides hoping to keep their fleeting attention by the odd second or two and in so doing increase the probability that they will watch the commercials, I can't really imagine what is being achieved. Instead, how about starting a conversation that begins the moment the weekly show ends and ends the moment the next week's show begins? CBS is doing this with shows like *The Amazing Race*, which sequesters the booted contestants into a house (a holding cell) for the duration of the tournament and allows viewers to interact, get bonus interviews, and so on.

### Conversation Is Not on Your Terms

One final point: If you give your consumers a voice, you have to be able to take the bad with the good. If you start a conversation, remember that it is going to take on a life of its own, and sometimes the results are going to be devastating, as the folks over at the *Washington Post* found out.

In June 2006, the *Washington Post* showed its hipness factor by opening up blogs, with comments no less. In one particularly memorable case, *Post* readers and visitors took particular issue with remarks made by the newspaper's ombudsman, Deborah Howell, who referred to Jack Abramoff in a January 15 column as having made "substantial campaign contributions to both major parties." What ensued was an explosion of vicious personal attacks against Deborah Howell.

Under a deluge of scathing comments, the *Post* yanked from the site all comments that were defamatory, inflammatory, or any other word ending with *-tory*. Of course, the *Post* was making a subjective assessment of what constituted inflammatory or defamatory comments versus good old-fashioned criticism. This, of course, only made matters worse.

The *Post* attempted to silence the conversation, but *fortunately* one reader (by Wikipedia's definition, also an ombudsman) performed the public service of keeping all the posts for the record.

For the most part, I am quite skeptical about the ability of established media brands to "go naked"—to invite and accept readers as co-authors and contributors. I guess it's one of those cases where you can't be half pregnant . . . but perhaps there is a middle ground. Surely this case would have been avoided had the *Post* utilized a moderated comment approach?

Perhaps, but ultimately even that solution would have backfired, since irate readers would have taken the conversation "outside" and spread it like wildfire. In fact, even if there had been no comments, the outcome would have been the same.

The learnings are quite profound. *If you give your consumers a voice, they will use it*, and it probably behooves you to channel their passion on your home turf, where at least you have some semblance of familiarity and comfort. And even if you choose not to give your consumers a voice, the fact is that they have one already and will use it at their discretion.

And so, whether or not you believe comments are required . . . whether or not you go the moderated route . . . hell, whether or not you have a blog . . . your readers/consumers are still going to express themselves—good, bad, or ugly. So I guess the real issue is this: Is it better for them to shit on your doorstep or their own? If the former, can it still be cleaned up?

It is (about) time to usher in an entirely new operating ethos and philosophy that hold the brand and its stewards to the highest possible standards of accountability.

AccuQuote started a conversation with its customers, not as a marketing effort per se, but as an expert lesson in customer service. The result was sheer branding nirvana. Incidentally, you can listen to a never-before-heard Across the Sound interview between myself, Sean Cheyney, and Tom Hespos on www.jointheconversation.us/accuquote

## A Case Study
## AccuQuote's Blogging Efforts
### Sean Cheyney, Vice President of
### Marketing and Business Development

In mid-2006 we had been dipping our toes in the blog pool when we finally decided to make a giant cannonball splash. We migrated the blog to its own domain, accuquoteblog.com, and we took a bold move: We shared our service philosophy with our customers and openly asked for their suggestions for how to improve our service.

### Simply Posting Wasn't Enough

After we started the thread, we packaged up the post into an e-mail and sent it to our entire customer database. The response was immediate, and the volume was much higher than expected. After mobilizing our internal blog response team (our CEO, our PR manager, and myself), we spent the next couple of days furiously responding back to everyone who had taken the time to post a comment. (See Figure 12.6.)

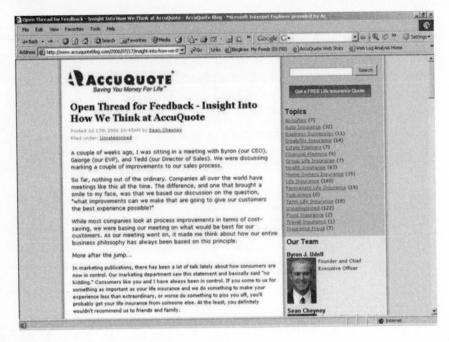

Figure 12.6    AccuQuote Screenshot #1

## You Need to Be Committed to the Conversation . . .
## Even if You Don't Like What You Hear

Before we started, we made the commitment to respond back within one business day to everyone who commented. Sure it's a lot of work, but it was well worth it. Of course, not all of the comments were positive, which was expected. We took the approach that we'd rather know about negative conversations than stick our head in the sand and pretend that our company was the model of perfection. How else can you expect to improve? Our constructive customers gave us valuable insights for improving our service levels as well as our overall process.

### A Funny Thing Happens When You Reach Out

As one of the country's largest direct-to-consumer life insurance brokerages, we do a great job of finding people the best value for their life insurance. The problem, as our customers vocally let us know, was that we weren't doing a good job keeping in touch with them consistently several years after they purchased their policy. We admitted that they were 100 percent correct, and they reached out to us for more life insurance coverage. In fact, so many of our existing customers took out additional life insurance on themselves and family members that this blog/e-mail combo proved to be the biggest revenue driver of any customer communication we ever did! (See Figure 12.7.)

**No One-Shot Wonders Here**

We were so excited by the conversation we were having with our customers that we extended the blog/e-mail combo strategy to our prospects as well as our customers. We've done this several times, with each one yielding a better and better response (one post had well over 300 comments) and more and more incremental sales. In addition to the e-mails, the number of subscribers to the blog continues to increase, and it's become a great platform to educate consumers on all aspects of insurance.

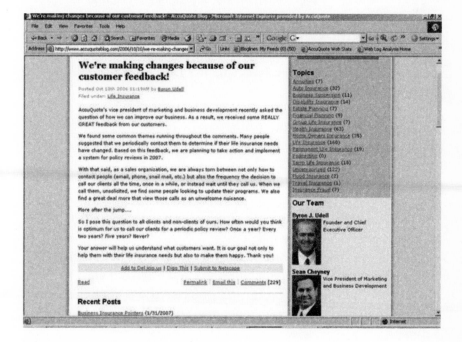

Figure 12.7   AccuQuote Screenshot #2

One of AccuQuote's latest blog posts asked customers what they would want (or expect) from the company as a means of expressing its thanks for their patronage and loyalty.[3]

> As a consumer, what would you want service companies, like Accu-Quote, to do in order to show you their appreciation?
>
> We struggle with this for a few reasons:
>
> First, we want to provide you with something that is valuable and meaningful because as customers of ours you are valuable and meaningful to us.
>
> Second, due to the nature of insurance regulations as implemented by the government, we are limited as to what we can and can do in regards to "free stuff" or "rebating."
>
> Here are two ideas we came up with, but we'd really like to hear yours:
>
> - Send you a *free copy* of a financial planning book or guide
> - Send you some token of our appreciation (a key chain, pen, calendar, etc.)
>
> So, tell us what you think. How would you want us to show you our appreciation for doing business with us? Leave us a comment and let us know.

When this book went to print, there were *over 300 comments*, including the likes of:

- A simple thank you is enough and goes a long way.

You'll also notice that many of these comments came from Sean Cheyney, which is exactly the point.

Sprint began an outreach program in late 2005 in which the company sought out influential bloggers and offered them a free cell phone, with fully loaded Sprint PCS service. I was included in the Sprint Ambassador program and, truthfully, was pretty chuffed

---

[3]See "How Can We Show You Our Appreciation?" at AccuQuote blog, http://www.accuquoteblog.com/2007/03/12/how-can-we-show-you-our-appreciation/2#comments.

when I found out I was included. All in all, 400 people signed up for the program. I gleefully accepted the role of "ambassador," created a separate section on my blog for any photographs I uploaded with my Sprint Ambassador phone, and even edited an audio vignette for my podcast. I even pitched the advertising trade publication *Brandweek* on a story about Sprint's program, which it ran.[4] Throughout the process, I watched live TV, downloaded MP3s, played games, checked the weather forecast, and used the GPS features when I was lost in downtown Manhattan. More importantly, I continue to talk about the program to anyone who will listen or read about it. As a savvy and skeptical blogger, I knew exactly what was going on here, but given Sprint's hands-off approach (perhaps too hands-off) and my transparency and disclosure about receiving the phone, I have had no problems talking about a landmark conversation starter.

Here's the kicker. I was not a Sprint customer then, and I am not a Sprint customer now. I may never become a Sprint customer. But in the game and spirit of community (my community), dialogue (between myself and my community), and partnership (Sprint as a direct catalyst and indirect starter), I became immensely valuable to Sprint.

It certainly wasn't the first time a prominent brand engaged the blogosphere with "free stuff." In 2004 Procter & Gamble gave free Mr. Clean Auto Dry kits to bloggers and asked for their honest appraisals. In 2005 Nokia handed out 1,800 Nokia 7710 phones in a way similar to the Sprint program.[5]

Whether you are listening to, responding to, joining, catalyzing, or starting a conversation, you are on a powerful path to honest, open, and productive dialogue that not only can make or break your brand but indeed can also transform your business and your consumers' lives.

Ultimately this does come down to truly believing that you fit

---

[4]Todd Wasserman, "New Media: Bloggers Come-a-Calling for Spring Swag Program," *Brandweek*, June 5, 2006.

[5]See the same *Brandweek* article I inspired (note 4).

into your consumers' lives, not the other way around. And if this is the case, then surely it is only logical that you have to be connected to the heart and soul, the passion and pain, the frenzy and fervor of your community—wholly and individually.

### Your Worst Chase Scenario?

One morning on the way into my New York office, I picked up a local paper (I believe it was *Metro*), and a full-page advertisement on the back cover caught my eye. (See Figure 12.8.) It was an absolutely brilliant move by J.P. Morgan Chase, just in time for the U.S. Open tennis tournament. The bank was asking its customers to volunteer their "Worst Chase Scenario"—their worst customer service experiences *with the bank*—as part of a competition. The winner would receive tickets to the women's semifinal. This offer made sense given that Chase is a major sponsor of the Grand Slam event.

This was neither an ad nor a promotion for Chase, but instead a rather subtly camouflaged attack on the company's labor practices by a trade union.[6] My exuberance turned to exasperation, not so much for what I was seeing but for what I could have been seeing. Can you imagine Chase (or any other company for that matter) opening the door for its most irate customers—not to mention lapsed customers—to actually share their horror stories with one another?

The company's potential vulnerability and openness would have been unprecedented, and of course, through this WYSIWYG (what you see is what you get) approach, such a campaign would have given Chase an equally unprecedented opportunity to address areas where there was room for improvement, turn them around, and even celebrate the process.

I don't expect you to understand this idea—nor do I expect any company to implement this extreme form of corporate nakedness anytime soon. That doesn't mean it's a bad idea. I dare each and

---

[6]The union was SEIU Local 32BJ, the largest building service workers' union in the United States.

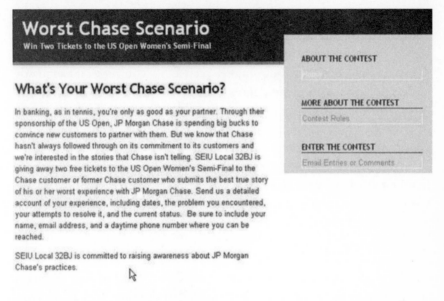

Figure 12.8   Worst Chase Scenario

every one of you to take this kind of chance not only to address a stark reality (hey, I didn't tick off your customers, you did) but to start the ultimate conversation—and relationship.

JetBlue CEO David Neeleman went on a damage control extravaganza when his darling airline left a couple of hundred people stranded on the tarmac at JFK airport for close to 11 hours following a snowstorm in February 2007. Neeleman appeared on *The Today Show*, purchased full-page advertisements in every major daily newspaper, uploaded apology videos to YouTube, and issued a bill of rights for passengers and a sliding penalty scale according to which JetBlue will pay customers based on the extent to which they are delayed in the future (hmmm). JetBlue also issued e-mail apologies to millions of (irrelevant at best: SPAM at worst) customers who weren't even affected.

What he didn't do, however, was allow his customers—particularly the ones affected—to vent. What he didn't do was allow them to get their tremendous frustration with their ordeal off their chests. What he didn't do was listen en masse and engage in a marketing conversation.

Whatever JetBlue does arguably will be too little too late . . . at least for those affected. Nothing will compensate the passengers affected directly. Certainly not the full refund and free round-trip ticket on JetBlue—which makes sense if you're a masochistic sucker for pain and more delays! JetBlue should have offered free tickets for an entire year to those affected. The airline had a moment of truth but blew it by not joining the conversation and embracing community, dialogue, and partnership.

Your worst chase scenario is also your best chase scenario depending on how you look at it. Unless you are David Neeleman, who is no longer with the company.

### Your Life—Your Card

Is there life after the 30-second Tahoe-spot? American Express seemed to think so, except that it shortened the time by half and appealed to sense and sensibility, with a less clunky and contrived brief *and* Academy Award winners (and fellow American Express commercial participants) Martin Scorsese and M. Night Shyamalan as judges (and in Scorsese's case, probably jury and executioner!).

By asking consumers to create a personal slice of their lives (their card), American Express gave them a way to express an authentic interpretation and internalization of the brand. This was CGC as opposed to CGM.

In addition, the RSS feed (http://clips.mylifemycard.com/index .xml which is no longer active—hmmm?) of the submissions, as they happened, not only was a nice touch but also put the creations in the public domain. Implication? People found out quickly whether or not they were hot based on a voting system . . . and this in turn put a little more (constructive) pressure on submitters to take this seriously (as if Martin and Night weren't incentive enough!). This community self-policing effort had a built-in quality-control mechanism to keep the effort honest.

What was really interesting about this program was the timing of it all. American Express primed the pump, months in advance through (gasp) largely traditional marketing and advertising, and once it had seeded an idea via communication, it was able to convert this interest into a conversation via community and participation.

## Starting a Conversation Works Both Ways

A final point needs to be made. Consumers are capable and just as likely to start a conversation themselves. In fact, this is one of those cases where we come full circle, where conversation rule number 5b says, "See rule number 1"—in other words, listen . . . then respond . . . then join . . . then catalyze. . . .

# 13

# When Conversation Isn't Conversation at All

As I said at the beginning of the last chapter, now is your chance to let your brand loose to run amok amid the chaotic and unpredictable. Sound appetizing or petrifying?

In reality, most brands' reactions and moves to date have been putrefying. For the most part, brands have gone about conversation all wrong. They've approached it like a piece of communication. A campaign. Controlled. Measured. Premeditated. Manipulated. Diluted. Misrepresented. Downright pathetic.

While there are emerging best practices when it comes to partnering and dialoguing with consumers and, most notably, your customers, there is also a list of worst practices. Here are five red flags that are surefire ways to isolate your brand (even more) from your community.

- Faking
- Manipulating
- Controlling
- Dominating
- Ignoring or avoiding

## FAKING THE CONVERSATION

Nobody likes a faker, and in this day and age of perfect information (or at the very minimum wise crowds), fake conversation stands out like a sore thumb.

Although it can be argued that most advertising is fake anyway, it is not held to the same high standard as any sociable form of communication (although it should be). Advertising is communication. Blogs, for example, are conversation.

For some inexplicable reason, marketers just don't seem to get the fact that faking or misrepresenting intentions or motivations and/or masking identity or disclosure are just not acceptable practices. Sony discovered this the hard way when it not only created a fake flog—the assumed account of an obsessed PSP fan regarding his Christmas gift wish list—but acted all smug and glib when it was found out:

> Busted. Nailed. Snagged. As many of you have figured out (maybe our speech was a little too funky fresh???), Peter isn't a real hip-hop maven and this site was actually developed by Sony. Guess we were trying to be just a little too clever. From this point forward, we will just stick to making cool products, and use this site to give you nothing but the facts on the PSP.
>
> —Sony Computer Entertainment America

The flog (or frog) in question, which was created by Zipatoni for Sony, begs these questions:

- Why did this need to be a blog . . . and a fake one at that?
- Surely there were *other* approaches that would have done the job equally well, if not better?
- And if not, why couldn't Sony go about this in a considered and authentic way?

It boggles my mind how many mainstream marketers/agencies look at new marketing through the same one-dimensional, traditional, advertising-based and biased lens. It's no wonder that the inevitable outcome every time is fakeness instead of authenticity.

Sony's apology, albeit quick on the draw (and that was only because it was found out!), was way too snide and snarky (note to marketers and their agencies: you don't do snarky well) and comes across only as arrogant and patronizing.

The flog also begs another question: Assuming Zipatoni was not complicit in the fakery of the whole effort (it claims to have warned its client about the possible pitfalls and minefields ahead), why did the agency not push back or push harder or refuse to sign off on the misguided attempt? For an agency that supposedly "gets it" (at least that's what its web site says), surely Zipatoni had (and surely we all have) a responsibility to do the right thing . . . even if it was the hardest thing.

## Reverse ROI

Another point: Is it even remotely possible that one of the reasons why Playstation 3 is lagging so far behind the new Nintendo Wii is because of efforts like these? We talk all the time about ROI, but what about reverse-ROI (I guess that would be IOR), namely, the negative effects of flawed attempts?

In their hearts, marketers really don't believe their consumers are intelligent, independent, and empowered citizens. "The consumer is boss" is just a cover-your-ass (CYA) lip-service flare to give the impression that marketers are "with it." In reality, they firmly buy into the belief that consumers are goldfish. The goldfish principle would certainly explain why we spam our consumers at the abusive frequency of 20 to 50 impressions per campaign (how many times have *you* seen one of those iPod commercials?). We figure they have short-term memory loss issues and so we need to keep reminding them all the time!

The same flawed assumption was applied in the Sony case. Marketers believe or hope (or pray) that consumers will forget about the way their intelligence is insulted and their integrity defiled. But consumers don't forget. Google doesn't either. It's like a Britney Spears tattoo of flaming lips: It's there for keeps, and it's going to sag and fade with time . . . but it ain't going away anytime soon (unless surgery is applied, but that's another metaphor for another day).

## The Difference between Fake Blogs and Character Blogs

Fake blogs are lies. Blatant lies and—even more egregious—masked or covered-up lies. Character blogs, on the other hand, represent real conversation by "fake" personas. Actually, there's nothing fake about the well-manicured blogs maintained, for example, by countless Second Life avatars. From the Second Life Herald, led by its narcissistic editor and publisher, Urizenus Sklar (a.k.a. Professor Peter Ludlow from the Department of Philosophy and Linguistics at the University of Michigan) to the exploits of Gideon Television SuperStar™ (a.k.a. *crayon*'s Chief Creative Officer, Steve Coulson), or even the sordid diaries of Second Life's supermodel (escort) Cardie Mahoney (identity: *unknown*), all three character blogs are very real—the posts are real, the engagement is real, and the conversation is real.

Truthfully, there never used to be a distinction between character and fake blogs. That was probably because there weren't yet so many fake blogs and because the quality of character blogs was so poor. What the two kinds of blogs had in common was that both were weak, contrived, and forced traditional attempts to emulate or imitate genuine conversation.

Frontier Airlines' ridiculous Flip the Dolphin blog chronicled the dolphin's frustrations in trying to secure a route to warmer Mexico. Give me a break. The blogosphere will annihilate you if you insult it with idiocy.

My advice to you if you're thinking about creating a character blog is to make sure you've checked the following mandatories:

- *Does the character have any right to blog?* Mickey Mouse, for example, should stick to shaking the hands of kids at theme parks.
- *Does the character have a unique point of view?* GEICO's gecko has earned the right to be a commentator.
- *Will the character add Relevance, Utility, and Entertainment (RUE) by blogging?* George Parker's blog, Adscam—the Horror, offers a particularly acidic dose of sobriety to the advertising world. What do you mean he's not a character? He most certainly is!
- *Does a corporation or brand with a character blog exercise full transparency and disclosure?* McDonald's 4railroads blog got pummeled for its lame and veiled attempt at selling its Monopoly promotion.

The 4railroads blog was quite harmless, but it got slaughtered through insufficient disclosure. It's not like we were talking about a 10-year-old 200-pound girl who insisted that her obesity was completely genetic and not influenced by the Big Macs she gorged on every day.

In fact, from a narrative standpoint, the idea—an "online journal/diary" of a possessed consumer, intent on winning McDonald's Monopoly game—was quite novel.

So what was the harm?

The problem was more about just plain pathos than about the lack of transparency. (I am torn between jumping on a holier-than-thou puritanical binge, which more often than not leads straight to the gates of hypocrisy, and demanding equally low or high standards for all media on the disclosure stakes before I go nutso on a nascent one, for example, product placement on television.)

The harm was the harmlessness.

There were no comments. There was no life. No nothing.

If anything, the transparency flare just exposed this for what it was: communication in a weak attempt at creating conversation.

From my perspective, the implications for marketers are twofold:

1. McDonald's could be investing better in blogs and really reaping the full power of conversation, dialogue, consumer-generated content, and networking.
2. Going back to the first-person narrative account, surely long-form content in some kind of episodic form would have been a better execution of this idea.

This is one of those cases where "social media" and "storytelling" are not necessarily one and the same. The former is dominated by PR people and the latter by advertising/marketing folk. I find myself somewhere in between (the "new marketing" middle—or is it the high ground?), longing for the days of good old-fashioned storytelling, with a sprinkle of authenticity and a drizzle of ROI to boot.

How about you?

My mom taught me when I was just five years old that lies always surface, so you think a corporation would know that they can't fool anyone. Plus, trying to trick your audience is insulting their intelligence and a violation of their trust. McDonald's . . . idea actually has a lot of potential, just be honest about it.

Posted by: Sue

The advice I give to clients considering unethical or nontransparent ventures into social media is that ersatz engagement carries risk (you get slated by bloggers) and where the attention is not negative it is usually nonexistent. As you point out, this blog was hardly connected: Despite a month of blogging there's only one link before people started writing about the fact the blog is fake: from the other fake blog.

Posted by: Antony Mayfield

I could argue that *most* of advertising is fake—the hyperbole, exaggeration, small print, disclaimers, etc. All I'm saying is that if we're going to judge or evaluate this in terms of evilness, shouldn't we be doing it across the board (raising the bar) . . . *or* . . . using the same low standards/bar that has been set across the miserable board as well?

Posted by: Joseph Jaffe

Fake blogs are wrong for so many reasons. Here's the real deal when it comes to an authentic McDonald's blog: The McChronicles (http://mcchronicles.blogspot.com). This blog is genuine, has never accepted a nickel, owes nothing to anyone, and remains true to its mission: "chronicling the McDonald's experience from the customers' point of view."

Posted by: McChronicles

## MANIPULATING THE CONVERSATION

There are way too many companies that infiltrate chat rooms and message boards, intercept passersby on the street with obvious fakery, post anonymous comments on blogs, and, oh yes, *advertise*.

In *Life After the 30-Second Spot*, I talk about the fact that consumers aren't as dumb as they used to be . . . put differently, consumers today are smarter than they used to be.

One example is the difference between (and perceived credibility of) movie critic reviews versus community (meaning you and me) reviews.

Exacerbating this is the borderline criminal misrepresentation of real reviews by studio frauds as misleading marketing propaganda.

As reported by the good folk at the Adrants blog, *Gelf* magazine put together a pretty telling exposé that reflected the disconnect, and in true new marketing fashion, I'm doing my part to spread it.

For example, marketers used a very selectively chosen quotation from Kevin Thomas's *Los Angeles Times* review of *Be Cool*: ". . . Travolta is as smooth as ever. . . ." Here's what Thomas actually wrote:

> [John Travolta's character Chili] Palmer is back in *Be Cool*, and although Travolta is as smooth as ever, the picture is a bust, a grimly unfunny comedy with no connection to reality, and worst of all, running on and on for two dismal hours.

Political advertising in the United States is disgraceful. The red side calls the blue side a liar, and the blue side calls the red side a liar. Only one side can be telling the truth. Except that both are most likely lying. Either way, voters have to decide which liar they want to represent them and their families. And people wonder why voter turnout is so low. I'd like to start a web site that lists all of the candidates' "integrated" advertising and evaluates the sum total of the messaging with a fact-based account of who the biggest rotten liar actually is.

Microsoft was just beginning to enjoy its newfound "underdog" status (relative to Apple) when along came Vista. To coincide with the launch of the new Windows operating system, Microsoft's PR agency devised a plan to send Acer computers preloaded with Windows Vista to a bunch of influential bloggers. The PCs were "gifts" (as in "yours to keep"), and the bloggers were told to write what they wanted, if they wanted. The only thing they *weren't* asked to do was to disclose that they were approached by Microsoft. One would think that the bloggers would have had enough common sense to state the obvious. Instead, giddily drunk on the freebie, they waxed lyrical about their brand-new PCs with Windows Vista . . . until they were "outed."

The lesson learned on this slippery slope to a painful fall was never to *overestimate* bloggers, who are *not* journalists. Even though neither Microsoft nor its PR agency set out to bribe the bloggers, there was manipulation-by-default in the sense of *not enough* control over the process. It's a bitter irony—but one that helps the next brand looking to get in on the conversation to set boundaries and thus manage its expectations accordingly.

## CONTROLLING THE CONVERSATION

Moderate conversation should be moderated. Healthy and productive conversation should be liberated. Make no mistake: There's no problem with structuring a dialogue in a somewhat logical and meaningful order, but when it is canned, boxed, neutered, and suppressed, the result is underwhelming at best and scorned at worst.

The folks over at General Motors' Chevrolet division found out the hard way when they invited their consumers to create Chevy Tahoe commercials on their behalf. The prize was not a new car (go figure) but some underwhelming and tangential and forgettable carrot.

The whole look and feel of the competition was very forced and contrived. Entrants had to choose a certain number of clips to drag into their mash-up. They had to specifically select clips from the three brand attribute buckets (ugggh), such as dependability or reliability. The terms and conditions were onerous.

I decided to create my own Tahoe commercial and gave the "Ad Management" (their words) folks at Chevy enough time to review and approve my spot, which was well within the rules set out by them. Surprise, surprise, my creation (or lack thereof) was not accepted (nor was it rejected . . . it was just sucked into the black hole of selective indifference), and I was not given the opportunity to share it with my friends (or readers). And so, as an

insurance policy, I crudely captured myself on video and uploaded it to YouTube, where it has been seen by over 1,000 clearly
deranged people.

While 1,000 permission-based views might not seem like a lot to
you, when you factor in a conservative amplification ratio of 1-to-
1,000 and multiply that by another 1,000 creations from people just
like me and my friends, you have what we in the ad game like to call
"critical mass."

Chevy's continued controlling of the situation did not allow it to
wake up and smell the hydrocarbons. There was no response to the
groundswell of backlash. There was no corporate Point Of View
(POV) or remote glimmer of humanity.

But I did receive this e-mail from Ed Peper of Chevy, which begins with the following words:

> You put in the effort. You made the most capable, most responsible,
> and most refined commercial you could for the 2007 Tahoe.

Indeed I did. Except that I never got to *see* my most capable,
most responsible, and most refined commercial, because it never got
most approved—or at least I never got the ability to most forward it
to a most friend or most view it myself (except on YouTube, that is).

Though there was a boardroom chat room (aligned with the *Apprentice* promotion, to which it was loosely tied) to discuss and an-
nounce the winners, it too was very carefully controlled.

On the complete flip side of the spectrum is the tremendous activation success of Mozilla's Firefox—the fierce alternative to Microsoft's Internet Explorer. Firefox has enjoyed a long-standing
healthy relationship with its fervent community by embracing its
creativity. A prolific amount of consumer-generated content has
been created; however, it hasn't been one-sided. Take the case of
Firefox Flicks.

On his blog, Ben Rowe offered up these reasons for why Firefox trumped Tahoe:

- Firefox had a creative brief.
- Firefox is a great product because:

- It has little negative downside (for example, it doesn't guzzle bandwidth).
- It has an immensely passionate consumer base.
- Foxfire had creative control, which it handed carte blanche to the community.[1]

The same creative brief proved successful for the dabbles of Al Gore's Current TV in consumer-generated content. The most notable result was 19-year-old Tyson Ibele's spot for Sony, entitled "Transformation." A creative brief offers an overarching framework against which to sculpt and mold, and provided the "mandatories" and various calls to action are not overly stifling and suffocating (you know, like advertising creative briefs!), consumers have room to move relatively freely with the framework.

The other lesson is to focus on your most loyal and passionate customers. Do you know who they are? Do you know them all by name? Are you aware of the 20 percent of your customers who are responsible for generating 80 percent of your revenues? Why is it that every morning, the guy who operates his kiosk on the corner of 57th and Broadway (his name is Abdul, by the way) remembers that I take my large coffee with skim milk and one and a half Equals and yet you cannot remember your loyal customers' names? He does not have the luxury of registration data or sophisticated CRM technology and yet—somehow—he successfully weaves through hundreds of daily transactions without losing a shred of his personal touch in the process.

And while we're at it, do you know the 1 percent of consumers who are responsible for 99 percent of your buzz? Figure out who they are and build bridges with them (partnership) without snuffing out the creative spirit in the process.

## DOMINATING THE CONVERSATION

As indicated earlier, good conversation is balanced between key participants and constituents. There is a natural equilibrium that is

[1]"Be Genuine," at Ben Rowe's blog, http://benrowesblog.wordpress.com (May 25, 2007).

disrupted when hotheads and bullies dominate a dialogue. Actually, in these cases it really is not a dialogue at all, but a monotonous monologue.

Bill O'Reilly of Fox News is an infamous bully. He doesn't interview his guests so much as interrogate them. And when they talk back, he shuts them up. Don Imus was likewise. Other celebrities, like Rosie O'Donnell and Mark Cuban, are making bigger and faster strides at partnering with their audiences and communities in order to stay close to them . . . learn from them . . . and build bridges and relationships with them. Their blogs are well read, and the connections made from them are without question boosting their own personal brands within the communities they serve. In several of these cases, we have witnessed a marked turning of the tide when it comes to the fate, fortitude, and prosperity afforded to those who unfairly dominate the conversation.

Companies and brands, however, aren't quite in the game yet. They tend to suffer from the all-too-common ailment of *conversatius extremititis* (except when it comes to communication, which falls somewhere on the fence: wishy-washy, bland, and mediocre to a fault). Companies are largely in the camp where command-and-control outweighs share-and-care. When in doubt, they leave it out. Those that do try to let go get stuck in mounds of lip service and superficial commitment.

Let me be a little less esoteric: Your consumers have a voice. A valuable voice. Acknowledge it. Give them a platform to speak. To you. To one another. Listen to what they say. Respond to it. Act on it.

All too often, brands solicit opinion, feedback, and expression from their consumers and yet they carefully prescreen, moderate, and manually select the best-sounding responses or entries. It is a *many-to-one* approach by which the few (and this includes consumers) are dominant. The communications profession has been indoctrinated with a methodology that is predicated on distilling the complex to the simple—a linear progression from general to specific. We oversimplify to the point where we are left with a pithy takeaway one-word equity—in other words, a chi-chi anemic serving of conversation that leaves most consumers walking away dissatisfied, discontented, and hungry for something better!

Brands have to know their role and place in conversation. Truthfully, it is an extremely loose, amorphous, and situational role that not only changes from case to case but indeed may evolve and shift within a single conversation. The art of conversation is absolutely an art, and the ability to deftly navigate the thin ice of tolerance, patience, emotion, and submission may very well mean the difference between connection and disconnection.

## IGNORING OR AVOIDING THE CONVERSATION

What conversation? There's a conversation going on? I had no idea!

I'm not sure which is worse: the companies that are completely oblivious to ongoing conversations or the ones that are acutely aware of them but choose (or are told) to ignore them.

Nike ignored the conversation when I posted my "viral video" to my blog. It was most definitely aware of the video, and I know this because an anonymous Nike employee posted comments on the thread informing me that my video had been sent around to all 7,000 employees in Nike's weekly marketing newsletter update. And yet they remained silent. Pity.

Coca-Cola remained silent for way too long when it came to acknowledging EepyBird's Stephen Voltz and Fritz Grobe, two ordinary consumers and yet artists in their own right who created somewhat of a sensation by dropping tubes of Mentos candy into two-liter bottles of Diet Coke.

The chemical reaction was explosive—a geyser of Diet Coke erupting in fountains and mountains of fizz. The reaction in the conversation was equally powerful and potent.

For the record, and thanks to the Steaming Pile blog (it takes all kinds), which credits Steve Spanger's science web site and Wikipedia, here is the method to the madness:

> Soda is bubbly because there is carbon dioxide ($CO_2$) gas dissolved in the sweetener/water/other chemical solution.
>
> The surface of a Mentos candy is covered with some huge number of itsy bitsy little pits and craters and spikes and stuff.

When the soda comes in contact with the sharp edges of the candy, *nucleation* sites are formed where the carbon dioxide comes out of solution with the rest of the soda and causes a chain reaction of rapidly expanding gas that forces the soda up and out of the bottle.

It's also handy that the candy sinks to the bottom of the bottle so that it has to force the soda up instead of just the gas coming out the top and foaming a bit (like when you drop ice cream into root beer).

So basically, it's just a physical reaction of the $CO_2$ and soda coming out of solution, not a real chemical explosion. The soda isn't really altered in any way, other than it comes out of the bottle and does not have any carbonation left.[2]

Now you know. Back to the story at hand. Two roads diverged in a wood and the Coca-Cola Company and Mentos took two distinct paths. Mentos embraced the phenomenon—and why wouldn't they? Mentos certainly had the least to lose, but by the same token Coca-Cola had the most to gain. Mentos seized the opportunity and catalyzed the conversation by buying up all impressions on Revver (the video-sharing web site that housed the original video). They also created a web site and promotion dedicated to consumers creating their own geysers—www.mentosgeysers.com (now defunct—hmmm!).

If I'm putting on a cynical hat for a moment, all Mentos did was take a gift horse and ride it to Triple Crown glory. It was opportunistic, and not really original at all. Just quick to act and certainly quicker than Coke. That said, speedy reaction has now become paramount, and it is still enough of a move to pull away from an otherwise indistinct chasing pack.

Coke's reaction, on the other hand, was nonexistent. In fact, only when prompted by the *Wall Street Journal* for an official response did the company's spokesperson give this:

It's an entertaining phenomenon. We would hope people want to drink [Diet Coke] more than try experiments with it.

---

[2]"Mentos Geyser—Diet Coke Eruption," at Steve Spangler Science, http://www.stevespangler science.com/experiment/00000109

Of course, that kind of reaction (or the lack thereof) was kind of like . . . I need a good metaphor . . . oh, here's one . . . like dropping Mentos candies into a two-liter bottle of Diet Coke. The blogosphere was not amused and berated the soft-drink brand for just not getting it.

Apple pretty much remains silent all the time unless an IMAX-sized screen, fireworks, video cameras, and Teleprompters appear and a turtlenecked and tortoise-spectacled Steve Jobs walks on-stage to do the talking. Apple has a massive opportunity—iPods aside—to convert consumers en masse from the very tired PC proposition to the liberated and unadulterated creativity engine that is Mac. Instead of opening up a dialogue and ongoing conversation with its most loyal customers, anointing them as silent sales-force emissaries or crusaders (you will not stop until you have converted every remaining PC infidel) or unleashing the power of consumer-generated content in the form of reviews, how-tos, step-by-step "conversion" guides, meet-ups, and so on, Apple chooses to perpetuate a carefully vetted and neatly produced series of communication-heavy commercials that, let's face it, do nothing but talk to themselves and their already converted customers. Worse still, Apple pretty overtly calls its entire universe of prospects nerds (using an actor who—surprise, surprise—has an uncanny likeness to one, William Gates). Smoooooooth.

As I've experienced on my own blog, Apple enthusiasts (zealots?) are incredibly active and proactive in terms of organizing themselves, helping others, and converting people to the cult of Mac. One might argue that Apple should, in fact, do nothing (i.e., keep out of the way of organic and natural collaboration). I would not argue this as I feel *some* kind of acknowledgment, gratitude, and/or enablement could go a disproportionately long way in return.

Credit where credit is due—Apple has been an unbelievable catalyst in promoting *other* people's conversations in the form of iTunes' podcasting-friendly interface, but when it comes to directly engaging its own consumers, Apple is so silent that you could hear a pin drop.

Ignoring the conversation is a flawed strategy. Inaction can do more damage than the worst imaginable scenario or outcome from doing something differently.

Ignoring a conversation by refusing to respond or join in has a catch-22 sucker-punch: There is the harm or damage from inaction as well as the opportunity cost of missing out on the benefit of what might have been.

> I recently heard a very profound statement: The biggest risk is not from trying something new but rather from spending $400 million or more on a campaign that nobody notices or remembers.

Remember, it is just as easy for your consumers to ignore you as it is for you to ignore them.

They already are.

## Conversation Evasion

When Starwood launched the aLoft hotel in Second Life, it received an outpouring of positive press. And deservedly so. What better way to pre-sensitize a lucrative audience to a future physical installation before ground had been broken? Enabling prospects to actually experience the hotel firsthand—its ambience, atmosphere, amenities, decor, design, and so on—was a brilliant way to raise purchase interest and intent to visit.

The problem was that after a while a few long-tailed avatars teleported their way to the hotel only to find it deserted—a ghost town. Not exactly the best way to portray a brand that was all about community, socialization, and activity. The brand was perfectly happy with all the good press, but when the tide turned, it was not prepared or willing to deal with the criticism and respond to its detractors. In fact, the hotel and its island were quickly taken offline and disappeared from the face of the virtual earth—possibly for renovation or refurbishment? No one knew.

As it turns out, I don't believe the detractors were detractors at all. They were of two camps: the constructive critics (people genuinely offering ideas and advice) and the downright playful, like Gideon Television–Superstar™, the storytelling avatar that turned the

## Gideon Shines at the aLoft

Figure 13.1   Gideon #1

I needed to get away. Somewhere far from the madding crowd, to get my head straight. And where better than Second Life's premium hotel destination, the aLoft. What a nice surprise. Bring your alibis. (Figure 13.1.)

Peace and quiet. Nice. (Figure 13.2.)

Figure 13.2   Gideon #2

I take a nap to quell the growing sense of unease that's creeping up on me—why the hell is it so quiet? And when I wake, I'm dressed, and there's mud on my boots, but I'm not sure from where, or when, or why. But I'm thinking clearer, as if logic now buzzes gently in my ear. Of course! It's Christmas! This place must be closed for the season, before the bad weather closes in. Maybe I should stay on and keep the boiler running. Like I'm the Caretaker.

. . .

The black buzzing was stronger now, like a thousand bees gnawing at my sinus. And I knew there was only one way to stop it—I needed to find those damn girls and "correct them." And if my wife tried to stop me from doing my god-fearing parental duty, I'd "correct" that bitch, too. (Figure 13.3.)

Figure 13.3   Gideon #3

too-quiet aLoft into a brilliant reincarnation of the Shining (see the full story and how it ends on www.jointheconversation.us/aloft).

Final word: Conversation doesn't count when you're talking to yourself, although it is a surefire way to get yourself committed.

In Super Bowl XLI, Rolling Rock, a bland and nondescript beer brand (true), took out a commercial (fake) in which it apologized for its original commercial, which had offended the public (fake) and was subsequently denounced and banned (fake). Rolling Rock followed this up with a series of full-page print advertisements in papers like *USA Today* on the Monday following the big game. The print ad was titled, "An Apology for Yesterday's Thong Ad." Here is an excerpt:

> This past Sunday we aired a commercial [fake] entitled "Man Thong," which evidently was not a big hit with consumers. The ad polls have confirmed we had one of the worst ads of the day, ranking us 61 out of a possible 62 [fake], which is disappointing to say the least, since we were hoping for a top-three finish.
>
> Keep in mind, however, this ad was not intended to amuse, but rather to provoke discussion and deliver a message of unity. [ultra fake]

The "letter" was signed by Ron Stablehorn, VP of marketing for Rolling Rock, who is most likely fake as well, but if for some inexplicable reason he is really running the show for Rolling Rock, it won't be for long.

This was a fake ad about a fake ad that faked a conversation. And for this excessive indulgence in self-gratuitous gluttony, we have to cut down trees, insult the intelligence of the viewing public, and desperately try to convince people to purchase more beer. Fat chance.

# 14

# Where Does Conversation Fit In?

Conversational marketing, or marketing as a conversation, is as nontraditional as any of the approaches I laid out in *Life After the 30-Second Spot* (interactive, gaming, on-demand consumption, experiential marketing, long-form content, consumer-generated content, search, music, mobile and things that make you go "Mmmmm," and finally, branded entertainment). In fact, conversation is as pervasive as the air we breathe. It can and does show up in all of the nontraditional approaches, is easily harnessed from the traditional approaches, and arguably deserves its own specialist category as well.

This is not an either/or—it's an *and*.

## WELCOME TO THE "AND ECONOMY"

Throughout my career I have witnessed the eternal swinging of the pendulum from one extreme to the other. It seems like we've been stuck in a professional purgatory where either branding or direct response rules; where the customer is either boss or buffoon; where we are either too accountable or not accountable enough. The list continues. . . .

To be able to win in today's fragmented and complex climate, companies have got to learn to draw from both extremes and yet end up in the middle. It's a delicate balancing act, and the idea is to end up with the best of both worlds without being a jack of all trades and master of none—to find order out of chaos and harmony and equilibrium within the very raging heart of the storm.

In the "And Economy," conversation is not an optional extra but a vital component in an ongoing process. It is both the logical progression and inevitable outcome of a truly consumer-centric approach to marketing—an approach that deeply values and respects the very lifeblood of the organization and its *life force*.

Shown here is a model that we use at *crayon*. We call this the "New Marketing Model," and it pretty much encapsulates everything we believe in and are striving to achieve. The New Marketing Model certainly helps to contextualize where conversation fits into the overall integrated picture; it also offers an iterative one-two-three guide to what we all (should) strive for: transformation—the transformation of businesses, business models, behaviors, and lives. (See Figure 14.1.)

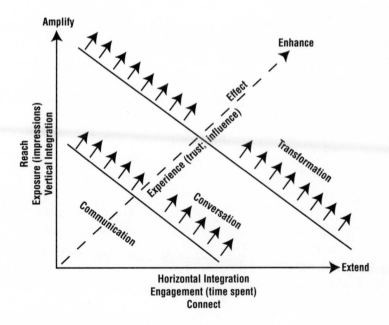

Figure 14.1   The New Marketing Model

## DISSECTING THE NEW MARKETING MODEL

Think of the model as a delectable deli sandwich from one of Manhattan's finest eateries, piled high with layers of nourishment:

Layer 1 — Objective: Reach-Connect-Effect

Layer 2 — Process: Expose-Engage-Experience

Layer 3 — Approach: Amplify-Extend-Enhance

Layer 4 — Result: Communication-Conversation-Transformation

**Reach-Connect-Effect**

Just because you can reach someone doesn't mean you will. And if you do reach them, will you connect with them? Will you get their attention, keep their attention, and be remembered for all the right reasons? And even if you do connect, will you "effect" with them? Will you effect change, insights, movement, and action?

That's the pretty systematic three-step process that, if left incomplete, denotes failure. In early 2007 the new marketing honcho of AFLAC, Jeff Herbert, announced that he would be phasing out the iconic and much-loved AFLAC duck. The primary reason? Simply put, everyone knew about AFLAC but nobody cared . . . or at least nobody cared enough to do anything about it. The AFLAC duck was finally going to be turned into duck pâté and not a moment too soon.[1] Eighty-three percent awareness (reach) just did not translate into a quest for more information and knowledge and ultimately sales. To the best of my knowledge, this "supplemental insurance" (which, if you think about it, would imply that primary insurance is deficient . . . gee, I wonder why they didn't talk about this at all?) required worker bees (you and me) to march into the offices of their human resources department and request or demand that their benefits plan include AFLAC.

---

[1] No animals were harmed in the writing of this book.

I don't know about you, but nowadays most employees avoid their HR people like the plague amid concerns about pink slips and cost cutting.

AFLAC would have done much better had it engaged the HR influencers and decision-makers in healthy and proactive dialogue. The answer lay in education, not entertainment.

Carl's Jr., the fast-food chicken chain, encountered the same outcome with its "racy" Paris Hilton "viral" commercials that associated chicken burgers with sex and Bentleys (I'm as stumped as you are), held together by the ambitious precarious thread of "That's hot," Paris's signature line as well as a quality of the spicy chicken burgers. The campaign got everyone talking, but not many people eating. So much for sex selling your product. . . .

## Expose-Engage-Experience

To achieve the trifecta of reach-connect-effect, the layer of exposure-engagement-experience can be applied. None of these three processes should be a surprise to you; however, what may be somewhat unexpected is how they are being applied today and how they should be applied tomorrow.

The biggest mistake being made today is the cramming of all three strategies into one Hail Mary push. The 30-second spot is an infamous culprit that desperately begs viewers to "be engaged" by a message without enabling them to interact, talk back, or act.

Compounding this career suicide attempt (CareerBuilder and its longtime agency parted ways when its Super Bowl XLI commercials failed to rate or rank highly among consumers) is the fact that mainstream marketing is barely keeping its head above water at getting the attention of consumers ("breaking through the clutter"), let alone engaging them.

*Exposure* can be as crude as streaking in front of a passerby. It is getting a foot in the door and gaining the consumer's awareness and with it the opportunity to earn precious attention and even concentration. Exposure does not always have to be one-sided. Your consumers are very much getting into the act as well. In fact, every day they are exposing themselves to you . . . either by coming out of hiding (or, as I call it, lurker mode) or by overtly prostrating themselves in front of you in the form of outreach (customer service), outrage (blogs), or outlandish behavior (consumer-generated content).

*Engagement*, on the other hand, hints at the beginnings of partnership—in this case, the passive viewer, listener, or reader is vesting himself or herself in the communication, either directly (lean-forward/proactive) or indirectly (lean-backwards/submission). Whereas exposure is typically marketer-driven but may also be initiated by consumers, engagement is wholeheartedly consumer-centric and permission-based. Exposure is a default, but engagement is very much earned. Marketers absolutely can influence the process and increase the probability of an earned connection, but ultimately it is the consumer's decision.

Fiat, the European automotive manufacturer, harnessed the community in an original way using Google Earth. The company created essentially a treasure hunt for four Fiats and one lil ole Ferrari buried underneath the snow in the Olympic area of Torino. Using Google Earth, registered users got to place a pushpin to mark their territory and, hopefully, drive away with an Italian Stallion.

It brought back fond memories of my childhood (sniff) when we used polystyrene, Play-Doh, paint, and push pins (the *other* four Ps) to achieve something similar—albeit decidedly lower-tech! (See Figure 14.2.)

What a great way to engage the community by working with it to activate this very novel repurposing of a classic game.

Then comes *experience*, which, according to Wikipedia, is an event or even an experiment (see Chapter 18) with buy-in, involvement, and/or learnings. I refer to experience as "engagement with context." Just as engagement naturally follows exposure, so experience follows engagement. Whereas engagement is associated with attention and concentration, experience is very much imbued with commitment and partnership. Engagement seems to differ from experience in that it focuses on the individual whereas experience assumes a certain amount of group or communal connectedness—whether on a pure referential scale or something a lot more profound.

Subservient Chicken, the irreverent mini-site by Burger King that allowed consumers to "have their way" with the chicken by typ-

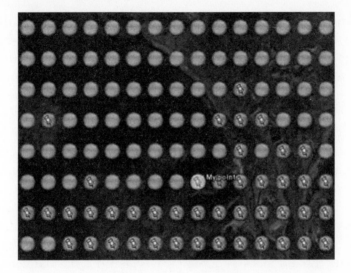

Figure 14.2 Fiat's Olympic-Sized Treasure Hunt. What you're seeing in this image is the Fiat treasure map overlay on top of an aerial view of Torino as depicted in Google Earth. Each dot represents a plot of land that participants can claim as their entry.

ing in various commands, most of which the chicken obligingly acted out, certainly hit the ball out of the park when it came to engagement—the average visitor spent seven and a half minutes interacting with the site—but was it necessarily an experience? Probably not. Burger King's wildly successful Xbox games (the fastest-selling Xbox games in history), however, do qualify.

## Welcome to Web 3.0: The Experience Web

The phrase "Web 2.0" has come to signify the "social Web"—the "read and write" web, which is designed to harness the network effects of communities. The social Web is all about discovery, sharing, searching, tagging, and self-policing meritocracies. Its predecessor (let's call it 1.0) was the commerce Web—a transactional, one-dimensional autocracy that combined glorified catalogs and brochure ware with oodles of text, static images, and buy-now buttons.

Enter Web 3.0 (or as purists call it, Web 3.d) — the *experience* Web. MMORPG (Massively Multiplayer Online Role-Playing Game) began the trend of connected gaming, and Playstation and Xbox took this communal activation to the next level in the form of console gaming. Now we have virtual worlds like Habbo Hotel, Cyworld, Webkinz and the very visible Second Life.

In Second Life, residents do not view, they do not surf, they do not browse (unless they're actually going shopping) — they experience, literally (or as literally as virtual allows). Take my book covers. Instead of posting the covers to a web site, I displayed them in the lobby of *crayon*'s island, crayonville (www.crayonvillesecondlife .com). Every Thursday morning from 9:00 to 9:30 A.M. EST, we have an informal social gathering where like-minded marketing enthusiasts discuss marketing topics over a cup of virtual coffee. It's called "Coffee with *crayon*" and you're all invited. During these sessions, I would often break away and give people a personal tour of the book covers. (See Figure 14.3.)

The world of Second Life (I describe it as the life you *were meant to lead*) may be virtual, but the connections made and relationships cultivated are very real. The shared experiences transcend alternative realities, and indeed, in a business where "perception is reality," Web 3.0 is no less real or relevant than any piece of communication

Figure 14.3   Experiencing Book Cover Candidates in the Crayon Lobby on Crayonville Island in Second Life

that is carefully constructed, controlled, and disseminated across the mainstream media waves.

## Amplify-Extend-Enhance

Which brings us to the third layer: amplification-extension-enhancement. Most traditional marketing communication is one form or another of *amplification*. The entire notion of integration for better or worse is just a means of amplifying a message — making it louder (or less easy to ignore, skip, or tune out). Integration is typically applied via tonnage (frequency) or persistence (presence). We surround our consumers to the point of smothering or stalking them. Perhaps this is why so many consumers are taking out restraining orders against us. . . .

Amplification is not about loudness. It is about *purity*. It is about fine-tuning or equalizing a message using a combination of viable approaches (what I call the 96 colors in Crayola's "Big Box") in a precise order, mix, combination, and quantity that is truly an art form. At times the tools or colors are served up on a silver platter; other times they are prostrated self-serve style, offered as a DIY tool for consumers to choose and use on demand.

Amplification does not refer only to communications — and certainly not only to paid communications. *Nonpaid* exposures or touch-points often yield that most credible and lasting "impression." Word of mouth and PR absolutely play an inextricable and important role in perfecting the harmony of integrated amplification.

Following on from the previous two points is the definition of an impression. Take the homepage of Google or the (iPod)[Red] that I carry around with me. Every time somebody visits Google or casts their gaze across the subway at a red Nano glistening in the poorly lit subway tunnels, there is most definitely an impression being registered (only it isn't being counted). Perhaps this is why design is playing such a critical role in marketing today — not just in the consideration and selection process but in the communication process as well.

*Extension*, on the other hand, can be applied in a variety of ways. It can be taken quite literally and applied like a line extension: for example, the extension to new consumers, communities, or constituencies. It can be applied to distribution platforms: for example, from a commercial to a console game or a full-length feature movie. It can be utilized to help repurpose a core idea across a variety of different interpretations or expressions. Or it can be used to convert an exposure into an event—one that has a collection of experience, permission, involvement, and conversation.

From a logical or iterative standpoint, amplifying an exposure would precede the gift of extending engagement; however, the link between the two is not—and should not be—assumed or guaranteed. There needs to be a bridge, with clear directional signage that helps a consumer navigate from a passive to a proactive state of vestment.

A simple call to action derives tremendous power from being automatically bundled with engagement. Consumers' ability to extend their time with a brand (anywhere on the continuum of exposure through experience) without forfeiting the right to choose and navigate on their own terms yields limitless possibilities. And yet the lowly URL is still as commonplace as the sighting of the Loch Ness Monster. I want to be clear about something: If you are not displaying a URL on every piece of communications, you are essentially embezzling money from investors, stakeholders, and the brand itself. If you are not devoting time to explaining to prospective or interested customers why they should consider taking the time to visit a web site, store, event, experience, or virtual gathering, or why they should send in an SMS or contribute to a community-powered wiki or blog—and the list goes on—*you are not doing your job*.

Beyond the basic "slap on a URL and give the consumer a reason to give a damn," think about ways you can extend an idea from a one-off exposure to an event. A rest stop. A halfway house. A place to chill. A meaningful hub for interested consumers to qualify themselves, find out more, connect with other like-minded consumers . . . and, yes, even purchase a product.

*The Biggest Loser* is a pretty good example of a television program (brand) that became a movement. Tens of thousands of inspired viewers (customers) are paying, registered subscribers in what has the *potential* to become a social phenomenon. Indeed, the difference between extend and enhance is the difference between superficial clicking and meaningful connecting—or put differently, a web site that is a shill to drive viewership tune-in versus a movement or tight-knit community that can change and transform lives. Weight Watchers should be kicking themselves (again) right about now. Why didn't they get in earlier? Hell, why didn't they *invent The Biggest Loser*?

As indicated earlier, the key metric here is time spent. Time spent is the one apples-to-apples comparison that can equate one medium with another and compare and contrast two or more competing messages, stories, or ideas. As it stands, 30 seconds is the cap or maximum time spent that is possible with a 30-second spot. Compare that with a television commercial with a strong Web-based call to action, which should be evaluated, valued, and monetized based on the total amount of time spent with the idea or story—and arguably penalized based on the *lack* of action or movement.

Total time spent is just the beginning. Time spent needs to be evaluated according to a methodology I call RFiD (not radio frequency identification): Recency, Frequency, Interactivity, and Duration.

> *Recency* refers to the amount of time elapsed between visits. All things being equal, a short gap between visits is usually a good predicator of overall satisfaction.

> *Frequency* refers to the number of visits in totality. The higher the number of visits, the more the chance of a favorable predisposition toward the offering.

> *Interactivity* is fairly self-explanatory. In this case, we'd be homing in on types of actions performed or sequences undertaken as a barometer of involvement and participation.

> *Duration* is more complicated. Total time spent should be subsegmented based on two primary variables:

> Voluntary time spent

> Quality time spent (positive versus negative experience)

Take the prototypical web-video view on a sharing site such as Break, Veoh, or Daily Motion. All things being equal, a creative video on television and the same one on YouTube.com have one thing—*and only one thing*—in common: 30 seconds. And that's about where it ends. A permission-based exposure or impression has got to be more valuable on so many levels. Now, if that piece of content has been recommended by a trusted friend or happens to be three or four minutes, multiply the sucker by a bunch of $x$'s.

I challenge you to argue that a linear, 30-second spot on television is in any way, shape, or form more valuable than the same product on an iPod nano. I'll give you a discount for "size of screen," but that's about it. The bottom line is that the entire pricing model is out of whack when it comes to the premium you place on *the same* product of *the same* length, delivered in *an inferior* manner (disruptive/intrusive/push-based).

Why wouldn't you heap your discretionary innovation time and money on obliterating the obstacle standing in the way between communication and conversation? If time spent is the great equalizer, then voluntary time spent is the great differentiator.

Voluntary time spent (VTS) focuses on quantity but needs to be counterbalanced with quality time spent as well. In most cases quality and quantity are proportionately linked. After all, why would anyone of sound mind choose to spend time in an environment that delivers a less than satisfactory experience? They wouldn't, but sometimes it happens nevertheless. Take a bad movie, for example, or poor navigation or usability on a web site.

Put it all together and you get Brawny Academy. Think BMW Films meets *Survivor*; although not as good as either, Brawny Academy outshines any average consumer packaged goods communication.

I watched the entire first episode and actually looked forward to the second. (See Figure 14.4.)

My position on judging these long-form efforts is very simple and very consistent: *At their very worst, they're no worse than 90 percent of the 30-second crap on TV.* Legendary ad critic and friend Bob Garfield wasn't as enamored as I was with Brawny Academy. He felt that no one would lean forward and watch all the episodes. I disagreed, because I didn't think the goal was to "reach" tens of millions of poten-

Figure 14.4  The Brawny Academy

tial consumers but rather to engage with a smaller subset of voluntary hand-raisers.

They even used RSS to alert viewers to updated episodes.

Even with the gratuitous product placement, which worked in a campy sort of way, the effect was a pretty warm personification of the Brawny brand through the Brawny Man. This, without question, humanized a brand I honestly never cared about before.

In fact, there's an exceptionally good chance that I'll purchase Brawny paper towels the next time I take the kids shopping while my wife gets a pedicure . . . just as soon as I go and put down that toilet seat.

After a pure message expressing a powerful idea becomes an event or series of events, held together by a positive mixture of RFiD, the final dimension of *enhancement* takes over. This is the ultimate expression of complete endorsement and total submission. The creation of an experience—a consumption experience that has the capability of leaving a lasting impression (as opposed to the fleeting one from a typical exposure).

Enhancement is larger than life. It is an idea whose time has come and whose potential has been realized. It is the cherry on top where the whole is greater than the sum of its parts. It is "Just Do It," which is no longer an advertising campaign featuring Tiger Woods, nor is it Niketown. It is perhaps "Run London."

"Run London" is an initiative that turned to thousands of normal Londoners and gave them the chance to "Just Do It" in the form of enrolling in a citywide series of fun runs, with a communal marketing central force of gravity that activated the passions and aspirations of its customers (existing and potential). (See Figure 14.5.)

Instead of talking about just doing it, Nike walked the talk—quite literally—and in doing so turned a brand promise into a branded experience with word of mouth and conversation bursting from the seams.

And Nike didn't stop there: It created an interactive application that allowed consumers to connect with others by uploading, tagging, and sharing their routes. New users could seek out a particular route based on unique search criteria such as distance, night lighting, and whether the terrain was hilly or "flat as Holland."

What a great way to create an unforgettable experience that delivered against both product (shoe as the hero) and brand (the fulfillment of a promise).

Measurement of enhancement goes back to the Net Promoter Score methodology, namely, the propensity or probability of someone voluntarily sharing the story, experience, idea, or message with someone else they know and value. That's right, a viral referral. A considered recommendation.

Sony's Blu-ray technology—yet *another* proprietary closed format from the beleaguered brand—could learn a thing or two about engaging influencers and organic referrals. According to a Cymfony report released in December 2006, positive discussions

Figure 14.5   My Triumphant Sister in Nike's "Run London"

about competition high-definition DVD players were 46 percent higher than for Blu-ray, with more than twice as many post authors stating that they were "impressed with HD DVD" versus "impressed with Blu-ray." As one prosumer quote  stated: "I'm kind of glad Sony is getting screwed. The laughing face of arrogance was suddenly slammed with the fist of reality."

## Communication-Conversation-Transformation

It all comes down to this, the moment of truth, the final mile. You're now in a position to plot your course and progress on the vertical, horizontal, and diagonal axes (which becomes a pretty telling competitive benchmarking exercise). It's a pretty unique way to gauge your resonance and innovation on a campaign-by-campaign basis. This 3D rendering of your latest and greatest creations will quickly cluster and, dare I say it, congeal in places you might not be entirely thrilled with.

I'm always asking some of the world's leading marketers how they would rate or grade their most successful campaigns on the basis of maximizing the potential of these ideas. "On a percentage scale of 1 to 100 percent," I ask them, "where would you score your progress in terms of getting the most out of the potential impact that could have been achieved?" For some reason, the responses are always unanimously in the region of 30 to 50 percent.

How is it possible in this day and age—when successes are dwarfed by failures and backfires—that by the time we finally get our act together we fizzle out and fade away before we properly hit our stride? I'll tell you why—because we are purveyors of the science of communication, not the art of conversation.

Our attempts to implement new marketing end up retro- or force-fitting a new approach into an old shell. In 2007 several marketers, including Doritos, Chevrolet, and the NFL, took consumer-generated content to the Super Bowl. Dove attempted it with the Academy Awards. With the Super Bowl, the CGC spots stole the show, but then again, that's not saying much nowadays. With Dove, the reaction was tepid at best. MasterCard attempted the same thing in two 30-second spots, "Sailboat" and "Typewriter," in which it invited consumers to fill in the blanks, as in: _____—$9; _____—$14; _____—priceless.

The top advertising blog, Adrants wondered whether consumers would get it, and also whether hungry freelance creatives would jump on board to get a job (that's not a bad thing). I wondered whether this attempt was the final concession that the creatives working in the business had finally run out of ideas and were waving the white flag at consumers, begging them to help them do their jobs.

Ultimately, the attempt invited interaction, which is never bad; nor was the fact that MasterCard stated that it would air the "winning entries," although to date I've never seen any of them. At the end of the day, however, was this the ideal way to draw attention and invite participation?

At a stretch, this was muted and highly controlled conversation. In reality, though, it was just a different communication approach and not conversation at all. Compare this campaign with the scores (and I mean scores) of incredibly funny MasterCard spoofs that circulate like wildfire over the Web. Why no acknowledgment of these from MasterCard? Why not create a museum or repository of this unofficial body of work?

Spoofs don't even need to be created by consumers to reflect the kind of edge that gets noticed. Comedy Central created a magnificent MasterCard commercial after the Boston Red Sox won the World Series (after an 86-year drought). I won't tell you more except that it involved Dennis Leary and nuts. Who needs a creative department when you have a brand idea that is a conversation factory?

Here's another example that reflects how all the amplification, extension, and enhancement in the world will remain grounded without the injection of community, dialogue, and partnership.

A recent commercial for Pontiac ended with the following voice-over and titles:

Don't take our word for it. Google "Pontiac" and discover for yourself.

The ad ended with a screenshot of Google's homepage, followed by the word "Pontiac" neatly typed into the search box for anyone who either didn't know how to use Google or couldn't remember the brand name (such as those who saw the famous car giveaway on Oprah but couldn't remember the brand concerned).

Here's a screenshot from Karl Long's blog. (See Figure 14.6.)

Figure 14.6    Pontiac's Google Stunt

Had you actually followed these directions, you would have been greeted with a host of paid-search listings for Mazda (short-lived), as well as this informative announcement:

> THE PONTIAC GRILLE is embarking on a major change in our menus and in our operations.
>
> Starting February 1, 2006 the first floor restaurant will become a STEAKHOUSE featuring top quality cuts of beef, pork and fish prepared to your order on our char-broiler. We will be open for dinner Monday through Thursday at 5 PM and serve until 10 PM. Friday we will open at 5 PM and serve until 11 PM. On Saturday and Sunday we will open for lunch at 11:30 AM and serve lunch until 5 PM from the menu below; then from 5PM until 11 PM on Saturday and 10 PM on Sunday we will serve dinner from our new Steakhouse menu.

Pontiac had a great opportunity to use this platform as a springboard to migrate from communication to conversation (and ultimately transformation). For starters, the search terms could have been a little more precise—for example, Pontiac + Reviews. But why stop there? If the company had felt that confident about the community's response to the car, why not create the means for consumers (just like you and me) to upload their own reviews to a growing database of *positivity*? Why not create a forum for interested parties to come together to talk about the new car? Or the opportunity to talk with the creator of the car?

Our challenge couldn't be more straightforward: As fast as we can, we need to get out of the communication space and into the transformation space. Our professional responsibility is to be in the transformational arena. After all, we're in the business of change. At our best, we change lives and make the world a better place. At our worst, we change nothing. Our business goal is to transform our business and our brands, and one way to achieve this goal is by building a bridge from communication to transformation. That bridge is conversation.

Where would your brand fit into the new marketing continuum using the amplify-extend-enhance methodology and then applying the communication-conversation-transformation assessment?

## THREE BRANDS, THREE MODELS

*Coca-Cola*'s status as one of the world's most loved and valuable brands is not going to be enough to sustain its leadership position into the foreseeable future. When it comes to conversation, the company historically has taken a backseat, and in fact, in the case of its enabling sponsorships, such as the World Cup, it has preferred to be a spectator and watch from the sidelines.

This is all changing. Fast. (See Figure 14.7.)

The web site weallspeakfootball.com was a step in the right direction. Uniting a global passion for football as only a global brand could, Coca-Cola sponsored a house during the 2006 World Cup in Germany in which guest and celebrity bloggers and podcasters could take turns staying and from which they could post.

Figure 14.7    We All Speak Conversation

The balance between transparency and control seems to have been comfortable and peaceful, as evidenced by this entry from one of the "current pro" bloggers, Lyssa (who posted a comment on my blog as well):

> Some of those at Coke responsible for this project (I didn't even know they had that many Global Directors and the like) dropped by today to take a look at the flat and talk to us. It was a really hot and sunny afternoon, everybody was casually dressed and quite relaxed. We were up on the rooftop admiring the great view when the Swedish guys staying at a hotel across the street (and partying all night) decided to put up the Swedish flag on the balcony.
>      Unfortunately one Swede wasn't only rather heavyset with an unhealthy pasty complexion, he was also almost naked. His only piece of

clothing was a tiny thong hardly visible underneath all that pale flesh. Welcome to Europe, Coke.

(And now I'm finally off to see what the Brazilians are wearing tonight.)

To me it works, and the quip about the "Global Directors" is quite endearing, especially to us industry geezers.

"Where do you want to go today?" asks *Microsoft*. My response would be met with the line uttered by Meryl Streep's character in *The Devil Wears Prada*: "That wasn't a question!" Microsoft's single biggest opportunity is to become a part of the lives of its community. Make a difference. A real difference. Every day it is winded by the quirky bitch-slaps of its archrival Apple, but really, this is not about advertising, is it? Rather, it is about purpose, conviction, and real dialogue (other than "cancel or allow?"). Microsoft is not in the software business anymore but rather in the conversation game (the *human network*, to borrow a phrase from another tech player, Cisco). Every day it enables conversation and real connections and yet is perceived as a cold, brittle, and sterile brand.

Figure 14.8   Google's Conversational Communication

And then there's *Google*. There's not much more to say about a company that pretty much bypassed "communication" en route to transformation central. And even when it does "advertise," it is with a strong conversational element built into the program. Take this billboard, which was in fact a pretty sublime recruitment effort. (See Figure 14.8.)

From a brand that is largely silent ("do" as opposed to "say"), Google sure is omnipresent across the Web, on the desktop, and beyond.

One might refer to this as "distributed conversation."

# 15

# Conversation through Community

*The Cluetrain Manifesto* defines community quite magnificently: "A community is a group of people who care about each other more than they should." There's something very special and quite intangible about the glue that binds members of a tribe together. Shared goals, beliefs, visions, ideals, hair color, religion, political leaning, marital status, color of iPod, or college (Go, Longhorns!) is enough to unite two or more people who otherwise might have passed each other like ships in the night.

And so it is quite strange when I attend or facilitate brainstorming sessions and hear participants eagerly whiteboarding ideas like "let's start a community" or "let's create a social network." Both follow the same tired formula: We the marketers initiate the program, pull the strings, and orchestrate the story on our terms. Just as this book suggests that "there are rich, powerful, authentic, and meaningful *conversations* going on," the same is true and then some for *community*.

Community is not a right. Community is a privilege.

You have to earn the right to be a part of a community.

The major media and the music and entertainment companies like Viacom or Disney just don't understand that the larger world does not revolve around them and their self-contained worlds (real or virtual) anymore. They see YouTube stealing their lunch and their logical gut reaction is (a) to sue and (b) to create a cheap imitation. Try as hard as they might, and no matter how much money they sink into the beast, what they will never have going for them is the intangible sense of belonging that is community.

I introduced the concept that "you are the community you keep" on my blog and asked my readers what they thought of it. Here are some of the responses:

The consumer owns your brand, not the company. So "the community you keep" defines you, defines the brand. The only thing I would disagree with in the phrase is that brands don't really decide the community they get to keep, either, the community chooses them. The brand's actions can influence that.

Posted by: Hashem Bajwa

So . . . "You are the community that keeps you."

Posted by: alp

Great observation and true. I wrote an article/post a while back for One Degree (www.onedegree.ca) titled "How Tennis Can Improve Your Marketing." The point: When you play with people who have game, yours improves. It is about accomplishing more around the brand of "you," improving your game in terms of who you are playing with. This has direct applicability to your thought about the community you keep. On a personal level and on a professional level, being a part of the digital community and connecting with others who have passion for the space and a desire to learn and share is an unbelievably good thing for all of us.

Posted by: Michael Seaton

What your phrase means to me: Your community determines what your brand ultimately is to become. A brand without validation from its community is like a tree falling in the woods . . . we would hardly know whether it is real. I also agree with Hashem—communities (market segments) have the power in choosing brands, and not the other way around. BrandIsLanguage.com.

Posted by: Monica Powers

I like the phrase. It encapsulates what great marketing today is all about. I think it goes deeper than brand, it's about how you create products and promote them, too. Instead of "converting prospects," one might think of promotional goals in terms of expanding community and improving one's service to their community. More difficult, much less expensive, and eminently more fun than traditional broadcast promotion.

Posted by: Doug Hudiburg

I think Nike is the best example . . . to prove this statement. Nike makes an assiduous effort to interact and live in the tastemaker/trendsetter community of New York. Nike ID is located in the very hip Nolita area and employs 20-somethings that are very involved in the New York "Cool Kids" nightlife scene. Nike ID is only available through invite, which furthers its exclusive coolness factor, in turn, making it more sought after by this community. How else are they involved in this community? They have art/gallery opening parties that are so common in this community (with open bar of course). And that's only "to name a few." Nike is also at the center of another more common community, sport.

Posted by Tyler Clemens — Self-Proclaimed Hipster Specialist

So, if you are the community you keep . . . or rather the community that keeps you . . . what about the company? Companies or brands together are the community they keep—or more accurately, the community that keeps them. Starbucks, the global chain of coffee shops, is the poster child of a premium-priced brand; it's a company that built its reputation and brand equity not by spending millions of dollars on advertising but rather on a powerful communal experience. (See Figure 15.1.)

Fan sites such as Starbucks Gossip sprouted up to document everything and anything there was to know about the coffee brand. And while there were detractors, too (there always are)—such as The Delocator, a clever web site where visitors punch in their zip code in order to find independently owned cafés other than the large corporate chain—life was generally good in java-bean land. (See Figure 15.2.)

Or was it? On Valentine's Day 2007, Howard Schultz penned a much-publicized memo to CEO Jim Donald with the subject

Figure 15.1    Starbucks Gossip Dot-Com

Figure 15.2    The Delocator

header: "The Commoditization of the Starbucks Experience" (the full transcript is on www.jointheconversation.us/starbucks).

Here's what my friend Robert Passikoff, founder and president of Brand Keys, Inc., a New York–based loyalty and engagement consultancy, and author of *Predicting Market Success: New Ways to Measure Customer Loyalty and Engage Consumers with Your Brand*, had to say about Starbucks:

### A Cup of Community to Go

The U.S. Department of Transportation discovered that a growing number of commuters—going out of their way to visit their favorite purveyors of caffeine and carbohydrates—have increasingly thwarted attempts to forecast travel patterns traditionally based on computer models that rely primarily on the predictability of the morning commute. Talk about behavior correlating with loyalty and engagement!

It turns out that what's true for a municipal community is also true for a brand community. In Brand Keys' 2007 Customer Loyalty Engagement Index—providing predictive, leading-indicator measures of customer and brand value buttressing—Starbucks was knocked out of first place in the Coffee and Doughnuts category by Dunkin' Donuts. That's the first time in five years Starbucks didn't dominate the category.

Generally speaking, companies that do dominate are those that are authentic. If people believe that they share values with a company, if they are having meaningful conversations with the brand, if they like living in the "neighborhood," they will stay loyal to a brand. It's hard to argue with that.

The results of the 2007 Brand Keys survey confirms [Howard] Schultz's self-assessment and the marketing tenet that while a commodity can transform itself into a premium-priced brand, if it isn't true to the community values that differentiated it from the competition, consumers will find a new community for themselves. In this category, perhaps more than many others, experience, dialogue, and a sense of community with customers—sometimes specifically articulated, other times just quietly shared with those around you—become the keys to loyalty and engagement success.

In his memo Mr. Schultz noted that the new automatic espresso machines don't require baristas to actually "pull" shots. "We achieved fresh-roasted bagged coffee, but at what cost?" Mr. Schultz asked.

Based on the Brand Keys findings: a good deal of customer discourse and loyalty and engagement.

Not to sound cynical, but if you assume that all these values (or lack thereof) have percolated to create the perfect tempest in a coffee pot affecting the bottom line, you'd be right. Starbucks shares have been off in five of the past seven sessions, including a 2.3 percent drop on the week the memo was revealed, with the stock down to $32.01 — 20 percent off its 52-week high. So it seems that Starbucks investors and customers alike are giving pause to the notion that diluting its strong brand identity as an experience-heavy, conversation-concentrated coffee shop ended up migrating the Starbucks brand closer to the commodity end of the brand continuum.

The Starbucks situation doesn't surprise us. Brand Keys has noted before that this is what happens when you take your eye off the brand and the community in which it lives and thrives. So many companies . . . end up process reengineering away their originality and differentiation, diluting the crispness of the brand experience, and stifling the conversation between the brand and the customer.

Talking with your customers should never be the conversational equivalent of an out-of-body experience. That's a sure and certain way of watering down a brand, whether it's coffee or anything else.


The writing had been on the wall for some time, and had the Starbucks marketing gurus been plugged into the conversation, or had they responded sooner, perhaps Schultz's memo would not have been necessary.

In late 2006 Starbucks issued an e-mail-based coupon for a free iced coffee. The regional offer, which was sent to a select group of employees and intended solely for pass-alongs, spread like wildfire and prompted the purveyors of intravenous caffeine to *suspend the offer*—and in so doing to turn away scores of legit customers (aren't all customers legit?) who showed up with the electronic offer.

The community was not impressed. (See Figure 15.3.)

Caribou Coffee picked up the ball that Starbucks had so clunkily dropped by accepting the voided coupons. It was a classic example of how being close to the conversation can allow marketers to capitalize on the lethargy, dysfunction, incrementalism, and shortsightedness that is traditional marketing.

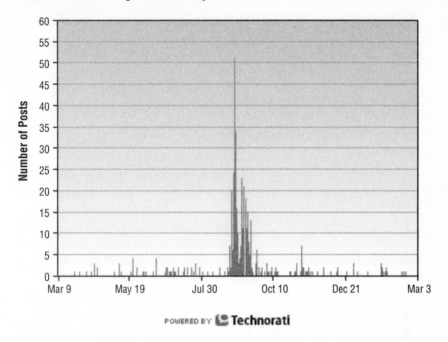

POWERED BY Technorati

Figure 15.3 Caribou 1, Starbucks 0: Posts by Day about Starbucks Iced Coffee Coupon, March 9, 2006, to March 3, 2007

It also proves two points:

1. There's no such thing as local or regional (this was a regional promo) anymore. The world is indeed flat.
2. Marketers want engagement and desperately look for signs of life from their customers, and yet, when their customers raise their hands and reach out to them, these customers get slapped with disdain, disrespect, and disapproval.

Starbucks' worst-case scenario—the alleged abuse or misuse of an innocuous coupon—was a blessing in disguise, but instead of capitalizing on this golden opportunity, Starbucks gifted it to a challenger brand and competitor.

It was a one-two sucker punch where *the opportunity cost was the opportunity lost.*

And then there's Winter. Nothing else. Just Winter, as his site, Starbucks Everywhere (www.starbuckseverywhere.net), explains. Winter and I have a lot in common: We both want to change the world, and we both love Starbucks, although admittedly Winter is a little more *enthusiastic* than I am.

Winter set out to drink a cup of coffee in *every single Starbucks store in the United States*. (See Figure 15.4.) As of February 2007, he had visited . . .

> . . . approximately 6,280 company-owned locations, of which at least 107 have closed or relocated, for a total of 6,173 active corporate-owned locations in North America of an estimated 6,741 or 91.8%. Internationally, 306 across England, Japan, Spain, France, and Quebec (not part of Canada in the Starbucks world). The estimated total locations excludes licensed stores, which I do not visit, because, with a few unusual exceptions, they are almost all mind-numbingly dull kiosks.[1]

Winter has been extensively written up, discussed, lauded, and interviewed (http://www.starbuckseverywhere.net/MediaAppearances .htm), and throughout this process Starbucks has been absent.

Many believed that Starbucks should have turned Winter into its version of Subway's Jared.[2] John Moore from the blog Brand Autopsy believes that Starbucks should have empowered Winter to complete his mission by sending him regular updates about newly opened stores, sponsoring his efforts in the form of a funded Starbucks card (Winter has spent over $30,000 of his own money on his quest), and inviting him to Starbucks headquarters in Seattle, Washington, for a personal tour and meet-and-greet with Mr. Memo.

So tell me. Coincidence or not that the watering down of the Starbucks experience correlates with an overarching neglect of the community that rallied so strongly to embrace and celebrate

---

[1] Excerpted from www.starbuckseverywhere.net.

[2] The Subway restaurant chain used Jared Fogle, a consumer who lost 245 pounds in just over a year by eating at Subway restaurants, as a corporate and advertising spokesperson.

Figure 15.4   The Winter of Starbucks' Discontent

the brand? Sure there were tangible missteps along the way, from the automated coffee-making machines to the issue of flavor-locked packaging over coffee beans, or plastic chairs over loungers, but ultimately this was about overall attitude and approach, and in the end everything is connected.

I'm discussing this case extensively to illustrate how even innovative and well-loved brands can be rejected over time, or even overnight, if they fail to stay connected and interconnected with the community that supported them in the first place. Starbucks failed to join the conversation—either by responding to it (iced coffee coupons), or catalyzing it (Winter).

I hope and trust by the time this book is out that Starbucks will have come to the party. I will most certainly continue to pay my premium for the Starbucks experience, which, automated or not, is still better than most.

Incidentally, instead of speculating about Winter, I approached him directly. And if I can do it, so can you. Here's a transcript of our brief Q&A:

**Q:** Why did you do it? What motivated you?

**A:** My primary reason and motivation were one and the same: to accomplish something singularly unique in the world. I've explored the deeper psychological motivations behind my desire to be unique with some reporters, but I am guessing that is beyond the scope of your interest.

**Q:** What did you learn about Starbucks?

**A:** I must emphasize that though I was a regular Starbucks customer for years before I set out to visit them all, my project has never been motivated by a love of Starbucks. As such, I tend to pay attention to just the details that are relevant to my project: where each store is located; the physical appearance of each store (because I photograph them); anything different about the interior design (so I can caption the photographs). Other details, like the coffee, other products, and the service, escape me. For me, Starbucks is really a vehicle through which I express my individuality.

**Q:** The million-dollar questions: Did Starbucks contact you? Did they reward you?

**A:** Starbucks' only official contact with me has been to determine my ultimate purpose. I have received no compensation from Starbucks, and I do not seek any. In fact, I want my project to remain independent, and I do not intend to ever promote the Starbucks brand.

What I do intend to promote is a philosophy of living a life that is oriented towards some purpose other than simply making a living.

**Q:** Would you do it again?

**A:** I would absolutely embark on my Starbucks project again, and I wish that I had known where it would lead when I conceived of the idea ten years ago. I would have started keeping records earlier, and I would have saved much of the money that I wasted before I started refining my process to maximize my travel resources.

**Q:** There's a lot of talk that the Starbucks experience has become tarnished/faded (with automatic machines, etc). What do you think?

**A:** I cannot comment on the specific reasons that Howard Schultz outlined in his February 14 memo, but I have noticed that the quality of baristas is not the same as it was 10 years ago, which makes complete sense considering how many new stores have opened. I hope that Starbucks slows its expansion and refocuses on recapturing the special feeling that Starbucks used to convey.

# 16

# Conversation through Dialogue

At first blush, one might confuse dialogue and conversation. Aren't they the same thing? On many levels they are, but I want to specifically call out what I think could quite possibly be the key philosophical shift in how we build relationships with our most valuable asset—our customers.

Ongoing dialogue, open lines of communications, response and responsiveness are all inextricably intertwined in a cultural sea change for organizations.

Every time I check into a Four Seasons resort, the front-desk manager welcomes me back by name and remarks on how recent my last stay was. Is that marketing? Is that sales? Is that branding? Is that customer service? The answer is yes.

## CUSTOMER SERVICE AS THE NEW MEDIA DEPARTMENT

My friend Pete Blackshaw, CMO of Nielsen-Buzzmetrics, talks about customer service as the new media department, and he couldn't be more right. With today's challenges, it would seem that all of our efforts are geared toward generating free impressions through things like "viral video," and yet we continue to invest all our dollars in bad old paid media and simultaneously ignore and neglect the most valuable nonpaid form of media know to humanity—our daily interactions with our customers.

By taking our eyes off the ball (assuming they ever were on it in the first place, which is a leap of faith all right), we tend to look beyond the most potent and undiluted conversational marketing weapon we have in our arsenal. This is what happened with AOL and Vincent Ferrari. It's what has been exposed with Get Human. It's the sad disarray of Comcast's abysmal customer service, not only to its customers but to its employees as well.

In 2006 a Comcast technician called on Brian Finkelstein to help restore his Internet service. During the visit the technician had to contact his service department and was left on hold for so long that he fell asleep in Brian's apartment. Brian used his video camera to share the sad reality of this experience with millions. The video reads something like this:

> A Comcast technician came to replace my cable modem.
> He spent over an hour on hold with Comcast.
> He fell asleep on my couch.
> Thanks, Comcast, for:
>
> - Two broken routers
> - Four-hour appointment blocks
> - Weeklong Internet outages
> - Long hold times
> - High prices
> - Three missed appointments
> - Promising to call back and then not calling
>
> Thanks, Comcast, for everything.

Unfortunately for Comcast, Brian Finkelstein was a blogger, and as if that wasn't enough, he was the blogger behind Snakes on a Blog, the wildly visible fan blog that was part of the unprecedented communal marketing extravaganza that happened for the movie *Snakes on a Plane*. You might read this and curse Comcast's luck for landing a whale of a consumer. After all, most consumers aren't bloggers, right? And of the allegedly 70 million blogs out there, only a fraction are considered highly authoritative. Yes and no. Today's new favorite pastime among consumers is finding out and exposing brands for hypocrisy, subpar service, inattentiveness, false and un-kept promises, and so on. And even if you aren't a blogger (or a prominent one at that), chances are that you know someone who knows someone who knows someone. *That* is the power of the social network—with only six pixels of separation (or less).

The blog Brandstorming had this advice for the folks over at Comcast:

1. Link to the video from the Comcast blog. Comcast screwed up, and admitting it is the first step to take. Link the video, admit how embarrassing it is, and call up Brian to personally apologize. Give him six months' worth of free service.
2. Work to correct the problem. The problem is not the poor tech. It's the fact that cable service is a mockery, and everyone from sitcoms to comedians to average customers makes fun of the service of cable guys. They even made a movie about it!
3. Don't fire the tech. Make him into a commercial where he drinks a lot of coffee. Turn this around. Use the guy as an example of how you are improving.
4. Highlight your successes by tracking progress. Highlight your successes. Make your improvements public.
5. Focus on other positive ways you can use blog marketing.

---

What would you have done? Air your views and free suggestions for companies like Comcast at www.jointheconversation.us/comcast

---

In fact, Comcast did respond. According to Snakes on a Blog:

On Wednesday evening I received a call from my regional Vice President at Comcast.

On Thursday evening I had a team of Comcast guys (including the head of the technical division in D.C.) working both outside and inside my home from 7:00 P.M. until midnight. After five hours of work, everything *appears* to be fully up and working. This crew was extremely professional, efficient, and they knew what they were talking about. It was great. If Comcast could provide this level of service for every person experiencing connection issues, they'd be the darling of the industry.

Sadly, however, the damage had already been done. I would suspect that of every 100 people who have seen the video or heard

YouTube - A **Comcast** Technician Sleeping on my Couch
Add **Video** to QuickList. The **Comcast** guy who feel asleep in my house ... Add **Video** to
QuickList. **Comcast** breaks into Red Bar Radio 01:48. From: deived420 ...
www.youtube.com/watch?v=CvVp7b5gzqU - 88k - Cached - Similar pages

Figure 16.1   Comcastic?

the story, fewer than five know (or care) how it turned out. Today, if
you type in phrases like "Comcast video" (which couldn't be more
relevant for a company providing cable television service, broadband Internet access, and the like) in search engines like Google,
your number-one result would be as shown in Figure 16.1.

## Every Day Is Crisis Management Central

JetBlue's response and responsiveness was tested to the limit following the 11-hour ordeal on the tarmac at JFK airport in February
2007. On both counts, the airline went by the book and to the letter
did what it was supposed to . . . and still it was not enough.

Ex-CEO David Neeleman was very quick to respond via the
traditional and nontraditional distribution platforms. And yet his
personal pseudo-blog, known as David Neeleman's Flight Log, wasn't
updated until a full week after this frenzy hit fever-pitch.

22 February 2007

Dear JetBlue Customers,

We are sorry and embarrassed. But most of all, we are deeply sorry.

Last week was the worst operational week in JetBlue's seven year
history. . . .

Most of this book focuses on events not capitalized on and inti-
mates that by being aware of what consumers are saying, an organization is better positioned to respond and therefore capitalize
on these fleeting moments of truth. On the upside, an opportunity
lost is an opportunity cost, but the flip side is equally pressing and

arguably even more imperative to the credibility and reputation of brands.

"This call may be monitored to improve customer service" is the statement you hear every time you dial in to a corporation's customer service center. Only now the roles have been reversed. The targeted have become the *targeters*, and every customer exchange runs the risk of becoming anything on the continuum from *Close Encounters of the Third Kind* to *War of the Worlds*.

Many people contend that Brian Finkelstein took advantage of the hapless Comcast technician and, at the very minimum, should have disclosed his intentions or efforts. Maybe so, but that still doesn't excuse the unforgivable and unacceptable attitudes, apathetic behaviors, and sloppiness exhibited in the name of customer service.

## CUSTOMER SERVICE IS NOW JUST A CLICK AWAY

A recent upgrade of the popular Internet Voiceover IP (VoIP)/telephony, Skype, comes with an Internet browser application plug-in that converts all recognized telephone numbers into a link, which, once clicked, initiates an outbound Skype call. Many Skype users already have software installed that automatically records all phone conversations. With disclosure formalities thus out of the way, we are talking about thousands of potential showcases of shoddy and embarrassing customer service on display for all.

There are seemingly two forces operating in separate directions right now. On the one hand, you have many—if not most—companies making it incredibly difficult to locate an actual telephone number on a web site; on the other hand, technology—like this Skype plug-in—is making it that much easier to close the gap between the search for help and the ability to actually get hold of a human being with the simple click of a mouse. (See Figure 16.2.) The implication is simple: If you're in the service game, be prepared to respond increasingly quickly and effectively, because your consumers are only a click away.

Figure 16.2    Customer Service Is Now Just a Click Away

## WHY YOUR WORST-CASE SCENARIO IS YOUR BEST-CASE SCENARIO (REPRISE)

Every single time one of your customers reaches out to you, you are being given a gift. Every single complaint is an invitation for dialogue. Every dissatisfied consumer is a gift-wrapped opportunity to right the wrongs, get a second chance, and solidify a customer for life. I keep on saying this to marketers and will continue to hammer home this point until there are no nails left: *Your biggest threat is not when customers complain or fight back against you—it's when they don't do anything; when they stop caring; when they give up on you.*

That's when you get ignored, forgotten, and discarded.

Here are five key pieces of advice for building effective conversation through dialogue:

1. *Plan for the worst-case scenario.* It's like walking into a pivotal sales pitch and having your computer crash on you midpresentation.

What, you didn't anticipate the possibility of PowerPoint spazzing out on you? Have you been living under a rock for the past 10 years? It boggles my mind how easily a competent professional is reduced to a babbling half-wit in the same amount of time it takes to say, "Blue screen of death." Similarly, companies need to anticipate the worst-case scenarios and make contingency plans accordingly. There really is no excuse when it comes to foreseeable outcomes and scenarios that most reasonable people could have identified in advance. That said, with a bit of lateral thinking and creative brainstorming, unforeseeable or unlikely contingencies based on — but not limited to — extraneous and uncontrollable circumstances or variables should be discussed and prepared for accordingly.

2. *Plan for the best-case scenario.* One of the more successful examples of viral nirvana came in the form of Tea Partay, an irreverent mash-up parody of New England meets Rap Life for Smirnoff's Raw Tea product. The original video has been viewed well over 3.6 million times and has been prolifically written up in the press as well as covered in the blogosphere. Who knew? The creators of Tea Partay certainly didn't. Perhaps that's why when people clicked through to the brand's web site, they received . . . nothing. Unless, of course, you consider an "under construction, come back soon" message something. Once upon a time a server crashing was an accolade worth cooing about, but not anymore.

3. *Be more reactive.* This sounds a bit counterintuitive, but it's not. Companies have got to learn to react — better, quicker, more decisively, and with more conviction — to their consumers. This is a different kind of reactivity in which a company truly catches up to its consumers, as opposed to *attempting* to catch up to them but always remaining one step behind. I would recommend the hiring and empowerment of a person dedicated to response and responsiveness.

4. *Dedicate a portion of budget to dialogue.* It's all well and good to have an effective conversation with one consumer at a time, but you're still in the scale business. At a time when people

like Winter or Tom Locke are serving up fresh brand equity daily, shouldn't you be thinking about ways to build people and, more importantly, ideas like theirs into your marketing communication?

5. *Integrate dialogue into ongoing plans.* Steps (or tips) 1 through 4 are all focused on mobilizing your organization to deal better (or cope better) with your consumers. Step 5 liberates your company from the back foot and propels it to the front foot. This is the part of the process where dialogue moves from an organizational process to a strategic imperative.

ESPN made the mistake of drinking one too many glasses of its own Kool-Aid when it uploaded its entertaining "This is *SportsCenter*" commercials to Apple's iTunes store . . . *and charged consumers $2 to download them!* Yes, I know, don't even say it. In fact, you needn't say anything, because consumers said it for you in the form of a litany of scathing "one-star" reviews.

To ESPN's credit, it quickly realized the error of its ways and pulled the price tag. Fortunately for ESPN, iTunes wiped the slate clean, and lo and behold, within days there was a new set of reviews — all five-star.

# 17

# Conversation through Partnership

Partnership is most certainly not overrated. If anything, it is taken for granted. Big time. If you think about it, you've been in partnership with your customers since the day you opened your doors. The thing is, though, it hasn't exactly been an equal partnership now, has it? Pretty one-sided at the end of the day when you factor in how closely you cooperate, collaborate, and interact with your "partners." Yours is a partnership of convenience: You call the shots and determine when it is acceptable to speak (in the form of crass and one-dimensional advertising) and when it is just fine and dandy to be a "silent partner."

Hear no evil. See no evil. Speak no evil.

You selectively filter and process what you want to hear and the extent to which you get close to consumers. These encounters are usually limited to fleeting photo opportunities with the "lucky winner" in competitions, focus groups, artificial copy testing exercises in futility, or the occasional challenge of being cornered in the local store by a persistent customer.

## IT'S ALL ABOUT CONTROL, ISN'T IT?

The number-one obstacle remaining in your path is that of control. It's the one aspect of your job that you cling to as a security blanket of salvation—which would make sense if you were still an infant or a growing brand, but unfortunately for you, you're 45 years old and wearing diapers. Awkwaaaard! Letting go may be quite possibly the hardest thing to do, but the results are beyond emancipating.

Why, then, are companies so reluctant or unable to let go of control? Is it the PR folks in corporate communications or the eagle-eyed vultures (mixed avian metaphor, I know) in legal affairs? What exactly are they afraid of? I've never heard anyone articulate *why* so many company-created barriers are erected between brand and consumer. Some of the reasons given are more often than not exceptions to the norm, worst-case scenarios, or pitiful excuses. In a game that is all about generalizing, numbers, and scale, it strikes me as somewhat odd that we are so sickly conservative in such a high-stakes game of winner-takes-all.

In addition to fear, too many companies are also experiencing an unhealthy dose of self-loathing. The inability to let go of control comes from a superiority complex that is deeply rooted in tremendous insecurity and lack of confidence. In every presentation I give, I ask my audience this question: "How many of you genuinely believe that you understand your brand better than your consumers do?" For some strange reason, there is always one person who raises his or her hand. I typically applaud that person for being courageous and remark that he or she is either the only honest person in the room (and thus, everyone else is a liar) or the biggest fool. The fact remains that if you genuinely believe your consumers understand and can define and articulate your brand better than you can, why on earth are you not deploying programs and solutions as such?

## From the Frying Pan into the Fire

Many companies (perhaps even yours) have started to take notice and concede that the power base is shifting a lot quicker than they expected.

Others have become so paranoid that they've overcompensated by *ceding too much control too soon*. The *Los Angeles Times* experimented with wikis to horrendous effect by allowing its consumers to edit — open-source style — an actual newspaper article. The result was abuse of the opportunity with such shocking intensity and force that the newspaper quickly took the wiki offline.

Many mainstream marketers are lost at sea (as Oliver Dooley's book cover submission suggests—see Chapter 19) when it comes to finding their place in an otherwise volatile and fluid landscape of shifting sands and expectations. When in doubt, the natural reaction is to hop from one extreme to the other. It's exactly what you see every day in the world, whether we're talking about national security or halftime performances at the Super Bowl. The And Economy suggests that instead of extreme marketing, the answer lies in balance and equilibrium. In other words, meet your consumers halfway. Work with them, not against them. Treat them as equals on some—but not all—levels. *Ultimately there is a difference between partners and partnership*, and it's up to you to find the sweet spot that resides somewhere in the middle of the continuum.

## Partnership Is Addictive

Frito-Lay is one company that has been bitten by the partnership bug. First there was Dorito's Crash the Super Bowl initiative, which invited people to submit their own spots for consideration. The creation of the eventual winner was aired during Super Bowl XLI in 2007. The winning spot cost $12 to make, of which $6 was spent on the product!

As it turns out, three of the final five spots were created by semi-professionals, that is, amateur filmmakers or small production or advertising boutiques. This fact drew some consternation, criticism, and debate, but at the end of the day true partnership does not discriminate.

I'll share here a couple of interesting learnings that came out of the Dorito's initiative:

1. By the end of October (when the campaign launched), only four entries had been submitted. November through December saw a jump to 400, and by the end of January over 2,000 entries had been submitted. The catalyst for this growth spurt was conversation—the ability to activate the influencers and get people excited and talking about the program. Frito-Lay divided its buzz targets into three distinct cate-

gories: makers, voters, and watchers. Note how neatly these three categories dovetail into Chapter 5's producer, prosumer, and consumer classification.

2. The number-one question asked of the brand by participants was the following: "Will you air what we produce and will you edit it?" The insight is clear: If you're asking your audience to contribute and participate in partnership, there needs to be a quid pro quo. Partnership can be one-sided (communication) or mutually beneficial (conversation).

Another Frito-Lay experiment was the launch of "Flavor X19R"—a new, unnamed variety of Doritos that was actually marketed and distributed in this incomplete format. The snack's packaging drew attention to the work-in-progress development and invited consumers to help name the product. Very smart.

Motorola partnered with its community via wiki to coincide with the launch of the Q.

Here's a quote from the Moto clan:

> Because the possible applications for the Q are always expanding, the "ideal user guide" would always grow and change. That can't happen on paper. With your help, this wiki can capture and share the ever-growing knowledge of the greater community of Q users.
>
> Frankly, Motorola can't possibly know how the Q will work in all situations—who could? But we love our Q users and want to learn from them, help them, and make our products better in the future.

What I *really* love about this is the numerator factor (that's for Len), as opposed to the denominator treatment. Companies are always trying to minimize cost or risk instead of maximizing return or reward. Case in point: Many companies are putting user guides on a CD or, worse still, making guides downloadable from a web site (rather than printing them).

Motorola, on the other hand, has opened itself up to allow its community to build a *human guide* (as opposed to a user guide), it no doubt will uncover rich, diverse, and incredibly valuable tips, tricks, tutorials, and so on.

Partnership does not always have to be an overt or explicit grant from a company to its community or consumer base. In many cases, the partnership is tacit or implicit. Put differently, it would behoove marketers to get the hell out of their own way and let their consumers talk among themselves without being watched over (like Big Brother), supervised, or spoon-fed. In other words, partnership can be between participating consumers or between brand and consumer (and *not* between brand marketer and consumer). One of my favorite examples (see Figure 17.1) is Virgin Digital's beautiful mash-up mosaic of bands (how many can you correctly identify?), which was promptly uploaded by a prosumer to Flickr and "solved" by the community. (See Figure 17.2.)

In the past, companies might have tried to block or deter the efforts of consumers to cheat or beat the system. But no longer. This kind of communal activation is exactly what we are so desperately seeking—it is pure, unadulterated engagement, and it's way cool.

Beating the system is a given today. It brings a sense of entitlement

Figure 17.1   Virgin Digital's Mash-up

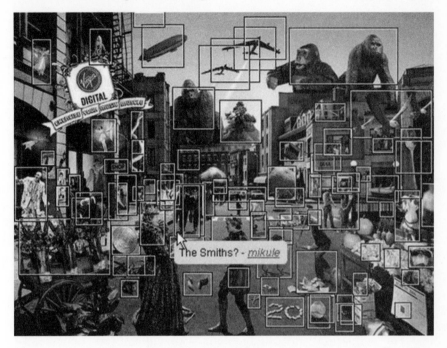

Figure 17.2    This Time with Communal Feeling

that both satisfies and exhilarates all who participate. However, I don't
believe these consumer responses even remotely constitute beating the
system, but rather are ways of embracing the system. Furthermore, it is
critical to note the differences between innovative and average consumers. Innovative consumers are your "mavens," your "connectors"
and "salespeople," as per Malcolm Gladwell's *The Tipping Point*. They
are the ones who will ultimately be responsible for seeding an idea to
the masses (and there you were puffing out your chest, patting yourself
on the back, and taking all the credit). They are the one in ten who influence the other nine ("the influentials"—see Chapter 20).

Innovative consumers are constantly beating the system, but
whatever you do, don't quash them. What they do is a sign of life
and proof of concept that bodes well for the endurance and health of
your efforts. Innovative consumers are not necessarily going to ruin
things for all who are yet to come (although they might). Rather,
they will talk among themselves and cross over to the masses when
the timing is right.

## IF THEY DON'T WANT BREAD, GIVE 'EM CHOICE

In the case of the musical mash-up, mainstream consumers most likely never saw the "solved" version of the mash-up mosaic on Flickr. Nor would they necessarily have wanted to. Hell, some of them might not even have realized this was solvable or cared enough, if they did, to take the time to identify the various bands or to stay the course. This mosaic, which was visually enticing and superficially engaging, worked rather well as a print ad. However, when activated by the community, the result was a stream of conversation via partnership.

In either scenario—whether as an ad (exposure) or as a mosaic (an engaging experience)—the idea worked. Consumers could choose and self-select how deep they wanted to go, how thorough they wanted to be in their pursuit of the solution, and how much they wanted to interact and connect with their fellow enthusiasts.

Arguably, this is one of the reasons why the Chevy Tahoe consumer-generated "advertising" attempt did not make it to the next level of activation and engagement. Consumers were not really given a choice at all. And they most certainly were not treated as partners, but rather as lackeys.

## PARTNERSHIP IS NOT AN ADVERTISING TACTIC

To build on the previous point, many consumers today have no interest in any kind of partnership whatsoever—at least not one that falls anywhere on the spectrum from telling-and-selling to commanding-and-controlling. To get consumers on board, you need to earn their trust and respect. Where better to start than the beginning of the process?

My advice to you is simple: Resist the urge to "be a more authentic *advertiser*," which at its core is an oxymoron (making you both the ox and the moron). Attempting to tell a more honest story is certainly a step in the right direction, but *it's not the ultimate step*. Your moment of truth lies in partnership, and it begins at the R&D phase—the place where true innovation resides—and continues through the insight-gathering process.

Everyone likes to beat up on General Motors, the Detroit behemoth that has fallen further and further behind its Japanese rivals in pretty much most key categories, from innovation to marketing, from sales to customer satisfaction. I've often said that if I were General Motors, my first action would be swift and decisive: I'd stop advertising. Period. I'd reinvest the entire advertising budget in my customers and my products. I'd make better cars. Cars that are relevant. Cars that are reliable. Cars that look great and drive great. Cars that don't guzzle gas and destroy the environment. Cars capable of credibly sponsoring the Live Earth concerts and global initiative.

I'd assemble unprecedented groups of consumers with a genuine interest in helping the company who would be willing to volunteer their opinions, suggestions, and recommendations. As this chart suggests, there's no shortage of opinion when it comes to General Motors. (See Figure 17.3.)

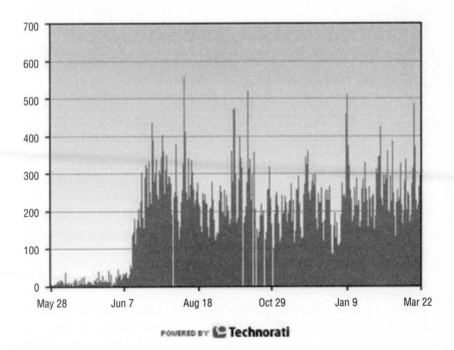

POWERED BY **Technorati**

Figure 17.3   Welcome to the Conversation! Posts by Day about General Motors, March 28, 2006, to March 22, 2007

To their credit, and as illustrated earlier in this book, GM is already engaging consumers through its blogs. Interestingly enough, it was the "rubbish" event (Chapter 11) that seems to have propelled GM into the forefront of healthy conversation. I'd recommend upping this intensity and formalizing the relationship from one-off consumer exchanges to ongoing advisory partnerships.

## INNOVATIVE FOCUS GROUPS

Think about it for a moment. We pull "typical" consumers into a room. Average Joes. People who represent the masses. But it isn't the masses or the "median consumers" who ultimately will be responsible for our success . . . it's the innovators and the opinion leaders.

These are the consumers we need to be talking to (and obviously not behind a one-way mirror, either): the ones who are leaders and the ones who are best at articulating and comprehending the abstract and conceptual.

That said, I often say that if you want to get the right answers, you need to ask the right questions. Think about "articulated needs" versus "unarticulated solutions." It's a given that consumers don't know what they don't know, but that leaves marketers stuck between a rock and a hard place, darting back and forth between two extreme positions: marketer as king (as in "we know better" or "we'll only hear what we want to hear") and consumer as king (as in giving the consumer too much latitude and leverage).

Ultimately, partnership is about *access*. To meet your consumers halfway, you have to be able to journey from your ivory tower to a neutral zone. And your consumers have to venture from their homes, blogs, and societies to meet you there.

To thrive, to grow . . . or to continue growing . . . access needs to increase, not decrease; the ability to gain access needs to be open, not closed. If you seriously want to build meaningful, enduring, and healthy *relationships* with your consumers, you'll have to abandon the old way of being detached, distant, and unavailable.

Establishing—and maintaining—a relationship (think about the words "personal," "personable," and "personalization") takes time, empathy, and commitment. Engaging audiences is not a point of differentiation anymore; it's standard operating procedure.

Brands that remain aloof, separate, and siloed will lose ground and momentum to consumers who are hungry for human contact. On the flip side, brands that open themselves up to their consumers—all of them, from enemies to prospects to customers to loyalists—will have the opportunity to be internalized, taken to heart, and essentially elevated to a new and very different place in consumers' hearts and minds and the collective consciousness.

## A New Definition of Creativity

In the many-to-many model and the And Economy, creativity is truly democratized. You no longer need the word "creative" in your job title to be a creative contributor. This is a difficult pill to swallow for advertising creatives, but it need not necessarily be looked at as an ultimatum; rather, it can be seen as a call to action. The lesson is not dissimilar from the one marketers are having to learn with respect to control, namely, that the balance of power has shifted from the one to the many. That said, once again the key to success lies in moderation and balance. Advertising creatives, with their tenure and expertise, are well positioned to be curators, connectors and conduits—influencers, if you will. They have the unprecedented opportunity to act as conductors—maestros who can harness the full power of the orchestra—but to do so they need to concede that their modus operandi has shifted from limited and veiled access to full-throttle collaboration.

Einstein defined insanity as doing the same thing over and over again expecting a different result. Dictionary.com defines "creativity" as "productive originality"—doing things differently and getting a result. In other words, creativity is the perfect antidote to insanity, and it is achieved by embracing both sides of the equation ("And")—both marketers and their consumers—to achieve the perfect harmony between selling and storytelling. If you think about it, this makes total sense. Consumers hate being constantly sold to, but when they have skin in the game—a vested interest—their buy-in and consent are almost guaranteed.

On July 23, 2007, a landmark and unprecedented event took place in the United States: A Democratic Party Debate with a conversational twist. Through the power of community, dialogue, and partnership (CNN and YouTube), ordinary consumers got to ask extraordinary questions directly to the 2008 candidates. All in all roughly 3,000 questions were submitted, and while only a fraction were able to be asked, those that did make it (including a talking snowman) injected an air of freshness, authenticity, and humanity into a mix that had for so long become nothing more than pomp and ceremony.

## PUTTING IT ALL TOGETHER—VIRTUAL THIRST

Coca-Cola's commitment for consumers to experience the "Coke Side of Life" led the company to build a presence in the online virtual world of Second Life. And it did it in a way that respected the established community: challenging residents to create a virtual Coca-Cola vending machine that would "dispense" the essence of the brand and a unique virtual experience. (See Figure 17.4.)

### Community

By giving the online public an opportunity to generate brand content, Coke aimed to encourage creative conversation with a new market of advanced consumers. Acknowledging the fact that hundreds of unofficial vending machines (i.e., tributes to the Coca-Cola brand equity) already existed in the SL world, Coke did not attempt to replace or beat the residents at their own game, but in fact joined in the brand conversation already in progress.

### Partnership

In order for the brand to build a relevant connection with the virtual community, an advisory panel of local leaders and influencers within SL was involved in all aspects of the program, from planning to the management of the contest.

Three in-world builders—or programmers—were also ap-

Figure 17.4 Coca-Cola Virtual Thirst Pavilion on Crayonville Island (www.crayonvillesecondlife.com)

proached with a broad brief to create virtual prototypes that would serve as inspiration for entries.

**Dialogue**

What made this program even more interesting was that most of the blog posts written by the community were personally responded to. In fact, after several concerns were expressed about the value of the prize, Coca-Cola's director of global interactive marketing, Michael Donnelly, not only personally responded to the critics, but actually upped the prize money.

You can view this video conversation at www.jointheconversation .us/virtualthirst

At the end of the day, even avatars get thirsty; however, this particular thirst was for conversation.

# 18

## Getting Started:
## The Manifesto for Experimentation

Author Seth Godin wrote a great post about defending the status quo.[1] Here are his 17 items; 18 through 30 are my additions. I've also provided some neat little boxes for you to score your own professional scenarios by putting a check mark next to the statements you've heard around your company:

1. "That will never work."  ❏
2. ". . . That said, the labor laws make it difficult for us to do a lot of the suggestions [you] put out. And we do live in a lawsuit-oriented society."  ❏
3. "Can you show me some research that demonstrates that this will work?"  ❏
4. "Well, if you had some real-world experience, then you would understand."  ❏
5. "I don't think our customers will go for that, and without them we'd never be able to afford to try this."  ❏
6. "It's fantastic, but the sales force won't like it."  ❏
7. "The sales force is willing to give it a try, but [major retailer] won't stock it."  ❏
8. "There are government regulations, and this won't be permitted."  ❏

---

[1]This chapter is excerpted from Joseph Jaffe, "The Manifesto for Experimentation," originally published January 9, 2007, at ChangeThis, http://www.changethis.com/30.06.Manifesto Experimentation.

9. "Well, this might work for other people, but I think we'll stick with what we've got." ❑
10. "We'll let someone else prove it works . . . it won't take long to catch up." ❑
11. "Our team doesn't have the technical chops to do this." ❑
12. "Maybe in the next budget cycle." ❑
13. "We need to finish this initiative first." ❑
14. "It's been done before." ❑
15. "It's never been done before." ❑
16. "We'll get back to you on this." ❑
17. "We're already doing it." ❑
18. "You have to understand: This is the [insert company name here] company." ❑
19. "Be patient with us." ❑
20. "We move slowly, but we'll get there." ❑
21. "You've obviously never worked in the [insert industry kind here] industry." ❑
22. "There just isn't enough budget for change." ❑
23. "Do you have best practices to go with that?" ❑
24. "No one ever got fired for putting TV on the plan" (yesterday's excuse). ❑
25. "No one ever got fired for putting [traditional] interactive on the plan" (today's excuse). ❑
26. "Our marketing mix modeling doesn't incorporate the approaches you're suggesting." ❑
27. "Well, that might work in [insert name of country A here], but this is [insert name of country B]." ❑
28. "What you say is terrific, but it would just be too hard to implement." ❑
29. "We need a certain amount of reach in order to be successful." ❑
30. "Change is good . . . but not on my watch." ❑

If you scored more than 1 out of 30, you might be throwing your hands in the air in despair, most notably over the challenges of where to start and what to do first. The good news is that changing the status quo is not that much different from losing weight. Every human possesses the intellect and common sense to recognize the need to lose weight; the hard part is self-discipline, focus, intensity, commitment, and ability to act on this need. And besides, there are way too many obese people out there!

I'm a big believer that the best place to start is at the beginning. Only this time, what you see before you is a fork in the road, and as legendary Yankees baseball catcher and captain Yogi Berra once said: "If you come to a fork in the road, take it!"

A July 2006 issue of *Wired* magazine introduced two distinct groups of *creatives*: "conceptual innovators" and "experimental innovators."

The article introduced economist David Galenson's "theory of artistic life cycles," an age-based methodology that essentially "reverse-engineered ingenuity to reveal the source code of the creative mind." It focused mainly on artists—for example, Picasso was a conceptual innovator, whereas Jackson Pollock was an experimental innovator—but posited that the same theory should equally apply across a much broader array of disciplines, including—but not limited to—business.

The article offered interesting insights into the concept of "genius," as well as the importance of finding happy mediums between left and right brain and extreme classifications. There are obvious implications for businesses, creativity, new marketing, and experimentation.

We are living through and operating in unprecedented times that are exciting, challenging, and anything but stagnant or predictable. To be successful, marketing organizations will need to foster and adopt an aggressive and intense culture of experimentation, risk-taking, change management (for communications), and creativity.

Anything less will result in relative business losses, competitive inferiority, and inefficient allocation of resources (and therefore suboptimal return on investment).

Wikipedia defines an "experiment" as a set of actions and observations performed in the context of solving a particular problem or question to support or falsify a hypothesis or research

To solve new and existing challenges associated with—but not limited to—the evolution and revolution of inevitable change, volatility, and flux, organizations need to adopt new, unique, original, creative, and different approaches.

The process through which these approaches are qualified, prioritized, and activated is called "new marketing experimentation," defined as the systematic and calculated ability to take risks, make mistakes, and implement unprecedented solutions on a concurrent cultural, organizational, strategic, and tactical basis.

concerning phenomena. The experiment is a cornerstone in the empirical approach to acquiring deeper knowledge about the physical world.

*It's what I've never seen before that I recognize.*
—Photographer Diane Arbus

Consumers are the same. As long as we continue to expose them to the same-old-same-old, they will continue to ignore us and get better at eliminating us from their lives.

Take your kids to a restaurant, and the waitress brings over the ubiquitous three-pack of crayons: red, yellow, blue—the three primary colors. If you think about it, there's an easy leap to media: red, yellow, blue—television, radio, print. Except that today Crayola has its Big Box, containing 96 colors (hence my earlier mentions).

- Are you still coloring in three colors?
- Do you begin with the default three-pack, or do you treat each color equally?
- Are you fully exploring the complete range of colors, with the full spectrum of permutations, combinations, and possibilities?
- Do you have a process in place to evaluate and select the variety of opportunities?

## PUTTING IT ALL TOGETHER LEADS TO A COHESIVE, INTEGRATED, AND MEASURABLE PLAN OF ACTION

Here are 10 critical insights to internalize that will help you on your journey:

1. *You can't be half pregnant.* Experimentation (like the word "test") is not about a halfhearted commitment. It's not about using negligible, leftover dollars . . . that approach ultimately puts too much pressure on a siloed and tactical one-off to overperform disproportionately against existing efforts.
2. *Call in the experts.* If there's one thing worse than not experimenting, it's experimenting poorly. Fake blogs (frogs), contrived and controlled environments, overly moderated forums for expression and creation, and the inability to respond in a hyper-timely fashion are all common mistakes.
3. *Swim upstream.* Tactics in search or absent of strategy are no better and no worse than the status quo. The earlier in the process you have the discussion and evaluation of alternatives, and the more aligned those alternatives are to brand and strategic equity, the better the chances of success.
4. *Strive toward implementing an integrated plan* in which your experimental components are allowed to feed off all possible opportunities and touchpoints and your untried and untested alternatives are allowed to flex their true potential.
5. *Develop fluid and nonlinear processes to allow a dynamic and opportunistic planning and development process.* Find a balance between fire-ready-aim and laborious and drawn-out conceptualization and ideation. Embrace a process where everyone is involved and allowed to contribute—and that, of course, means consumers as well as every department of your organization. Reject territorialized and compartmentalized hierarchies and fiefdoms.
6. *Cultural buy-in is critical.* This cannot be accentuated and emphasized enough. There has got to be buy-in from the highest level and a commitment to aggressively upping the spending/budget allocation based on results.

7. *Measurement: Nothing escapes without a layer of evaluation.* Be sure to spend considerable time developing key metrics and fair evaluation criteria in order to fully encapsulate the benefits and pitfalls of your plan. Remember: Negative lessons learned are just as valuable as positive ones. Depending on your level of risk, you might even want to err on the side of qualitative "proof of experiment" above quantitative. Handicapping your experimentation may be exactly what you need to help move from embryonic to independent status.

> **To get the right answers, you need to ask the right questions.**

8. *Trust your gut.* And trust that your competitors are keeping their successes close to their chests. This is about doing the right thing—this is about truth—and you will know when you're on the right path or not. (And rest assured, your consumers are only too happy to lead you back to the path should you stray.)

9. *Be responsive, be humble, be open to co-creation and open-source contributions from freelancers, bloggers, consumers.* You will get feedback whether you like it or not—and lots of it. Make sure you respond. Build in processes whereby you reward contributions with a combination of fame (recognition) and fortune (compensation).

10. *Be prepared to make mistakes.* Embrace your ability to strike out. This may seem disingenuous, but it's not. There's no way you're going to hit the ground with a "Hall of Fame" ratio of hits-to-misses. Facilitate a culture in which bold decisions are made by risk-inclined teams. This is not a license to let loose with a series of Hail Marys, but rather with earnest attempts to encourage a culture of change in which the brand is continuously mixing it up and adapting to the dynamic and organic environment in which it lives and breathes.

## MAKING EXPERIMENTATION A REALITY: A FIVE-STEP PLAN

The following is a five-step guide to determining an experimentation roadmap or path forward.

## STEP 1: ORGANIZATIONAL STRUCTURE

Experimentation should not be charged to any existing internal or external partners. Anyone with an existing mandate or with a day-to-day portfolio that is tied to and grounded in short-term metrics or deliverables is going to be biased, clouded, or at the very minimum distracted.

### Special Teams versus Black Ops

Experimentation is best conducted by a separated team—a nimble, independent, empowered, and intense group of individuals who report straight to the top.

Depending on your anticipated level of risk and your comfort level, this team could be assembled as a "Delta Force" or "black ops" group . . . unaccountable throughout but ready and prepared to pay the ultimate price upon failure.

### Sourcing Your Delta Force

- Model 1: Internal existing (a mash-up of individuals from various internal departments)
- Model 2: External existing (a mash-up of individuals from various partners/agencies)
- Model 3: External specialists (a company specializing in experimentation/new approaches)
- Model 4: Mash-up (a task force consisting of a combination of these three models, led by an external specialist—either an individual or a team)

**Reporting Structure**

Your experimentation team will report to the chief executive officer, the chief marketing officer, or the appropriate counterpart.

**An Integrated Silo**

The ideal experimentation team remains separate (in terms of autonomy and independence) and yet connected (that is, integrated and holistic) to the organization. It is critical (and should be self-evident) that the ideal special teams will interface regularly with the day-to-day departments in order to execute "experiments with context."

## STEP 2: PROCESS

If experimentation is like the systematic tossing of pasta against the wall to see if it sticks and is al dente, then there had better be a recipe in mind to cook up a storm or there's going to be a hell of a mess left over.

Butchered mixed metaphors aside, you're going to need to "connect the dots" and put it all together with some kind of a structure and process that will help imbed and integrate the experimentation imperative into the very fiber and DNA of the organization.

You'll need a structure that helps you do the following:

- Determine which brands or geographies are right and ripe for experimentation
- Set the intensity level of experimentation in terms of budget/ sufficiency commitment against the number of experiments over a defined time period, as well as some kind of multiple that will allow you to scale and step up accordingly
- Evaluate *which* experiments should be utilized in which order
- Choose your rules of engagement against which all key constituencies sign off
- Find evaluation/measurement criteria to determine efficacy and key learnings/insights; establish knowledge management methodology to help capture and share "different practices"

Put simply, experimentation without purpose, overarching objectives, defined metrics, organizational structure and process, and cultural buy-in will inevitably run out of steam and momentum and run the risk of being marginalized or minimized from a priority, investment, and commitment perspective.

---

**Experiment or be experimented on.**

---

## STEP 3: ALLOCATION/INVESTMENT

- *Yesterday (circa 2005)*: What percentage of my budget should I allocate to interactive?
- *Today (circa 2007)*: What percentage of my budget should I allocate to search or video?
- *Tomorrow*: What percentage of my budget should I allocate to experimentation?

---

**Unless you're Neil Armstrong, you're not going to achieve exponential results by taking incremental steps.**

---

There is some precedent, but in fact we are in uncharted territory here. Can you imagine Christopher Columbus asking for a map before embarking on his discovery of America?

How much should you be spending on experimentation? According to triangulated anecdotes,[2] that percentage is in the low to mid 20s.

Google's CEO, Eric Schmidt, is a proponent of the 70:20:10 rule, where up to 30 percent of the company's budget goes toward experimentation. The catch here is that when budget cuts arise (as they inevitably do), normally the first to go is the innovation or experimental allocation. You need to change this. Quickly. Forever.

---

[2]Blackfriars communications and McKinsey reports.

## STEP 4: CATEGORIZATION

What should you be experimenting on?

- *Layer 1: Tweaking the existing paradigm (communication)*. The application of new/nontraditional techniques to existing/traditional approaches/media. Example: KFC's hidden coupon code in a 30-second spot that was only visible in slow-motion mode (and ultimately via the Web).
- *Layer 2: Deploying a new paradigm (conversation)*. The incorporation of new techniques, approaches, and alternatives. Simply put—using an approach you've never used before. Example: VOD or social media (blogs, podcasts, and so on).
- *Layer 3: Creating a new paradigm (transformation)*. This is "Windows Registry" territory: Proceed with an experienced guide, with caution, and at your own risk. Focus on your business model and your overall and overarching relationship with your consumers, going beyond media, communication, and even conversation into a "transformation" or innovation space.

## STEP 5: EVALUATION/MEASUREMENT

### Time Frame

Overheard in the halls of an advertising agency:

STAFFER 1:
This stuff is hard. It's too complicated. I've been doing the same thing for twenty years, and all I want to do is just see out the next three years and then retire.

STAFFER 2:
Don't you understand? By embracing [new marketing], you'll keep your job for the next three years.

## The Three-Year Plan

One suggested path forward is to put together and execute a phased three-year plan focused on the systematic installation and integration of experimentation into the very core of the organization.

This process would follow a "focused chaos" methodology, that is, being clear and rigorous about managing expectations, ascertaining the real ROI (learnings, metrics, insights), integrating programs into the larger "mother ship," and ultimately closing the loop on each iteration in order to evolve, improve, and innovate on the next go-round.

In other words, such a plan would manage expectations through an appropriate investment of time, money, energy, and efforts (together with cultural and corporate buy-in) over a sustained period of time.

Three years is a placeholder. Your optimal time frame will be directly influenced by your category, corporate culture, objectives, business cycles, and propensity or openness to change.


## Return on Experimentation (ROE)

Short-term goals (goals oriented more toward direct response) should not overpower and cloud the real reasons why you are experimenting in the first place. Your goal is to learn. Your goal is to learn (and learn from your mistakes) before your competitors do. Your goal is to move on to the next level/experiment when your competitors are making the same mistakes you made long in the past.

Instead of a traditional linear and binary ROI focus, employ an ROE layer of evaluation: Return On Experimentation.

This is an opportune time to put flesh and directional guidelines around both new metrics (such as time spent, engagement, influence, organic referrals, and behavioral shifts) and more qualitative and sometimes intangible gauges of success, including—but not limited to—buzz, press coverage, relevance, resonance, and motivation (internal).

## Do It While You Can Before You Have To

Those were nine words of wisdom spoken to me at a conference in Toronto by a fellow blogger, the new marketing evangelist Kate Tgovac.

The bottom line is that you simply cannot afford to be in the chasing pack (the ones who have to). You need to be in the while-you-can clan. You've been given an unprecedented array of bold, new approaches, alternatives to the staid, tried-and-tested mainstream outlets.

Along the way, you're going to make mistakes—plenty of them—but be sure to make the good kind of mistakes, as opposed to the bad kind.

Good mistakes are mistakes you learn from, the kind you get smarter from, the kind that you'll be making before your competitors so that when they get around to making the same mistakes you'll be way ahead . . . possibly making new mistakes, but probably not. Bad mistakes are the kind that leave a lasting stain, the kind that may very well poison the waters for future drinking, the kind that you simply cannot afford to make.

So how do you differentiate between good and bad mistakes? How do you determine how to make the right kinds of mistakes? This is the "art" and expertise aspect of the new marketing experimentation equation.

With a nod to Monopoly, your options are characterized by a mash-up of risk and return that spans the full gamut of success and failure. The point of this chapter is that there will be two phases of new marketing investment, hallmarked against the two types of mistakes. (See Figure 18.1.)

At the end of the day, it really comes down to the importance you're placing, or will place, on the various change elements associated with the business and brand-building worlds, the ever-increasing challenge of reaching-connecting-effecting today's elusive, marketing-weary, and increasingly empowered consumers, and the ability to utilize and incorporate these approaches in order to stand out, resonate, and convert.

Whether you look at it from a tactical (blog, podcast, consumer-generated content, gaming, virtual world), strategic (experience,

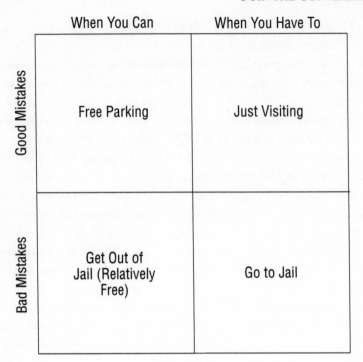

Figure 18.1    Good Mistakes and Bad Mistakes

permission, involvement, conversation), organizational (process, nonlinear responsiveness, fluid contingencies), or cultural (part of the company's DNA, the holistic-commitment across every single internal or external constituency or touchpoint; R&D; innovation) perspective, you control your future. If you truly believe that the health, growth, and prosperity of your brand will pivot around the extent to which you are able to seize and capitalize on the limitless possibilities out there, then it comes down to when you're going to do something while you can, rather than when you have to.

## FAILURE *IS* AN OPTION

In early 2007, in a social event/experience called "Bumrush the Charts," bloggers, podcasters, citizens, humans, and so on, attempted to propel—flash mob style—a particular track from an unsigned and independent band into the iTunes stratosphere. The band in question was Black Lab, and the track was "Mine Again." At the end of the day (literally), "Mine Again" did not hit the number-one spot on iTunes, but it did hit number 99 overall and number 11 in the "U.S. rock" category. And in countries like the Netherlands and Norway, "Mine Again" reached number 15 and number 55 overall, respectively. So was it a success or a failure? I chatted with one of the organizers, Christopher Penn, and you can listen and respond to our conversation on www.jointheconversation.us/bumrush

I'm sure there are many variations on the story, but the way I remember it, legendary NFL coach Vince Lombardi was once questioned after losing a game and said something to the effect, *"In my entire career, I never lost a single game . . . I just ran out of time."*

It struck me as a sublime way to help us cope with the whole notion of failure versus success.

What seems like today's failure is often tomorrow's delayed success.

Being quick to judge is bad enough, but in today's volatile climate, where job tenure is as fickle as ever—where both mainstream media and bloggers suffer from either schizophrenic journalism or premature speculation (there are drugs to treat this disorder)—it is incumbent upon us to think big picture, long term, and stay the course, especially when naysayers jump on the bandwagon and try to derail innovation and progress.

Vince Lombardi was a visionary, being both optimistic and pragmatic. He realized that failure is only failure when it is seen as an end unto itself—when there is no learning or insight that can be realized the next time round.

It is not that dissimilar from new marketing experimentation.

## Lessons in Conversation
### *Tom Hespos, President and CEO, Underscore Marketing*

Agreeing to a conversational marketing campaign is simple in principle.

Most advertisers are eager to hop on the blogging and social networking bandwagons, and if you ask most decision-makers on the client side whether they plan to market within the social networking space in the coming year, roughly half will say they plan to do so, according to Jupiter Research.

But there is a vast minefield between conceptual buy-in and actual execution of a successful conversational marketing initiative.

Once a company agrees that conversational marketing is something they want to explore or implement, they must understand that the effort they're about to undertake isn't something easily handled by the existing marketing team, customer service, or a bunch of college interns. Nor can it be wholly outsourced. The setting of expectations is critical.

## Selling Conversational Marketing

My bet is that if Jupiter Research asked the 48 percent of brand marketers who said they want to get into social marketing what, specifically, they'll implement within the social marketing space, most of them would shrug or give clueless looks.

For a lot of larger companies, the task of responding to comments and addressing customer concerns is overwhelming. Customer service may already be overwhelmed. Most marketing departments aren't big enough to devote sufficient time to following things up on a one-to-one basis. So who gets the responsibility for dealing with the incoming questions and concerns?

This is the first land mine you're likely to encounter. It's where most conversational marketing initiatives immediately die.

## Understanding the Depth of Commitment

Failing to address comments in a timely manner fails to deliver on the expectation of having a forum in the first place. Most people who participate in two-way dialogue on the Internet expect rigorous follow-up, and if they don't get a response within a reasonable length of time, they assume no one on the other end of the conversation is listening. They're then likely to assume an online forum set up by a company is just another channel for corporate happy-talk or image enhancement, and they'll move on, usually after dropping some additional comments about how the company doesn't think their business is important.

Having outsiders comment on behalf of a company is worse. It sends the message that customer service isn't important enough to be taken seriously. Worse still, when a customer connects with someone who isn't a part of the company they're claiming to represent, a backlash typically results. Such an act is seen as grounds for mistrust and an attempt to keep the customer at arm's length, much like when a customer talks with a clueless outsourced customer service rep located somewhere in another country where labor is cheap. Using representatives who aren't familiar with the situation on the ground can also be counterproductive, since unfamiliarity breeds situations in which representatives can't intelligently discuss the matters confronting them.

The best representatives of a company are the people who work for it. They're the best people to handle the job of communicating directly with customers.

Unfortunately, they're also the people who, when speaking to the public, need to attend "press training" or run their press releases through the corporate communications department before they see the light of day. Most large companies have been trained to keep their communications controlled, "on message," and manufactured.

This stands in stark contrast to the type of conversation most people want to have with people at a company. They want to hear from the engineer at Ford who is hard at work trying to build a Corvette-killer. They want to hear from the Microsoft guys about what it was like starting out in a garage. They want to know whether the clothing a company makes will be sold at JC Penney in their particular size. And they want to hear about these things directly from a company, in real human speech, and not in the language of press releases, form letters, or preapproved snippets from a company's customer service manuals.

The success of a conversational marketing initiative thus depends not only on the ability of a company to loosen the reins and let its people speak more freely but also on the ability of the people involved to shed the notion of "staying on message." For many people working in corporate environments, this is a very difficult thing to do.

Companies that want to launch conversational marketing initiatives but are unprepared to adequately address the three challenges I've listed here should avoid conversational marketing altogether. Doing this halfheartedly is more likely to result in a customer backlash than anything else, so cutting corners is not an option.

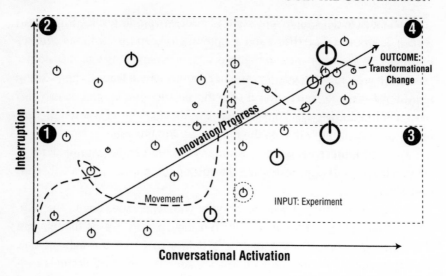

Figure 18.2    X Marks the Spot

## Putting Experimentation into Action

The overwhelming challenge at hand right now is not in the sell-through, but rather in the implementation and the execution. Everybody wants process and methodology. This is my attempt[1] to put it all together, using the well-structured experiment as the weapon of choice (input) and transformational change as the goal (outcome). (See Figure 18.2.)

Using a generalist-specialist 1-2 punch of interruption and conversation as the two axes that frame the playing field, what emerges is a pretty straightforward path from here (status quo) to there (future).

In a perfect world, the fruits of innovation would resemble a straight line (the shortest distance between two points), but the reality is anything but. The reality is an unpredictable force of momentum, which over time should triangulate and smoothen out close to — or around — the diagonal line of innovation.

---

[1]With the help of my friend, Richard Beaven.

What I've witnessed in many organizations is a spiraling—and out-of-control—line that is certainly moving, but almost always veering off course.

Your success will be determined in your ability to balance the complementary forces of art (the experiment) and science (the ability to build on successes and learn from failures). In this process, failure is an absolutely vital ingredient in the recipe of transformational change. Without it, course correction is practically impossible.

Like all good consulting matrices, four quadrants are visibly evident in this process:

1. *Status quo.* This quadrant represents low interruption and low conversation. That's where most of the world is stuck.

2. *Communication.* This quadrant represents advertising at its best. The craft of being able to birth highly disruptive and creative ideas, built around unique consumer insights, is a grand, yet increasingly elusive prize.

3. *Conversation.* This quadrant represents PR at its best. Getting people to talk without necessarily buying them in the process (earned or nonpaid versus paid media) is almost always perceived as more credible.

4. *Transformation.* This quadrant represents high interruption and high conversation—the new marketing realization of mashing-up community, dialogue and partnership in a red bow of conversation, unlike quadrant 2 (the fireworks display that is short-lived and, as quickly as it explodes, fades away and sinks back down to earth) and quadrant 3 (solidly rooted in the rock face and reality of communal engagement, but without the brand's creative flair and holistic clout—like the ratites—unable to take flight).

This is a continuum that is fluid and always changing, but it does have structure, form, and a framework that can be benchmarked, plotted, and measured against to ensure forward movement, innovation, and progress.

# 19

## Does Conversation Work?

At the end of the day, it's all going to come down to return on investment, isn't it? And why not. The central hypothesis of this entire book is that conversation trumps communication *every time*, and if this is true, then the results should be self-evident.

That's the easy part. The tougher part is proving it. Now, that said, you probably have all the proof you need inside the hallowed walls of your own company. Whether you represent a media company, an advertising or PR agency, or a brand marketer, you probably have a good idea of what's working and what isn't, and I would suspect that the status quo falls into the latter category, whereas the untried and untested may fall neatly into the former category.

Audi gave it a go with its much-publicized Art of the Heist campaign. By being a part of its consumers' conversations, the automaker boosted its chances of being discovered and trafficked. In fact, 29 percent of traffic to the campaign came via blog advertising. The kicker is that 29 percent was achieved with just one half of 1 percent of the overall media budget. To give you a sense of how ridiculously efficient and effective Audi's engagement with its consumers was, the media cost for the entire blog ad buy was less than the cost for one banner ad on a mainstream site such as Yahoo! Forget comparisons between new marketing and more traditional approaches—conversation trumped communication even within the digital and interactive arena.

### IT DEPENDS ON YOUR DEFINITION OF "WORK"

Before I continue, I want to quickly address one of the most preposterous arguments I sometimes hear about the disproportionate business impact that comes from investment in the "untried and untested." "If I get that kind of results from a minuscule spend, why would I need to increase my investment?" This is quite possibly the most absurd and warped logic I have ever encountered. It excuses the negligent exponential wastage piled on top of the status quo and scrutinizes the hyper-efficient. The playing field is a constant moving target, and what works today might work better tomorrow or it might not work at all. Ultimately, if something is delivering disproportionate results, it is well worth your time and your money to accentuate the positive. Don't confuse first mover advantage (the 100-meter sprint) with sustainable competitive advantage (the marathon).

There's no question that conversational marketing is "cheap" right now in terms of dollars expended or invested. That's definitely going to change, however, as more and more companies get in on the act and inevitably drive up pricing. Take the MommyCast: This popular podcast, according to the film's distributors, was responsible for one out of every four tickets sold for the movie *March of the Penguins*! That's essentially $25 million out of a total of $100 million in movie and DVD sales.[1]

Their rates—and the rates of similarly growing podcasts and blogs—will continue to rise.

That said (and the conversational marketing survey definitely seems to support this), conversational marketing is never going to be about usurping majority shares of current marketing communications budgets. If it ever did do that, it would become the very same spam that it helped to force out of the limelight. Conversational marketing is—and always will be—about quality dialogue, meaningful exchanges, and relevant investments of time.

## CONVERSATION CARPET-BOMBING THIS IS NOT

The SNCR survey seems to back up the assertion that the conversational imperative is not about tonnage. While a hefty chunk (41 percent) of the sample predicts they will be spending over 10 percent of

---

[1]See "Podcasting Moms Making Money from Home," CBS News *Early Show*, August 17, 2006, http://www.cbsnews.com/stories/2006/08/17/earlyshow/main1904502.shtml.

their budget on conversation, only 16 percent estimate they will be spending over 25 percent. I absolutely could argue that everything will be about conversation in five year's time . . . because it already is. If anything, what you are seeing here is a representation of a conversation silo—that is, a dedicated budget allocated exclusively to conversation. I absolutely could argue that conversation needs its own budget. (See Figure 19.1.)

This is another case of "and" versus "or." You are absolutely going to need to devote specific and specialized resources to conversation (beginning right now), *and* you are absolutely going to need to build conversation around every single integrated effort that you birth from here on out as well.

The real art is going to be in deciding *when* to silo and when to integrate. And when you integrate, you will be tested and challenged on how and how early you build in layers of conversation around your creative idea, your content, your consumer, and your community.

There are no silver bullets here—only bullets of varying shades of gray. A great way to look at the impact of conversational marketing is in terms of *relative efficacy*. Instead of swinging for the fences in an all-or-nothing effort, consider how quality shifts will lead to quantity results—disproportionate positive business impact. If you were previously spending $100 million to get back $150 million,

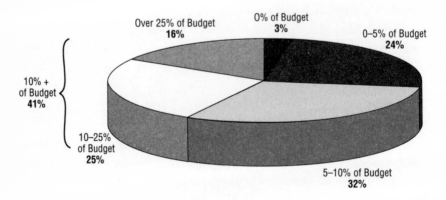

Figure 19.1   Conversation Marketing Spend (% Budget) in Five Years' Time

would you now pass up the opportunity to spend $95 million in order to get back $155 million? Of course you wouldn't. And built into the $10 million differential lift is the ability to better reward or compensate all participants—end consumers and interim service providers (such as agencies) alike.

## SOAP BUBBLE

Jim Nail, Cymfony's chief strategic and marketing officer, wrote this post about relative efficacy on his blog, Influence 2.0, which addressed the perceived disappointed reaction to the unprecedented social media frenzy that accompanied the pre-release conversation around *Snakes on a Plane* www.blog.cymfony.com/2006/08/index.html

> New Line Cinema's apparent disappointment with the box office take of *Snakes on a Plane* shows they have missed the point . . . (via the *New York Times*):
>
> - "The film was still the No. 1 draw at the box office during the weekend."
> - "It basically performed like a normal horror movie," said David Tuckerman, president for theatrical distribution for New Line.
> - The article notes they only spent $20 million on marketing.
> - Box office was $15.2 million on the opening weekend.
>
> So let me get this right—New Line spent about half the marketing budget they normally would (Hollywood Reporter notes $36.5 million is average[2]), drove the same amount of revenue they would expect from this type of movie, and still grabbed the #1 slot for the weekend.
>
> And they're disappointed?
>
> They make a consciously low-budget B-movie and are surprised when the alchemy of [word of mouth] doesn't turn this lead into gold. Duh!
>
> Count your profits, go home, and plan the word-of-mouth campaign for your next movie! (And fire half of your marketing staff, since you don't need them anymore.)

---

[2]See Stephen Galloway, "Movies and the Media," at The Hollywood Reporter, July 1, 2006, http://www.hollywoodreporter.com/thr/film/feature_display.jsp?vnu_content_id=1002464344

## A Case Study
## Novell on Conversational Marketing
*Bruce Lowry, Director of Global PR, Novell and Research Fellow,*
*Society for New Communications Research*

As a leading commercial Linux distributor, Novell is getting increasingly involved in open source, and open source requires open communication. What we do and what we say are finely parsed on the blogs and messages boards of the open-source community. When the community presses for an answer to questions it has, we respond. The community is only one constituency among many, of course, but it's the one where conversational marketing is the most prevalent.

Our chief marketing and technology officers blog on issues in their respective areas. In addition, Novell's PR team has a group blog. The PR blog launched first, in September 2005, while the executive blogs launched in spring 2006. Also in early 2006, we started a series of product-focused blogs, Novell Cool Blogs, which are group blogs by the engineering leads for the various Novell products. Finally, in mid-2006, we initiated a regular podcast series, Novell Open Audio.

While it probably isn't a surprise, we found the blogs have attracted a fair amount of negative comment. This reflects human nature to some degree, in that people are more likely to take the time to complain about something they don't like than weigh in positively on something they do. We also found, at least initially, that comments posted to the blogs tended to simply be a platform for that individual's position and were often unrelated to the content of the blog postings themselves. That has diminished over time.

In general, people appreciate the fact that the avenues for communication exist, even if they may take issue with the content or, more broadly, may disagree with a Novell policy or practice.

Controversy draws eyeballs. Our most commented-upon blog posting had to do with two different graphical user interface options for the Linux desktop, which generated some heated exchanges between the two opposing camps. This is a bit tricky for a public company, in that we don't necessarily want to create controversy. A corporate blog is restrained by regulatory issues and corporate policy from being a forum for a pure free-for-all. That said, the blog does allow us to jump in quickly to comment on issues that come up. It has allowed us to correct inaccuracies in the media and to put out statements about industry developments quickly. There are many occasions when people might be interested in knowing the company's position on an issue but the occasion doesn't warrant a formal press release. The blog is great for that.

We haven't faced internal hurdles. We needed initial finance and legal buyoff to launch the blogs, but since then we've had no opposition. The toughest part is maintaining frequency, finding the time in the day to look at what's happening in the market and to post something relevant and interesting. The press of business makes it easy for the blog to take a backseat. That said, it also is simply a challenge of training oneself. Blogs don't require long, thought-out postings to be interesting. It's more about having the blog in mind throughout the day and thinking, "Hey, this is interesting and worth a blog," when the right topic presents itself.

It's hard to quantify that [conversational marketing works]. I think blogging provides value as a source of content and a communications channel to stakeholders in the company. I suspect the product blogs provide useful information to customers directly. There is also a positive overall image effect for a company like Novell, involved in open source, in that it conveys a greater openness to dialogue.

[At this time] we don't have any explicit metrics measuring the conversational marketing initiatives at Novell.

From Nikon to Stormhoek, from Nike to Novell, from Dove to Audi. Throughout this book, I've offered a slew of examples—from the good to the bad to the ugly (mostly ugly). You can take their word for it . . . you can take my word for it . . . but ultimately you're going to have to experiment yourself in order to *put the walk into talk*.

I'm essentially doing the same with this book. The communal wiki chapter (Chapter 10) was one way of engaging my own community of like-minded influencers. So too was the book jacket initiative, which I will reflect on here as a case study in and of itself.

## THE REVOLUTION HAS A FACE—ACTUALLY 2,000 FACES

Not everyone likes to write, and so I threw down the gauntlet to the more visual artists among us, challenging them to design the jacket of this very book. All in all I received 10 unique designs (including one from Wiley as an insurance policy).

During the process, I had an epiphany. I discovered another initiative afoot, entitled The 2,000 Bloggers. It was a classic "link-baiting" exercise, as we call it in the blogosphere. Everybody loves a list, right? And through *this* list, every blogger who joined the fame-and-fortune bandwagon would—if the honor code was observed—link back to the original post and blog belonging to Tino Buntic. As intimated by Tino's e-mail signature, "sales leads without cold calling," this was a pretty sublime way of getting noticed without bashing down the door.

As Tino was building up his list, one member of the burgeoning community decided to put faces behind the names, and a magnificent tapestry of human voices began to dynamically assemble itself. Surely this was the ideal jacket for the book—a diverse mosaic of cat, boss, and viral blogs[3] of personal and professional passions all neatly shrink-wrapped into the very epitome of the conversation already in progress (the same one that the book's title suggests is worth joining).

Instead of unilaterally anteing up the new jacket, I put the idea out to the community, and the response was a unanimous and overwhelming affirmative.

As the submission deadline passed, I put the designs on display in our island in the virtual world of Second Life and then opened up the voting process. Over 750 responses poured in, with three jackets competing neck-and-neck for eventual honors.

Truth be told, there was foul play afoot as the voting process went through several iterations of exponential surges in votes. The wisdom of crowds suggests that the crowd should always get it right when it comes to reaching a consensus on the unknown. That, of course, assumes that no passion is involved.

[3]One classification as per Seth Godin.

Could I have created a foolproof process in order to make sure that nobody voted twice? Of course, but then I would have been the biggest fool of the bunch, taking the fun out of the game. Five seasons deep, *American Idol* is still plagued by Vote for the Worst (www.votefortheworst.com), which rallies the contrarians to keep the weakest links in the competition (and make the greedy producers' jobs a little more challenging). Sanjaya Malakar might not have won the whole competition, but he sure came close!

As it turns out, the motif of 2,000 bloggers made a dramatic last-minute surge to pip the two leading candidates at the post. Content with the results, I closed the survey knowing full well that there were going to be tears, shock, awe, jubilation, and commiseration no matter how the voting turned out—and that would just be my emotions!

As far as I'm concerned, everyone who participated was a winner, and so to celebrate the efforts from all who contributed, I'm going to list them all with full attribution and my deepest gratitude.

### First Place: The 2,000 Bloggers

To all 2,000 bloggers[4] (of whom I am two): Your daily contributions to the conversation are a muse to us all. I hope you can find yourselves and your several pixels of fame among the covers. You can view all of the book cover submissions at www.jointheconversation .us/bookcovers

## The Twist: Does Conversation Sell?

Time will tell whether 2,000 bloggers will purchase the book and blog about it to their respective audiences. At the very minimum, they represent a load of links. Several people who have been following the thread have very astutely noted the obvious business connection between display and sales. Others (including some of the 2,000 bloggers) have already stated that they will purchase the book.

---

[4]Attributed back to http://www.2kbloggers.com/photo-montage

Then there's the approval process. In this case, I took the position of *trusting the crowd* based on overwhelming consent. *The reasons why people blog are the very same reasons why this kind of initiative can only be embraced. Any moves to quash such an effort go against the very motivations behind blogging in the first place.*

So, does conversational marketing actually work? We'll see how many people talk about, review, and buy this book, won't we?

# 20

## Do You Speak Conversation?
## Take the Test

If you're still reading at this point, you're pretty much on board with the fundamental belief that two-way community, dialogue, and partnership have replaced one-way monologue. You understand that the dialogue isn't just about giving consumers the ability to interact with or react to your communications. It's not about letting them design your next Super Bowl commercial, and it's not about generating artificial or negative buzz in order to "get people talking."

Marketing as a conversation is primarily focused on enriching, deep, relevant, and meaningful conversations that more often than not are consumer-centric, not marketer-driven. When marketing becomes part of the conversation, it begins to hint at realizing what it was always supposed to stand for: meaning and purpose—the ability to change behavior, attitudes, perceptions, and, more substantially, lives.

Marketing (as a face and a voice) does not have to be a spectator. It does not have to be silent on the sidelines, and it certainly does not have to be a victim (especially at its own hands). Marketing at its purest can and should and does and will be a conduit, a catalyst, a means to an end.

A confidant.

A role model.

A friend.

Now is the time for you to act and *put your money where your ears are*.

Now is the time for you to demonstrate the substance behind your bravado.

Now is the time to be put to the test. To gauge conversations already in progress and "what has stuck"—the al dente ideas that resonate in your communities.

Compare the conversation audit to your garden-variety communication or competitive audit. Think about it: To date you've been measuring how you stack up based on message tonnage. Your "share of voice" or presence is nothing more than a crude representation of clutter. It's a lose-lose situation: Whether you are being outspent by your competitors or you're the one doing the outspending, you're either lost in the clutter or the one responsible for it in the first place. In either scenario, your consumers are turning away from you.

If you want to be a part of your consumers' lives, you need to be listening to them and responding to them. You need to be a part of *their* conversation in order to be able to determine what *your* role should be. Sure you can put your consumers in a confined room and bias them (uh, "guide" them) with a set of predetermined path-of-least-resistance questions designed to deliver against your self-serving agenda. But why wouldn't you just tear down the walls and embrace them directly?

Talk to them. Listen to them. Laugh with them and cry with them. They are, at the end of the day . . . you! (as *Time* magazine attested with its 2006 end-of-year cover).

Look in the mirror: If you don't like what you see, it's time to apply an extreme makeover to your marketing efforts.

To help you determine whether you're ready for conversational rehab, here is one portion of the expanded methodology we use at *crayon* that is something like a self-assessment test you can take right now.

*Question 1:* Do you know how many times you were mentioned on blogs, message boards, podcasts, or forums last month? Use the following chart to determine the number and percentages of mentions of your company, your brand, your brand positioning, or your key messages for, say, video sharing.

| Video Sharing | Your Company | | Your Brand | | Your Brand Positioning | | Your Key Messages | |
|---|---|---|---|---|---|---|---|---|
| | # | % | # | % | # | % | # | % |
| Total mentions | | | | | | | | |
| Brand-initiated mentions | | | | | | | | |
| Consumer-initiated mentions | | | | | | | | |
| Estimated total impressions | | | | | | | | |
| Brand-initiated impressions | | | | | | | | |
| Consumer-initiated impressions | | | | | | | | |
| Brand: CGC ratio | | | | | | | | |
| Distribution sites [embedded html] | | | | | | | | |
| Comments | | | | | | | | |
| Links to | | | | | | | | |
| Favorited | | | | | | | | |
| Tags | | | | | | | | |
| Responses | | | | | | | | |
| Honors | | | | | | | | |
| Spoofs | | | | | | | | |
| Distribution sites (embed HTML) | | | | | | | | |

*Question 2:* Do you know how many times *your competitors' brands* were mentioned on blogs, message boards, podcasts, or forums last month? Fill out the chart, once again starting with the example of video sharing.

| Video Sharing | Your Brand # | % | Your #1 Competitor # | % | Your #2 Competitor # | % | Your #3 Competitor # | % |
|---|---|---|---|---|---|---|---|---|
| Total mentions | | | | | | | | |
| Brand-initiated mentions | | | | | | | | |
| Consumer-initiated mentions | | | | | | | | |
| Estimated total impressions | | | | | | | | |
| Brand-initiated impressions | | | | | | | | |
| Consumer-initiated impressions | | | | | | | | |
| Brand: CGC ratio | | | | | | | | |
| Distribution sites [embedded html] | | | | | | | | |
| Comments | | | | | | | | |
| Links to | | | | | | | | |
| Favorited | | | | | | | | |
| Tags | | | | | | | | |
| Responses | | | | | | | | |
| Honors | | | | | | | | |
| Spoofs | | | | | | | | |
| Distribution sites (embed HTML) | | | | | | | | |

Now perform the same exercise for your company and competition for each of the following:

- Message boards and forms
- Blogs
- Product hits
- Podcasts (audio and video)
- Chat
- Review sites
- Photo-sharing web sites
- Social networking sites
- Search results
- Virtual worlds
- Presence applications (Twitter, etc.)

You are just getting started. Now answer the following questions:

## Community

*Question 3:* Can you break down *who* is doing the talking based on levels of influence?

*Question 4:* Can you break down *who* is doing the talking based on their relationship to your company (prospect, customer, loyalist, lapsed customer, detractor)?

*Question 5:* Can you segment based on *what* is being said?

*Question 6:* Can you subdivide what is being said based on the following categorizations: positive, positive-neutral, neutral, neutral-negative, negative?

*Question 7:* What clusters are evident and what patterns are emerging?

*Question 8:* How does this stack up relative to your competitors?

*Question 9:* How does this stack up relative to other industries?

## Dialogue

*Question 10:* How many people called your customer service lines last month?

*Question 11:* How many people wrote your company via mail or by electronic means (e-mail, the Web)?

*Question 12:* To what extent did you respond to these consumers or customers in a timely fashion?

*Question 13:* How adequately did you respond to these consumers or customers?

*Question 14:* To what extent did you fully satisfy or resolve the needs of these consumers or customers?

*Question 15:* How many consumers or customers voluntarily shared some positive news or information about your company or brand?

*Question 16:* How many consumers or customers voluntarily shared some negative news or information about your company or brand?

## Partnership

*Question 17:* How many consumers or customers directly or indirectly approached you with specific marketing ideas or suggestions?

*Question 18:* What did you learn from consumers or your customers that you otherwise did not know or were not aware of?

*Question 19:* In any capacity, did you take what you may have observed or learned and incorporate these insights/learnings into your ongoing communications or conversational efforts?

*Question 20:* Can you name three (3) key learnings and/or insights you gained from recent successful and "failed" experiments?

1. _____

2. _____

3. _____

Now that you have completed this introspective self-assessment, are you able to identify three (3) specific next steps for your organization and/or brand(s)?

1. _____

2. _____

3. _____

> **Pay it forward: Why don't you share your next steps with the community at www.jointheconversation.us/nextsteps**

In one conversational audit we did for a single-serve coffee brewing brand (Brand X), we found that while it was being outspent by only *some* of its competitors, it was in fact being outsmarted by *all* of its competitors. Brand X just wasn't part of the conversation, and the results (or lack thereof) were overwhelming. (See Figure 20.1.)

The advertising trade publication *Ad Age* releases its "Leading National Advertisers" report every year, and what always strikes me is the extent to which the so-called leaders are in fact not. Take interactive, for example: Interactive grew from 2.4 percent to 2.6 percent of budget from 2004 to 2005 among the top 100 LNAs, compared to an increase from 2.8 percent to 3.1 percent among all advertisers during the same period. Or how about the fact that the

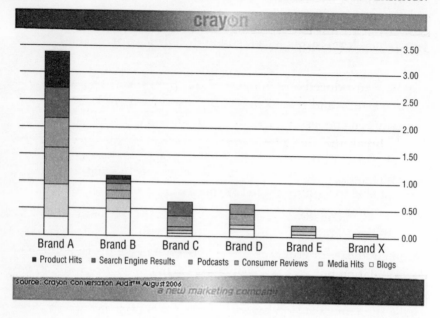

Figure 20.1　Don't Drown Out the Conversation — Join In!

100 top LNAs' television spend, in all shapes and forms (network, spot, syndicated, cable network, cable local spot), represented 57 percent of total measured media?

I could have my math horribly screwed up, but ultimately what I see in the "Leading National Advertisers" is an acute *lack* of leadership, openness to experimentation, and ability to change. Mitigating risk is no longer a best practice. On the one hand, the argument could be put forward that these blue-chip brands have the least to gain by virtue of their superior or established or mature market share, vested equity, and proven track record. By the same token, they also have the most to lose when they get beaten by another 800-pound gorilla — or, more realistically, by a swarm of challenger brands. Risk is relative, and return is most certainly going to be more and more a function of outthinking and out-smarting, compared to outspending and outlasting. Add the con-sumer into the mix as the new "x" factor and the entire dynamic changes irrevocably.

## WITH INCREASED CONVERSATION COMES INCREASED CONSIDERATION

Earlier I introduced a hypothesis about time spent. Closely related to time spent—and specifically voluntary time spent (VTS)—is the link between conversation, consideration, and conversion.

I'd break this out into two phases of conversation. The first is the belief that to the extent that you're a part of the conversations that consumers have among themselves, you increase the chances of being on a short list of consideration.

A report sponsored by Manning Selvage & Lee and released by the Keller Fay Group in 2007 identified consumers called "conversation catalysts," a group of consumers who make up 15 percent of the population but are responsible for 1.5 billion word-of-mouth impressions per day, or one-third of all word-of-mouth conversations. That's the equivalent of 184 unique conversations per catalyst per week—a full one and a half times more than the rest of the pack. These *influentials* have certain demographic commonalities and yet are not necessarily bound or defined by variables such as age, gender, or income.

According to the report, the following 10 brands are talked about the most positively:

1. Pepsi
2. Coke
3. Target
4. Honda
5. Sony
6. Apple/iPod
7. Toyota
8. Wal-Mart
9. HP
10. Budweiser

The report also mentions that a full 54 percent of the conversations of catalysts cite marketing and media, which introduces the notion of brands *themselves* as catalysts or conduits.

> *The more people talk **about** you, the more likely the **possibility** of them purchasing you.*
>
> *The more people talk **with** you, the more likely the **probability** of them purchasing you.*

## TALK IS CHEAP

Literally. There's no premium on consumers talking among themselves, but there is a price to pay when the tide turns and the conversation isn't 100 percent glowing. In reality, this is how it's going to be—flawed, nonlinear, impassioned, inaccurate. Consumers will talk freely with one another, and often they'll have the facts completely backwards. It's a costly game of broken telephones, and if you're not in it, you most certainly will not win it.

Part of the art of conversation is in the *timing*. Knowing exactly when to intercede or ask permission to join is critical and can make all the difference. Perfecting your timing will come with considerable practice and, no doubt, many mistakes, much trial and error, and a host of revisions.

## PEOPLE DON'T CARE HOW MUCH YOU KNOW . . .

. . . until they know how much you care.

This is one of the most universal truths and fundamental lessons in any relationship-building business (which is really every business category). The entire damned media business—where heads of broadcast networks are godparents to the children of the media-buying C-suite—runs on this central premise. With all the data, proprietary research, mix modeling, and negotiations, it all comes down to a partnership based on trust, rapport, dependability, and Super Bowl tickets (I couldn't resist). My point here is simple: If this insight applies so wholeheartedly to the business-to-business (B2B) space, why on earth have we not put it into practice in the business-to-consumer (B2C) arena?

When consumers have a vested interest in a company or a brand, they're almost always going to rally behind it, defend it, and speak up on its behalf. If you don't already believe this, I'm not sure this book or any other book (even the good one) is going to help you. I'm more interested in those of you who do believe but either aren't doing anything about it or don't know how to go about putting it into practice.

If you take away one thing and only one thing from reading this book, it should be this: It's never too late to join the conversation. Especially when you can do so with a healthy dose of humility. If Target had been plugged into the conversation, it would have had ample time to not just respond to Tom Locke but overdeliver in a big way.

## A Case Study:
## Dell Joins the Conversation
### John Cass, Research Fellow,
### Society for New Communications Research

Direct2Dell (http://direct2dell.com/) was like its name suggests—a direct line of conversation between company and consumers. It was launched in July 2006 AJ (after Jarvis) with a doctrine that includes the idea that "Direct2Dell is all about conversations."

Here is the case study transcript from an interview with Richard Binhammer (corporate communications, digital media), John Pope (communication strategist), and Lionel Menchaca (digital media) at Dell, conducted by the SNCR fellows exclusively for *Join the Conversation*:

"[What] we realized is that there were a lot of issues, a lot of conversations going on around us, and a lot of those conversations had to deal with regular, basic, customer support issues. So that's where we started to focus.

"As we grew the program, we went from customer support to the direct Dell blog to the generally blogging response and monitoring. We were already monitoring lots of blogs, but then we started to engage in the conversations that are on the blogs.

"There [was] some skepticism from customers [who thought] it may not really be a Dell person ... [but] the thing that surprised all of us was that once people accept that you're there, they're very prepared to hear you, and nine times out of ten it's a positive response that results in new information [and] any negative commentary is significantly slowed down.

"Sometimes the conversation turns totally. Many times we have the opportunity to engage to get our point of view for balance in a conversation. We viewed that as a win, and sometimes we will impart some new information to a blogger or their readers that was previously unknown, and it just totally shifts the tone ... because you're engaged in that dialogue ... because if you're not there to converse ... people talk about you ... you don't have a chance. *Other people will be talking for you.*"

## Example: Ed Bott

"Ed Bott had a pretty aggressive posting saying Dell isn't listening. It was a letter to Kevin Rollins about how badly we were doing on customer services, etc. And we waited and said, 'Yes, we are listening. And in fact, we see your open letter to Kevin Rollins and Michael Dell. Did you know that we're doing the following things to change our customer support and our customer experience, and this includes blogger outreach. If there are any concerns or complaints about our customer service, we'll be happy to solve them. Please have them e-mail us directly at this e-mail address.' And he posted that, and he also posted a new blog posting that said Dell gets 'clueful 2.0' or something like that. And he referred all the customer complaints in to us, and we basically solved the problems that were current and existing on that Web page, and he closed down the Web page because we solved them, and the address for resolutions was now posted on his blog. Then he went and met with Michael at CES, where he wrote on his blog that his message was that while we weren't perfect we had sure come a long way and we're going in the right direction."

## Scope and Scale

"Between the people doing the customer outreach and the other people doing the general blog outreach, we're looking at over 1,500 blogs every day.

"Sometimes there are things that we can't comment on. And then sometimes there are things that we will jump on. For instance, when we went through our battery problems.

"We pinpointed that problem first, and we came to know that [it] was really much wider than just Dell. But early on it appeared that it was just us, and there were a number of bloggers out there speculating that it was inherent to our product designs, that we were doing things in the product design arena that resulted in battery failures, and that was just bogus information. It was just not true. The fact of the matter was that there was a third-party supplier to Dell and others that had a manufacturing defect with their batteries.

"And it was an industry problem. So we jumped on the boat of speculation quite aggressively.

"We [also] went out and proactively approached people on the battery issue and said, 'Hey, we've got a battery recall under way. Just wanted to make sure you got the direct link to it so that you can. . . .'"

## Does Conversation Work?

"One of the things is that we have ourselves a new early warning system or issue management system.

"We identify sooner, and we probably respond sooner, and we respond better. So that's, I think, one of our successes."

## Learnings and Surprises

"One of our surprises was the minute you enter the conversation and provide additional information or open yourself up for the dialogue or apologize for the mistake and try and fix it or say, 'We're sorry that did not live up to Dell standards. It shouldn't have happened that way. Let's see what we can do here,' the conversation changes. It's not the big bad company anymore. And we have seen a decline in the first six months of over 18 percent in negative commentary.

"You start to see customers who are very angry with us and very upset instantly saying, 'Wow, this is great. I can't believe a big company like Dell is actually doing this.' And those customers are quickly turning from people who were very frustrated with this to people who are becoming strong advocates. And these same people who were threatening to sell their systems or to never buy Dell again are now, because of our offer, saying, 'Hey, this is something I didn't expect. Now that you guys are doing this, I'm a Dell fan again. I'm just waiting for you to execute.' It's where we are right now.

"We were surprised in some respects that when you weigh in with factual information in a conversational kind of way with the blogs and talk to people about these things, nine times out of ten you're bringing information to the party. The information seems to be accepted and respected.

"You have to be transparent. You have to be fact-based. You must be conversational. And you have to be rapid with your response; otherwise, the conversation's on to other things.

"And you have to be willing to take your lumps, too. You have to be very open.

"But having these tools themselves doesn't ensure success. It requires commitment not only from the people who are directly supporting the tools but the business behind it."

### Culture and Morale

"If you look at Dell, 23 years ago Michael Dell redefined how computers were sold, and that was basically cutting out the middleman and dealing directly with customers. And that became the Dell direct model, so to speak. And if you look behind that and Web 2.0 and dealing directly with customers, what we're doing today is really a logical extension of that direct model. And we have tremendous support from the top of our business to pull out all the stops and be as creative as we can possibly be.

"I've definitely seen that [conversational engagement] has energized folks, and they're excited about it because it's different. It's pretty clear to employees that what we're doing goes beyond a lot of companies."

### Conversation at Dell

Dell came around to the realization that conversation trumps communication. The company has initiated programs in Second Life, including a very friendly and valuable orientation to help virtual-world newcomers get their bearings (before disappearing into the black hole of porn). In 2007 Dell also launched Ideastorm (think message boards meet Digg), a program that reaches out to consumers to allow them to give Dell ideas and feedback on what *they* want in the next generation of Dell computers. The community then votes for what they think are the most compelling ideas, and Dell's strategy team takes the most popular ideas and looks at ways to implement them. What a revelation—actually asking consumers what they want instead of telling them!

In a work session with a consumer packaged-good company, a very interesting question was raised: Surely this would open up several pathways to abuse—especially by competitors? What would stop a competitor from suggesting (and voting on) something blatantly off strategy or off target? The answer is, of course, nothing; however, I think the questioner might have missed the point of Ideastorm. For starters, the wisdom of crowds would be likely to sort the wheat from the chaff. And if not, Dell would always be able to say yes or no to an idea.

I explained that the real danger or threat would lie in Dell's competitors lurking and eavesdropping for free R&D. Linux as a standard feature? Great idea. I'll get right on that.... Again, this might not be the point, either. Instead, consider a company—tortured for its inability to partner with its consumers—doing almost a full 180, showing some vulnerability, reaching out to its customers, and being prepared to listen to and learn from them. *That's* the kind of goodwill that just can't be purchased.

In early 2007 I was in Atlanta at my client, Coca-Cola. During lunch everyone made their way to the outside quad and gathered around a very busy platform with tables, strings, pipes, and tons of two-liter bottles of Diet Coke. Two gentlemen appeared with goggles and white coats and then the magic began. . . .

Stephen Voltz and Fritz Grobe, a.k.a. EepyBird, performed Experiment #214, "The Domino Effect," *in front of the entire Coca-Cola Company.* Chairman Neville Isdell was in town, and although I can't confirm that he watched, I'll bet he did. (See Figure 20.2.)

I was like a kid in a candy store as I watched in awe as the new celebrities (aka consumers like you and me) did their thing.

Figure 20.2    The Eepy-Center of Coca-Cola

At the end of the performance, the sound heard was not the sound of silence but rounds of cheers and applause.

This moment was the realization of blood, sweat, and tears-and the passionate belief that new marketing is here to stay.

Think about it: Two talented yet normal citizens of planet earth (actually Buckfield, Maine) became the poster children for the rise of CGC and, more importantly, the democratization of creativity. Not only did they get the attention of the Coca-Cola Company, but they received acknowledgment and respect in the process.

I spend a lot of time blogging about companies and brands that get it and those that don't get it. Generally, I'm on the outside specu-lating about what goes on inside; on this wintry day in February, however, I got to witness a completely different perspective from the inside out (or the Eepy-Center).

I specifically requested permission to talk about this seminal moment and share this experience and my feelings with *you*. I even got a blessing to use a photograph from a colleague's cell phone (as opposed to a hi-res image from a professional photographer). Coke did not ask me to do this, nor did it stand in my way. How different this was from its earlier reaction and response. Who knows . . . soon enough companies like Coca-Cola will be making certain that bloggers are present at events like these. Microsoft has already started doing this by flying in highly influential bloggers to hang out with Bill Gates.

I should add that several readers were not convinced and continued to criticize the company's efforts, describing the event as "too little too late." I beg to differ and prefer to take a "better late than never" point of view. I mention this to remind you that all responses are valued and valuable. It's all part of the new deal of conversation. No more retreating. No more throwing in the towel. No more pulling the plug or gagging the conversation. Who knows, by the time you read this perhaps even Neville Isdell himself will have commented on my blog.

And when all the dust has settled, not only will the benefits of open, honest, and direct conversation outweigh the cost, but, indeed, the impact will be profound. Customers will feel a renewed sense of loyalty. Consumers will feel a strong sense of belonging. Communities, feeling emboldened, will thrive. Citizens will be empowered to effect change. Companies will converse more freely and fluidly throughout the many, no longer being shut out or on the outside looking in.

Marketing will be conversations, brands will be catalysts, consumers will be willing participants, and the world will be a thriving stage of stories that move hearts, minds, mountains, and business.

Trent Reznor, founder of the industrial rock group Nine Inch Nails, harnessed the power of conversational marketing to launch the group's new album, *Year Zero*. Using an alternate-reality game consisting of riddles, clues, rabbit holes, and Easter eggs, Reznor architected an elaborate experiential panacea that partnered with his fervent fan-base community, shrink-wrapped in a throbbing skin of dialogue.

*In February, a fan noticed that highlighted letters on a Nine Inch Nails tour T-shirt spelled "I am trying to believe," leading to the first web site. A*

*USB drive found in a bathroom in Lisbon, Portugal, contained an MP3 of "My Violent Heart" and instantly spread online. Spectrographic analysis of the song's closing static revealed an image of "The Presence," a hand reaching from the sky. Another memory stick yielded a phone number and additional evidence. A digital brushfire ensued. Sites multiplied. Fans built databases and message boards.*

Results in both online buzz and album sales seem to reflect this game-changing approach, within an industry hell-bent on communication status quo and control.[1]

Reznor, like my Mom and Abdul, the coffee guy, are all experts in conversational marketing. In varying degrees, capacities, and contexts, they've all experienced the benefits of community, dialogue, and partnership. Now comes the test. Are you prepared to step up and join them? Are you ready to join the myriads of thriving conversations going on even as you complete reading this book? Everything is at stake and everything is on the table. Join in.

What are you waiting for?

It's now time for you to join the conversation, because at the end of the day, this is *your* conversation as much as it is mine.

Register to become an author on the Join the Conversation blog (www.jointheconversation.us/blog).

Join the JTC Facebook group and connect with others around conversational marketing.

And don't forget my blog and podcast, Jaffe Juice (www.jaffe juice.com), where you can work with me on book number three (like a Bond film, Joseph Jaffe will return in . . .).

---

[1]*USA Today* (http://www.usatoday.com/life/music/news/2007-04-18-nine-inch-nails_N.htm).

# Index